Escape from Manchuria

The Rescue of 1.7 Million Japanese Civilians Trapped in Soviet-occupied Manchuria Following the End of World War II

Paul K. Maruyama

iUniverse, Inc.
New York Bloomington

iUniverse books may be ordered through booksellers or by contacting:

iUniverse
1663 Liberty Drive
Bloomington, IN 47403
www.iuniverse.com
1-800-Authors (1-800-288-4677)

ISBN: 978-1-4502-0579-5 (sc)
ISBN: 978-1-4502-0580-1 (ebook)
ISBN: 978-1-4502-0581-8 (dj)

Printed in the United States of America

iUniverse rev. date: 03/03/2010

In memory of Kunio and Mary Maruyama,
my father and mother.
In memory, also, of Masamichi Musashi who passed
away as this book went into print.

About the Cover

The illustration on the cover is from the cover of a small pamphlet that was published in Japan in June 1946 and sold (or often given away) mainly at train station kiosks. The 35-page booklet by Kunio Maruyama was the first published document that detailed to the people of Japan the miserable conditions of the nearly 1.7 million Japanese civilians still trapped in Soviet-occupied Manchuria since the end of World War II. The illustration shows a group of weary travelers who seem to be waiting to catch a train or board a ship. A mother carrying a baby on her back is sitting on her suitcase; a young boy and an elderly man behind her are similarly seated. Two other young boys are standing in front of the mother. All are bundled up in winter clothing. The mother looks anxious as she holds the arm of the younger of the two boys standing in front of her; the baby on her back appears to be asleep. Many years later, Maruyama explained that the illustration depicted his own family left behind in Dalian, awaiting transportation home: his wife Mary, Robert (then nine), Joseph (seven), Paul (five), and Xavier (the baby, two years old, on Mary's back). The elderly man in the illustration was a stranger, simply another Japanese awaiting repatriation.

Contents

Acknowledgments

If my late father Kunio Maruyama had not written, in Japanese, his book *Yutopia wo Mezashite (Aiming at Utopia)* in 1970, this book would not have been written. *Yutopia wo Mezashite* was my father's memoir describing several significant crises and triumphs in his life that he rarely talked about, even to his own children. The major portion of the book described the story of his role in escaping to Japan from Manchuria in 1946 with two companions. Thus, first and foremost, I am grateful to my father for having left a detailed record that allowed me to write this book.

Another important resource for this book was Masamichi Musashi's *Ajia no Akebono—Shisen wo Koete (The Dawning of Asia—Crossing the Lines of Death)*. Masamichi Musashi was the youngest of the three men who fled Manchuria and the only one who survives today. In particular, *Ajia no Akebono* allowed me to relate in chapter 22 the horrendous ordeal that Mr. Musashi suffered at the hands of the Nationalist Chinese Army for more than seventy days when he was mistakenly arrested as a Communist spy. He also told me a great deal about the admirable character of Kunio Maruyama that I, his own son, had not fully appreciated.

It would probably not be an exaggeration to say that this book is a collaborative effort on the part of all my siblings: Robert, Joseph, Xavier, Marianne, and Roseanne. I sincerely and humbly thank all my brothers and sisters who contributed their memories and knowledge as I worked on my manuscript.

I am especially grateful to my younger sister Marianne Maruyama who spent many hours meticulously proofreading and correcting the many, many errors in spelling, grammar, and sentence structure in my manuscript.

I also owe much to my younger brother Xavier Maruyama who accompanied me in the summer of 2008 to conduct research at various archives. His expertise and experience as the owner and publisher of a newspaper were invaluable in locating obscure and scantily recorded documents.

The staff at Asian Complex, which produced an NHK (Japan Broadcasting Corporation) documentary in 2008, entitled *This Was How Repatriation Happened—The Former Manchuria: The Road to Koroto*, was especially helpful to me at every step of the way as I struggled to collect documentation from Japanese publications. I am especially thankful to the kindness of Ms. Ai Hirano and Mr. Mitsunori Sato who never faltered in their encouragement to me throughout the project.

I owe much gratitude to my friend, Mr. Tohru Takahashi, managing director of Starting Place in Tokyo, who assisted me with research in Japan and offered me much helpful advice (and encouragement) as I labored at my manuscript. I must admit that it was the spirit of Japanese–American relationship and friendship which Mr. Takahashi represents that inspired me to relate to the world this courageous story of three brave Japanese men whose success was due mostly to the magnanimity and compassion of the United States of America, primarily embodied by General Douglas MacArthur and his staff as well as the American Catholic order, the Maryknoll Mission of New York.

I have asked for, and graciously received, much help from many other people without whose wise counsel, advice, and criticism I would not have been able to complete this book. Among them are Mrs. Seiko Green; best-selling author Ms. Lisa

Bergren; Father Michael Walsh, the curator at the Maryknoll Mission Archives; and Mr. James W. Zobel, the archivist at the MacArthur Memorial Library. I owe a debt of gratitude to my employer, Colorado College, for providing a grant that allowed me to travel to various archives to conduct research in the summer of 2008. I sincerely thank my good friend, Mr. Robert Strout, who encouraged me from the outset many years ago as I took on this project and who offered many valuable suggestions as I began writing.

Finally, I am most grateful (more than she may realize) to my wife LaRae, who has put up with my often impatient ways, offered incomparable advice to improve the manuscript, and never failed to stand behind and support me through the many ups and downs of translating, researching, and composing as I plugged away at this book.

I can only hope that this book, written by a novice author, does justice to all who have helped me along the way to completion. But, most of all, I can only pray that the book does justice in letting the world know about the amazing undertaking of my father and his two companions to whom my brothers and I (and the nearly 1.7 million repatriates and their descendants) owe our lives.

Introduction

This is the true story of three courageous men whose secret escape in 1946 from northern China, then called Manchuria, saved the lives of one million seven hundred thousand of their fellow Japanese. The three men, Kunio Maruyama, Hachiro Shinpo, and Masamichi Musashi, departed surreptitiously from Anshan to Dalian, then to Shenyang (known then as Mukden), then on by rail to Shanhaiguan where the Great Wall of China separated Manchuria from China, and finally to Tanggu on the China side. They departed on their risky journey without the help, or for the most part the knowledge, of other Japanese. At Tanggu, the three boarded a United States LST (a Landing Ship, Tank amphibious vessel), one of the many United States Navy ships then engaged in the evacuation to Japan of more than two million Japanese who had been stranded in mainland China at the end of World War II.

Upon returning to Japan, the three men engaged in a single-minded, vigorous campaign to inform the Japanese people and their government about the tragic situation that had befallen their fellow citizens in Manchuria and to bring about their return to their homeland. Already, millions of Japanese from China, Indonesia, and the Philippines, who had similarly been stranded overseas when Japan surrendered, had been repatriated, but none from Manchuria. In those days, the only entity that could execute repatriation on such a massive scale was the United States military under the command of General

Douglas MacArthur, Supreme Commander for Allied Powers (SCAP). The three Japanese men eventually met face to face with General MacArthur who, shortly after their meeting in April 1946, issued an order to dispatch ships to the Manchurian port of Koroto (its Chinese name was Huludao), the only navigable port in all of Manchuria not under Soviet control. Koroto was under the control of the anti-Communist Chinese Nationalist army of Generalissimo Chiang Kai-shek.

Thanks to the humanitarian efforts of the United States military and to the understanding of General MacArthur personally, more than a million of the 1.7 million stranded Japanese were evacuated from Manchuria and safely returned to Japan by the end of 1946 on board United States naval and Japanese civilian vessels (all vessels were crewed by the Japanese). However, the Soviet Union continued to prevent the evacuation of hundreds of thousands of Japanese still under Soviet occupation in Manchuria and other territories even as repatriation from Koroto was nearing completion near the end of 1946. Thus, the three men relentlessly continued their efforts to focus the attention of the Japanese nation and of the General Headquarters of SCAP (simply referred to as GHQ) on repatriation from Manchuria until negotiations between the United States and the Soviet Union were finally concluded. In December 1946, the Soviets relented to allow the repatriation of Japanese from Soviet-controlled ports of Manchuria.

Although the courageous and single-handed efforts of the three brave men could not save all the lives of the thousands of Japanese—many died from starvation, illness, bitter cold, neglect and, in many cases, from violence at the hands of gangs, mobs, and soldiers (of both the Soviet and Chinese Communist armies)—a catastrophe beyond imagination might have resulted had not the three men acted.

The Soviet Union Invades Manchuria

On August 8, 1945, only one week before Japan unconditionally surrendered, the Soviet Union declared war on Japan, and a few hours later, at 1:00 AM on August 9, the Soviet Union launched a massive attack on Manchuria in an operation code-named "August Storm." More than one and a half million Soviet soldiers, accompanied by tanks, planes, and heavy artillery, invaded Manchuria from the west, the north, and the east, beginning in the dark of the night.

The world, including the Japanese nation, had no idea what was happening in Manchuria. The Japanese army in Manchuria, then called the Kwantung Army, was totally unprepared for the onslaught. The world did not learn until much later that the Soviets in Manchuria forcibly transported to Siberia those Japanese soldiers who surrendered in the onslaught; they systematically dismantled entire factories, schools, hospitals, cultural structures, and other assets in Manchuria, using Japanese soldiers and civilians as slave laborers; and they transported all the dismantled assets as spoils of war to the Soviet Union. The world did not know because the Soviet Union completely and effectively severed all communications across Manchuria's borders.

The nonmilitary, civilian Japanese residents in Manchuria were now made to pay the price as the losers in a war. They were immediately thrown out of work and became permanently unemployed. All means of exit from Manchuria were blocked. All bank accounts held by Japanese were frozen. Women (as well as men) lived in constant fear of assault by Soviet soldiers. No house was safe from incursion and robbery by Soviet soldiers and roving gangs and mobs intent on exacting revenge on the Japanese. Civil order vanished. It was not only the Japanese who suffered; many innocent Chinese also suffered at the hands of the ruthless Soviet army.

The Beginning of a Long, Dark Night

It was under these circumstances that the three men, Masamichi Musashi (then twenty-four years old), Hachiro Shinpo (thirty-one), and Kunio Maruyama (thirty-seven), secretly conspired to escape to Japan to bring about the rescue of their 1.7 million fellow noncombatant Japanese citizens stranded in Manchuria, who had seemingly been abandoned and forgotten by their government. While this story must necessarily relate historical chronology that may interrupt the flow of the narration, the intent of the author is not to present a history book per se. Rather, the intent is to narrate the courageous actions of the three brave Japanese and to set the record straight on how repatriation of Japanese civilians from Manchuria proceeded.

When word was communicated to Japanese associations in various parts of Manchuria in mid-1946 that Japanese citizens should make their way to Koroto (Huludao in Chinese) because the long-awaited repatriation ships were finally coming from Japan to pick them up, no Japanese objected to the long and perilous journey they encountered in getting to Koroto. Erratic trains sometimes took weeks to reach their destination, and some perished on their journey to Koroto. When they finally scrambled on to the American naval vessels and Japanese merchant ships to return at last to their native land, hardly a soul ever knew (or had the strength to wonder in those desperate times) why those particular ships came to that port to rescue them. For the most part, the repatriated Japanese only had the strength to curse the land they were leaving behind and give thanks that they were finally able to return home alive, to reunite with families, relatives, and anxiously waiting cherished friends. Hardly a soul was aware that their return home was possible in large part because of the courage, tenacity, and perseverance of three brave men who appealed directly to General Douglas MacArthur. He in turn ordered the dispatch of rescue ships to the little-known Manchurian Port of Koroto.

Primary Sources: Maruyama's and Musashi's Books

While the story related here is about the selflessness, doggedness, and bravery demonstrated equally by all three men, the main character of this narration is Kunio Maruyama. There are several reasons why the author focuses on Maruyama in the following pages: First, he wrote a book (*Why Was Koroto Opened*, Tokyo: Nagata Shobo), published in 1970, that detailed for the first time the exploits of the three men, and this author relies heavily on that book for facts, quotes, and episodes.[1]

Second, Maruyama was the originator and organizer of the audacious plan to escape from Manchuria, and he recruited Shinpo and Musashi to be accomplices in that extremely risky undertaking. Third, while the role of each of the three men was equally important and critical to the overall success of their heroic mission, Maruyama acted as the unofficial spokesman for the group. Moreover, his English-speaking ability was crucial to opening many doors, including that of GHQ, and he ultimately prevailed on General MacArthur to order the dispatch of repatriation ships to Manchuria. As a final reason, he was this author's father.

Masamichi Musashi, who is the only one of the three men alive at the time of this writing, also wrote a book in Japanese several years ago from his own perspectives about the undertaking of the three brave men (*The Dawning of Asia—Crossing the Lines of Death*, Tokyo: Jiyusha, 2000). Musashi went back from Japan to Manchuria in May 1946 on the first repatriation ship, to help deliver vital documents and pharmaceutical supplies to Japanese associations throughout Manchuria and to assist in organizing the daunting task of repatriation. It was thanks in great part to Musashi that Japanese residents in Manchuria (not under direct Soviet control) were able to make the journey from throughout Manchuria in an orderly manner to the Port of Koroto on Bohai Bay to board the waiting repatriation ships. During that endeavor, he endured a horrific ordeal when he was arrested by the Nationalist army as a spy, incarcerated, and tortured for seventy days before he was finally released.

Major Entities Crucial to the Success of the Repatriation Effort

There were three major entities that had critical roles in allowing the three men to accomplish so miraculously the mission to rescue 1.7 million Japanese from Soviet control in the now extinct empire of Manchuria. One was General MacArthur and his GHQ staff, United States military officers and men engaged in carrying out the Allied occupation policies following Japan's defeat. No other entity, including the defeated and helpless Japanese government, had the resources to carry out the massive operation to return so many people to Japanese soil.

The Nationalist Chinese forces under the command of Generalissimo Chiang Kai-shek were another major player. When the three men were working up the plan to escape, it was the staff of the underground Nationalist Chinese army that had quietly and secretly advanced into the Soviet- and Communist Chinese-controlled region of Shenyang who collaborated in the plot of the three Japanese. The Nationalist Chinese provided vital documents to the three men, thereby allowing them safe passage into China. The underground headquarters even provided two Nationalist officers disguised as civilians to act as escorts for them.

Finally, the Catholic Church's Maryknoll Mission in Dalian under the leadership of American bishop Raymond Lane lent immeasurable help in the escape, not only by providing documents and letters that proved invaluable in Japan but also by taking the families of Shinpo and Maruyama under its wing and providing protection when the three men made their escape. (If the Soviets or Communist Chinese had discovered that someone had escaped to Japan and that their families still remained in Manchuria, the retaliation against the families undoubtedly would have been deadly.) The help from Maryknoll and the Catholic Church continued on in Japan through invaluable help from Father (later Bishop) Patrick James Byrne of Kyoto and the papal emissary in Japan, Archbishop Paul Marella, who both lent their considerable prestige and assistance in urging GHQ and MacArthur to take necessary action to commence repatriation.

The Unsung Heroine

Throughout this book, this author (the third of four siblings who remained in Manchuria with their mother while their father escaped to Japan) will refer to his own father as *Maruyama* or *Kunio* in order to keep the narration relatively impersonal. In Japanese culture (from which this author derives originally), one should never refer to one's parents simply by name; they are always referred to by title (e.g., "my father," "my mother," "Dad," "Mom"). However, the reader is requested to realize that no impudence or disrespect is meant by using simply their first or last name. This author has the greatest respect, admiration, and love for both his parents, now deceased.

Perhaps the unsung hero, or heroine in this case, was Kunio's wife, Mary Mariko Maruyama. When Kunio began formulating his plans to flee the clutches of the Soviet bear, his wife was the only living person to whom he could confide. The mother of four young boys, she was the only person in the world who shared his secrets and gave him courage, suppressing her own fears and worries for what her husband was about to undertake.

Mary, a Seattle-born American citizen, had met and married Kunio while he was a graduate student in the United States. Because Mary was an American, the four Maruyama boys were also American citizens. When Kunio departed on his secret mission to Japan, it would be months before she would find out if Kunio and his companions had succeeded in their escape. As the author and his siblings like to say, "Dad saved 1.7 million Japanese; Mom saved the four of us."

The Author's Motives in Writing the Book

While the intent of this book is to inform the readers about three courageous Japanese men who risked their lives on behalf of their fellow countrymen in a unique chain of events probably unknown to most readers, it is the author's hope that this account will enable readers to appreciate the humanitarian and heroic roles played by General Douglas MacArthur and his staff at GHQ, by the Maryknoll Mission as well as the Catholic Church itself, and by the Nationalist army of Chiang Kai-shek.

The author feels that a gesture of gratitude to the three men by the emperor of Japan, even today, is long overdue and would represent the Japanese nation's sincere gratitude for the safe return of so many of her citizens who went to Manchuria, unwittingly believing they were acting out of patriotism. Such a gesture would also honor those thousands of Japanese souls who never returned from the land of the Manchus, to forever become a part of the red soil of a land with beautiful summers and cruel winters, a land which in the end meted out terrible punishment to those unwelcome visitors from the Land of the Rising Sun, who, after all, were only obeying the wishes of their living god, Emperor Hirohito.

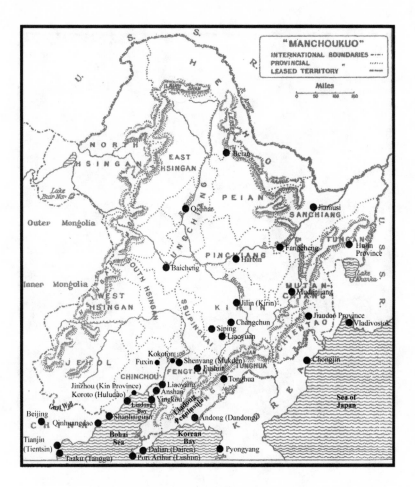

Map of Manchuria (Manchukuo)

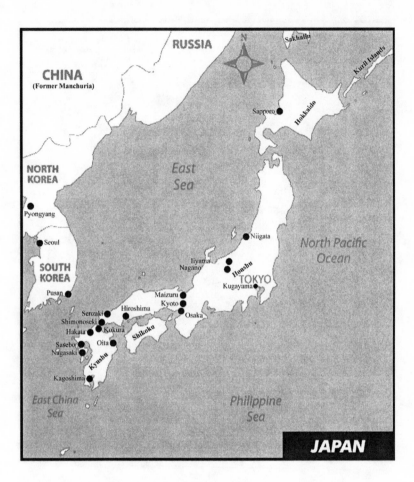

Map of Japan

Chapter 1

The Battle against a Discriminatory Act

The Immigration Act of 1924

Kunio Maruyama was born on June 28 in the thirty-sixth year of the Meiji emperor (1903) in the mountainous district of Tomikura (now called Iiyama) in Yanagihara Village in Nagano Prefecture, about 150 miles northwest of Tokyo. From early in his youth, he loved to study, learn, and read books. He left home after high school to attend Meiji University in Tokyo and graduated from its undergraduate law department. He wasted no time in continuing his education, crossing the Pacific Ocean to arrive in the United States at Seattle, Washington, in 1930. There he enrolled at the University of Puget Sound in Tacoma to pursue a BA in political science and economics.

Several years before Maruyama departed Japan, the United States Congress had passed the Immigration Act of 1924 which contained a provision banning future immigration of Japanese to the United States. Although President Coolidge tried to postpone the exclusion provision for two years, congressional sentiment resulted in rejecting the delay. The act was signed into law by Coolidge on May 26, 1924, even though the president deplored the discriminatory provision contained in it.[1] Due mainly to the paranoia of farmers in California, who feared that the success of hardworking Japanese immigrant farmers would eventually have an adverse effect on American farms and farmers, pressure was brought to bear upon congress to pass the legislation that prohibited immigration from Japan. Among other reasons for the law, it was deemed that Japanese culture was "unassimilable" into American culture.

This law had an enormous and shocking impact on the Japanese people. Only the year before, when Japan suffered catastrophic damage as a result of the Great Kanto Earthquake, it was the United States of America that came to Japan's rescue with unprecedented financial and material relief. Never had U.S.–Japan relations been better. The Japanese people were therefore at a loss to comprehend the unexpected slap in the face by the nation which they had come to admire so greatly, toward which they had felt such gratitude. The law remained on the books until Lyndon Johnson's administration (1965).

The anti-Japanese immigration act had a profound and adverse effect on exchange students from Japan studying in various parts of the United States. They were not allowed to work, even part-time, while studying in America. All money for their tuition, board, living expenses, books, and other necessities had to be sent from Japan. In fact, when Maruyama received his visa to study in the United States, he purchased the more costly second-class passage (which he could ill afford, but at least it was not as expensive as a first-class ticket) on the ship that brought him to America. A Japanese student with the more expensive second-class ticket was less likely to draw the unwanted attention of U.S. immigration officials than a student with a third-class ticket who might be refused entry if the officials felt the student was not carrying enough money to sustain him until more money arrived from Japan.

Since all overseas mail, parcels, and packages in those days were carried by ships, delays in delivery, including money from home, were common. Immigration agents frequently exercised the right to check up on Japanese students to ascertain if they had sufficient deposits in the bank. While in the state of Washington, Maruyama himself witnessed several occasions of injustice inflicted upon other Japanese exchange students. The immigration law was vigorously enforced against Japanese students who were required to register to prove to authorities that they indeed were receiving their money from their homeland and not from working in America. Immigration officials scrutinized a few of Maruyama's acquaintances between the time their money ran out and the next delivery. They were arrested and deported under the discriminatory 1924 law. No amount of reasoning to explain that money had been delayed because ships did not arrive from Japan on time was accepted as excuses by immigration officials.

To a student from Japan studying abroad, there was no humiliation and loss of face worse than to be forcibly deported back to Japan. His life was forever ruined (and most Japanese exchange students in those days were men). Those who went to study abroad in those days were the absolute "cream of the crop" among Japanese students; most became the future political, business, and academic leaders of Japan. A deported student often could not even face his own parents upon returning to Japan. The shame was so great that he dared not face his friends and mentors who had helped him to get the opportunity to study in the United States. Some students even committed suicide in despair.

Unable to silently stand by witnessing these injustices, Maruyama decided to move to the center of power of the United States to work on righting the wrongs he had witnessed. Therefore, upon graduating with a BA from the University of Puget Sound in 1934, he moved to Washington, DC, and

3

he enrolled at George Washington University to continue his studies as a graduate student.

This would, of course, not be the only time that Maruyama would personally feel the need and the calling to do something about an injustice. He loved to read books, particularly in English, and a book that had a most profound influence on his life was Sir Thomas More's *Utopia,* which the later-to-be-canonized Catholic saint wrote in 1516. Maruyama, a Buddhist, took Saint Thomas More's philosophy to heart: throughout his life, he always sought Utopia, which he understood to be an ideal place, a place of perfection that would never exist in this world.

Maruyama wrote an autobiographical book entitled *Aiming at Utopia* in 1970 in which he wrote that "according to a person's circumstance, each individual's Utopia is born. Based on this point, therefore, Utopia is a dream that everyone carries within his bosom, and all people aim for Utopia."[2] Maruyama, much like Don Quixote, could never turn a blind eye when he saw the need to aim for Utopia, to right an injustice. This personal characteristic would manifest itself time and again, but never as dramatically as in the years following the end of World War II.

Founding the Nipponese Student League of America

Upon moving to Washington, DC, and enrolling at George Washington University, Maruyama formed the first ever nationwide association of Japanese students studying in the United States. Called the Nipponese Student League of America, the organization had membership and support not only of Japanese students throughout the United States, but of many non-student Japanese as well as of Japanese-Americans living in the United States who had been seeking ways to raise their voices against the discriminatory law. While combating the Immigration Act of 1924, the Nipponese Student League also served as a support organization for all Japanese students

4

studying in the United States, and Maruyama served as the equivalent of its first executive director. A prominent member of the association was Kenzaburo Hara, who remained one of Maruyama's closest life-long friends. He later became one of the longest-serving members of Japan's parliament and served as Minister of Labor in the 1970s.

Maruyama's (and the Nipponese Student League's) primary objective was to raise awareness among those in authority about the injustice and discrimination that Japanese students were facing daily from the discriminatory act of 1924. Thus, he began a campaign of meeting with as many United States congressmen and senators as possible. Ultimately, he wanted to speak directly with the Secretary of Labor under whose jurisdiction all immigration issues fell. His first meeting was with Senator Elbert Thomas of Utah who had taught for five months in Japan and whose daughter (she was born in Japan) had been given the name Chiyoko. From the outset, the senator had denounced the discriminatory act as "an idiotic and evil act." Needless to say, Senator Thomas was most sympathetic to Maruyama's viewpoint. Others he met with were the Who's Who of the United States Congress of that time, including Senator Hiram Johnson of California, who had tremendous respect for the Japanese and said "I would not be able to eat fresh vegetables every day were it not for the Japanese farmers in California"; Louisiana's Senator Huey Long, though he expressed no great knowledge or interest in U.S.–Japan affairs, he nevertheless considered the Japanese an outstanding people; Senator William King of California, who was more pro-Chinese than pro-Japanese but felt that the act could eventually spill over to discriminate against Chinese as well and thus was sympathetic to Maruyama's entreaties; Representative Virginia Jenckes of Indiana, a great supporter of students from abroad who was against the act (she later arranged for Maruyama's meeting with Secretary of Labor Frances Perkins); and many others. In all, Maruyama personally met with twenty-three senators and congressmen to alert them about the unfair and sad consequences brought about by the anti-Japanese immigration act.

One of the stories that Maruyama told the lawmakers he met usually drew an appreciative chuckle. He said that Japan owed much to the United States of America, mainly because Commodore Matthew Perry forcibly opened the closed doors of feudal Japan in 1853 that resulted in Japan joining the ranks of modern nations. However, America owed much to Japan as well. The reason was, he would explain, Christopher Columbus had read the adventures of Marco Polo, which related the wonders and riches of an island nation called Cipangu. (Marco Polo himself had never visited Cipangu, or Japan.) Determined to reach Cipangu, Columbus set out on his great adventure, only to take a wrong turn on the Atlantic and end up discovering America. That clearly demonstrates, concluded Maruyama, that Japan was the reason that America was discovered, and Americans should always be thankful to Japan, just as the Japanese are thankful to America for sending Perry.

In all his meetings with the many "movers and shakers" of the United States, the one thing that impressed Maruyama the most was that each received him (a mere graduate exchange student from Japan) cordially, politely, and without affectation, so unlike most Japanese politicians and men of influence who usually made known their importance.

The Meeting with Madame Secretary

One day, a phone call came from Congresswoman Jenckes' secretary to summon Maruyama to the legislator's office. He was informed by the congresswoman that Frances Perkins, U.S. Secretary of Labor, would see him on October 3, 1934. (Secretary of Labor Frances Perkins, the first woman ever to be appointed as a Cabinet member, was one of the most trusted advisors to President Franklin Roosevelt. She remained in her post throughout Roosevelt's long tenure as president and on into Truman's administration. She died at age eighty-three in 1965.)

When Maruyama arrived at Secretary Perkins's office at the appointed time, she confirmed in reply to his first question that she could allow one hour for the meeting. Having carefully prepared for this meeting, Maruyama described the injustice of the law and how a Japanese student had to have almost two thousand dollars in the bank merely as security to continue studying without fear of deportation. At the end of this narration, Secretary Perkins expressed surprise about the consequences of the law and apologized for her ignorance regarding the vigor with which her immigration officials were applying the law. On the spot, she called in several senior immigration officers to her office while Maruyama was still there and confirmed the truths of Maruyama's allegations.

After the officials had departed, Frances Perkins turned to Maruyama and said, "Mr. Maruyama, as a result of your detailed and clear explanations, I have been enlightened. From here on, I will make sure that we fully understand the intent of the immigration law and I will make sure all concerned agencies also fully understand. I intend to deal with this properly."[3] After spending a few more relaxed and pleasant minutes conversing socially about Japanese woodblock prints (which fascinated the secretary), the two parted amicably, exchanging firm handshakes and smiles. Again, Maruyama thought, "If only Japanese executives could be so honest and humble!" From that time on, Maruyama notes, there were no cases of unfair harassment and deportation of Japanese students enrolled in the United States.

Mary Takeda Takes Charge

While still a student at the University of Puget Sound in Tacoma, Washington, Maruyama met an attractive young

Nisei (second generation Japanese-American) girl named Mary Mariko Takeda. Mary was born in Seattle in 1911, the daughter of Seijuro Takeda, who emigrated to the United States from Japan's Yamaguchi Prefecture at age fifteen and was the founder of the first Japanese language newspaper in Seattle. Mary had gone to Japan during her youth and attended Hofu Girls High School in Yamaguchi Prefecture, the home of her parents. Upon her return, she graduated from Broadway High School in Seattle, and then enrolled at the University of Washington where she began her studies in home economics. While a coed, she taught Japanese at the Maryknoll School in Seattle, where her lifelong relationship with the Catholic Church, and Maryknoll in particular, began. (Mary later converted to Catholicism while in Manchuria, while Kunio stayed a Buddhist until shortly before he died, when he also was baptized a Catholic.)

Maruyama and Mary met during a speech event sponsored by Japanese students studying in the western United States. Maruyama fell in love with this intelligent and vivacious girl, and the two became engaged just before he departed for Washington, DC. She remained in Seattle to finish her undergraduate studies while he went east.

Maruyama's life as a student in Washington, DC, was indeed a hectic one. Living alone in an apartment, he tried his best to balance his studies with his activities in the causes of the Nipponese Student League of America. Never much of a cook and always busy, he often lived for days just on milk and ice cream, a diet on which he lost much weight. By chance, a friend of Mary Takeda visited Maruyama at his apartment and witnessed the unhealthy way Maruyama lived. The friend returned to Seattle and reported to Mary that "Maruyama is completely underweight due to overwork so that I fear that his health will be endangered if he keeps going the way he is." For a brief time, Mary worried greatly. Soon, however, she dropped out of her university courses and headed straight for Washington,

DC, to take charge of Maruyama's health. Not only did she make sure he ate well, she became his full-time assistant as she took over all his typing, correspondence, and other office work. Maruyama was now able to concentrate wholly on his studies and his activities in the student league. In effect, Mary became the executive secretary for the Nipponese Student League of America. Thanks to Mary, whom he married shortly thereafter (March 28, 1935), he completed and turned in an outstanding master's thesis to George Washington University.

Maruyama stayed on as de facto leader of the Nipponese Student League of America until 1936, when he graduated from George Washington University with an MA in political science and then enrolled at Columbia University in New York to continue his studies. Since no further problems had been encountered by Japanese students studying in the United States after his meeting with Secretary of Labor Frances Perkins who promised there would be reform, Maruyama handed over his leadership position in the student organization to others upon his transfer to New York. He continued his studies at Columbia University until September of 1937.

A Tour of Europe

It had always been in Maruyama's plan to go on a journey to Europe and visit several countries as an important element of his education. Thus, he bade farewell to his bride, who was now pregnant with their first child, and set out alone on his journey to Europe while Mary traveled to Los Angeles to await the birth of their first son, whom they named Robert.

After a yearlong journey through many European countries, Maruyama returned to Japan in 1938 to be reunited with his parents, older brother Tadao, and younger brother Katsuei, who all still lived in Nagano, Maruyama's birthplace. Tragically, his youngest brother Kiyoshi had died while Maruyama was studying in the United States. While Kiyoshi lay in bed during his long illness, he often talked to those who came to see him at his bedside about his older brother Kunio's activities in the United States, fighting for justice in the struggle against the Immigration Act of 1924. When Maruyama finally visited Kiyoshi's grave, he silently and tearfully reported to his younger brother about his success in bringing about just treatment for Japanese students in the United States.

Shortly after his family visit in Nagano, Maruyama returned to Tokyo to welcome his wife and his new son Robert to Japan. They were now ready to start a new life. But sadly, the atmosphere in Japan was ominous: the Japanese government seemed to have lost all control over its military, particularly in Manchuria. Anyone returning from the United States, especially one with an American wife, came under the close scrutiny of the military. The Maruyama couple and their infant son were embarking on a new family life in a nation where basic freedom had all but completely disappeared.

(Note: On October 3, 1965, President Lyndon Johnson signed a new law under the gaze of the Statue of Liberty that finally abolished the Immigration Act of 1924. Under the new law, immigration was no longer to be based on one's country of origin. Immigration was given preference to keeping the families of Americans together and preference was also given to immigrants who possessed skills vital to the United States. After forty-one years, in Kunio Maruyama's view, Utopia had finally arrived!)

Kunio and Mary Maruyama pose for a photo shortly after Kunio ended
his studies at Columbia University (1937). Kunio soon departed on a
yearlong tour of Europe, leaving his now pregnant wife in Los Angeles
where she gave birth to their first child, Robert. They reunited in Japan
the following year. (Kunio Maruyama Collection)

Chapter 2

Darkness Falls on Manchuria

Japan under Total Military Rule

Maruyama had always dreamed that, after his studies in the United States, he would return to Japan and enter the life of an academic. In fact, his mentors and advisors in Japan, who gave him counsel before he set off for the United States in 1930, had high hopes that he would return to take up the mantle of teaching, and Maruyama had every intention of repaying the kindness to his professors by teaching at his alma mater, Meiji University. However, Japan's political mood made him hesitate.

The Japanese military had initiated its plan to eventually dominate China by causing problems in Manchuria. These actions gave the all-but-autonomous Japanese power in the region, the Japanese Imperial Army (which was known as the Kwantung Army), the excuse to usurp and exercise complete control. In 1932, a puppet government was set up by Japan that installed the last emperor of China, Pu Yi, as the emperor of Manchuria, which the Japanese renamed "Manchukuo."

The Lytton Commission, appointed by the League of Nations, investigated and found Japan to be at fault for military excesses in Manchuria. As a result of the commission's rebuke in 1933, Japan withdrew from the League of Nations. The following year, the Amau Doctrine (sometimes referred to as the "Asiatic Monroe Doctrine") was issued by the Japanese Foreign Ministry. It stated that Japan would take full responsibility for peace in East Asia and would act as overseer of China's relations with Western powers. As the Kwantung Army became increasingly bold in its military engagements in Manchuria against the Chinese, the people of Japan were whipped into a frenzy of patriotism and nationalism with each military success and resented the international community, which criticized the actions of their military.

Within the Japanese army itself, incidents of assassinations and attempted coups by radical officers became frequent, with the "February 26 Incident" representing the most notable of these crises. On February 26, 1936, an army division of nearly 1,400 men followed the leadership of a group of radical officers in a bloody coup attempt with intent to capture the Japanese government to "safeguard the Fatherland by killing all those responsible for impeding the Showa Restoration and slurring the Imperial prestige." For three days, the rebellious troops occupied the police headquarters, the general staff headquarters of the War Ministry, and the Diet building. Eventually, the attempted coup was put down, but the February 26 Incident was a serious and ominous sign that the military was spinning out of control.[1] On the international front, Japan signed an anti-Communist pact with Hitler's Germany in November 1936, that pledged cooperation in defending against the spread of Soviet influence. In reality, this pact was looked upon by the world as a military alliance and as the creation of a sphere of Japanese influence in the western Pacific and the East Indies.[2] From there, things got worse for democracy in Japan.

This was the atmosphere that awaited Maruyama on his return to Japan. He knew that he carried the label of a "liberalist" (one who believed in democracy and freedom) upon his return

13

from America. He did not mind that label. In fact, he was proud of it since he had always believed in the inherent human freedoms and firmly opposed despotism and totalitarianism that suppressed an individual's will or ignored a person's character. Those were Maruyama's core beliefs. But the Japan of 1936 was ruled by the might of the military, which emphasized a national clarity of theory based on nonscientific ideology. The military imposed a totalitarian ideology that was identical to that of Germany and Italy.

To teach in such a climate meant that he would have to suppress his thoughts and pay blind obedience to the nationalistic ideology. Maruyama's conscience and character would simply not have allowed him to stand in a university classroom full of students and adhere blindly to military dictates. He simply could not divorce himself from democratic principles to comply with popular views. He decided to forgo his dream of teaching for the time being and seek another means of living.

As a result of discussions with and recommendations from many of his mentors during his university days, he became an employee of Rokuho Shokai Company, an international trading firm. In those days, as Japan became increasingly isolated from the West, and in particular from the United States, importing goods from foreign countries became extremely difficult. Although he was concerned about the direction Japan was taking politically and diplomatically, he did feel a need to be in a position where he could be useful to Japan and work to the utmost on behalf of the Japanese people. Using his skills in English, he immersed himself in commerce and busied himself primarily in writing letters to foreign businesses day after day in an attempt to bring into Japan needed merchandise. However, the commercial trade industry for Japan shrank dramatically day by day and Maruyama felt as if he were on a sinking ship.

Working in Anshan, Manchuria

One day, a close friend from his Meiji University days (in Japan, relationships built up during college days remain important throughout one's life) happened to visit Tokyo and came to see Maruyama. Shozo Kubota, also a native of Nagano Prefecture, was then the managing director of Showa Steel Manufacturing Company, a major steel firm whose head office was located in Anshan, Manchuria, with a branch office in Tokyo. As talk turned to Maruyama's chosen career in the trade industry, Kubota said, "Maruyama-san, you did the right thing in not taking up the whip as an educator, since the times are not right. But foreign trade such as you are presently involved with is now in its death throes, and I predict you will not be able to accomplish anything significant for quite some time. Whatever you do, you must always stay alert to the winds of change. My suggestion to you is that you should go to Manchuria rather than continue to struggle in Japan. Why not go to Manchuria and breathe in the fresh air of the continent and find the opportunities to continue your studies?"[3] Never having considered such an idea, Maruyama was intrigued by the suggestion.

Manchuria was regarded by most Japanese during those times as a land of great opportunity and a place to contribute patriotically to Japan's national goals. Maruyama began to seriously mull over the idea of working in the northern Chinese territory that had become so vital to Japan's national goals. For years, government propaganda had been encouraging Japanese immigration into Manchuria, to cultivate its land and to populate its territories. Maruyama made a visit to another college-era friend, Eiichi Nakamura, from whom Maruyama had often sought advice even while he was studying in the United States. By coincidence, Nakamura at that time happened to be the secretary to the executive director of Kubota's very same Showa Steel Manufacturing Company. Nakamura greeted his old friend with warmth and kindness and encouraged Maruyama to seek employment with Showa Steel. With a promise from Nakamura that he would find a position for Maruyama that would fully take advantage of his bilingual talent, Maruyama bade Nakamura adieu and entrusted his future to his old friend. A few weeks later, Maruyama became an employee of Showa Steel Manufacturing Company.

For some time, although he visited his employer's head office in Manchuria from time to time beginning in 1939, Maruyama worked mainly in the Tokyo office. The Tokyo office was engaged in a major construction project partnered with an American company in Chicago that specialized in construction technologies. With the outbreak of World War II, the project came to an abrupt halt as relations with the American company were terminated. Maruyama was then transferred to the head office at Anshan, an industrial center located about 180 miles northwest of Dalian, site of Port Arthur and the largest city in Manchuria. Maruyama was placed in charge of conducting economic research on all the nations Showa Steel dealt with and was also made the company's public information officer. Additionally, "breathing in the fresh air of the continent" as Kubota had suggested, he was assigned duties as an instructor for company employees at its education facility, which gave him the opportunity to indulge his most cherished passion, teaching.

Kunio (sitting in second row, fourth from right) and his fellow employees at Showa Steel Manufacturing Company in Anshan, Manchuria around 1943. In spite of the ominous large cannon guarding the region, life was calm in Manchuria as Japanese news reports announced victory after victory for the glorious Imperial Army throughout Asia. (Kunio Maruyama Collection)

Manchuria under Japanese Occupation and Rule

It may be useful at this time to explain more fully the history of Japanese occupation of Manchuria, the role it played in Japan's march toward World War II, and why so many Japanese were in Manchuria at the time of Japan's surrender on August 15, 1945.

Until the arrival in 1853 of Commodore Matthew Perry and his fleet of "Black Ships" into the Bay of Edo (as Tokyo was then called), Japan had been a completely isolated, feudal samurai nation whose laws forbade its government and citizens from carrying on foreign exchange; punishment for violating those laws was death. (The only exception for foreign trade was at a tiny island off Nagasaki in southern Japan where the Dutch and Chinese were allowed to engage in limited commercial exchange.) The arrival of Perry in the Land of the Rising Sun caused an upheaval in the closed nation that changed her forever, often accompanied by violence and assassinations. It resulted in the toppling of the Shogun and abolition of the feudal system of government, the restoration of Emperor Meiji as the head of the land, the end of the samurai class, and declaration of relative equality and freedom for all Japanese. Unable to resist the many trade and diplomatic concessions that were forced, initially by Perry, then followed by other Western countries, upon the still backward nation of Japan, the island nation quickly realized that, among other considerations, one critical way to gain equal status with the west was to build up its military. Under the slogan *"fukoku kyohei"* ("prosperous nation, strong military"), Japan began as early as 1873 to earnestly strengthen its military.

In 1894, Japan declared war on China and took possession of northern China's (Manchuria's) Liaodong Peninsula, including Port Arthur. However, pressure from Russia, Germany, and France forced Japan to cede the peninsula back to China. In 1904, Japan declared war on Russia, and after two years of savage warfare, Japan emerged as the first Asian country to defeat a European nation. Once again, Port Arthur returned to Japanese control. The Treaty of Portsmouth, brokered by President Theodore Roosevelt and signed in Portsmouth, New Hampshire, by Japanese and Russian diplomats on September 1, 1905, formally ended the Russo-Japanese War.

Under the treaty, the Russians conceded to Japan the right to occupy the Kwantung Territory on the southern tip of Liaodong, along with the right to operate a portion of the Russian-built Chinese Eastern Railway running from Port Arthur to Changchun. The Japanese promptly renamed it the South Manchurian Railway. This gave Japan the right to exercise administrative and jurisdictional control over all territories adjacent to the railroad tracks. The Japanese created the Kwantung Army, a part of the Imperial Army, to carry out all the multiple responsibilities ceded by Russia under the Portsmouth Treaty and to defend all the new rights in Manchuria. To operate the railway, the South Manchurian Railway Company was established as both a commercial company and an agency of the Japanese government.

In a short time, the colonization and commercializing efforts of the South Manchurian Railway Company made the Kwantung Territory a booming success as the region became the most industrialized part of continental Asia. The railroads were vastly improved and expanded, modern express train services were installed, hotels and other commercial services were built near stations on the rail system, and agricultural and industrial enterprises (including soybean production, coal mines and ironworks, petroleum refineries, electric power plants, and other major undertakings) were initiated or subsidized by the South Manchurian Railway Company. Dalian became one of the world's leading and most modern ports.

At the same time, investments in schools, parks, hospitals, and libraries were not neglected. Japanese from the homeland began populating the area so that the number of Japanese in southern Manchuria grew from 25,000 in 1907 to 220,000 in 1930, and there was no end in sight to the boom.[4] By 1930, Japan's Kwantung Army numbered ten thousand personnel.

In Japan, meanwhile, one fanatical army lieutenant colonel named Kanji Ishiwara believed that a clash was inevitable between the United States, which had emerged across the Pacific to become the most powerful nation among Western societies, and Japan, which was emerging as the undisputed leader of Asian civilization. Lieutenant Colonel Ishiwara managed to have himself transferred from Tokyo to Manchuria to serve as part of the Kwantung Army. Espousing the belief that it was necessary for Japan to control and harness all the natural resources that lay in Manchuria and Inner Mongolia in preparation for a decisive and final war against the United States and the Soviet Union, Ishiwara and his allies took matters into their own hands to start the process, which many believe was the match that lit the fuse leading Japan into the catastrophic war in China and the Pacific, which the Japanese eventually called the Greater East Asia War. On September 18, 1931, Ishiwara and a group of fellow officers blew up a railway line near Mukden (now Shenyang) to make it appear as if the Chinese were responsible for the act. This created a convenient pretext for the Kwantung Army to intervene. What followed was an eruption of violence by the Japanese military in Manchuria that the Tokyo government could not control.

The Manchurian Incident, as the event came be known, resulted in the domination and occupation of all of Manchuria by the Kwantung Army. The people of Japan, who had been hungering for good news after years of economic depression and collectively had been harboring an inferiority complex among the races of the world, began hearing nothing but glorious news of victory after victory by the Kwantung Army. The public sentiment was such that the Japanese government was forced to meekly endorse the unsanctioned adventures of its army in Manchuria. Thus, when the Lytton Commission appointed by the League of Nations condemned the military excesses by the Japanese army in Manchuria, Japan withdrew from the League of Nations in 1933.

Control of Manchuria gave the Japanese military the opportunity to develop the territory into a vital industrialized state and to make it a testing ground where the Japanese military experimented with its concept for a planned economy. With its abundance of natural resources (coal, steel, petroleum, etc.) and fertile land, Manchuria was the new frontier for Japan. On March 1, 1932, after the Kwantung Army occupied most of southwestern Manchuria, including Harbin, an independent nation called Manchukuo was created by Japan. The last emperor of China, Henry Pu Yi, was placed as head of state and was crowned the Emperor of Manchukuo in 1934. In reality,

Pu Yi had very little power, and Manchukuo was nothing more than a puppet state of Japan.

The real power rested in the hands of the commander of the Kwantung Army, who was concurrently the Japanese Ambassador to Manchukuo and ruler of the new nation from behind the scenes. Between 1930 and 1939, the number of military personnel in the Kwantung Army grew from 10,000 to 270,000, a formidable force consisting of 9 divisions, 560 aircraft, and 200 tanks.[5] The Japanese army in Manchuria operated all but autonomously, often ignoring Tokyo's (and occasionally even the Japanese emperor's) directives. With the outbreak of World War II, major cities along the South Manchurian Railway, from the Harbin region southward to Fushun, Shenyang (Mukden), Anshan, and the port area of Dalian, were developed into a huge complex of coal, petroleum, metallurgical, and chemical enterprises.

Chapter 3

Life under Soviet Occupation

War Hits Close to Home

Maruyama's employer, Showa Steel Manufacturing Company, was one of those industrial entities that was a major player supporting the war efforts of Japan. As war progressed and Japan's victories began turning to defeats, life in Tokyo became difficult for the ordinary citizen as everything was rationed and food became scarce, Allied bombings increased, and the Japanese military took away the most basic freedoms from its citizens. Life in Manchuria, in contrast, was not too bad. Food was plentiful, necessities such as fuel to heat homes were not rationed, the life of the average Japanese was relatively comfortable, and fear of Allied bombings was not a concern—until July 29, 1944.

For the first time in their lives, Japanese (and Chinese) in the industrial city of Anshan experienced what had become an all-too-frequent nightmare in Japan. Just past noon on that July day, when the sun was burning hot, Maruyama happened to look up at the blue sky over Anshan to see a formation of silver airplanes, their wings gleaming, heading toward his company's factory complex. It was a formation of more than ten American

B-29 bombers. Just then, the eerie sirens of the factory began wailing loudly, and everyone around Maruyama looked up, visibly nervous and afraid.

"How bold they look, all lined up in a perfect and elegant formation," Maruyama thought, mesmerized by the oncoming silver wings. But as the planes flew over the Showa Steel Manufacturing compound, they dropped their bombs, all aimed at the factories and, thought Maruyama, at him. As he scrambled for cover, one of the bombs dropped only a few yards away (or so it seemed). The blast hurled him some thirty feet, and he crashed to the ground hard, dazed but unhurt. The American planes dropped wave after wave of bombs in just a few minutes, and the factory area was soon enveloped in black smoke and fierce fire. Heartrending screams could be heard amid the dark smoke, which made it impossible to pinpoint their sources.

About the time the American planes began dropping their bombs, several fighters of the Kwantung Army based in Anshan appeared in the sky and began pursuing the bombers. But as the B-29s flew away, seemingly at leisure, after finishing their deadly mission, the pursuing fighters with the bright red rising sun emblazoned on their sides began to fall behind with each passing second. The gap between the large bombers and the Japanese fighters widened quickly as thousands of Japanese and Manchurians watched the drama. There was a collective sigh of exasperation as those on the ground looked on, some mumbling, "What? Can't catch up?" At that instant, the morale of the Japanese people plummeted as they realized the helplessness of the Japanese army, whose propaganda had made them out to be invincible.

From that day on, the attitude of ordinary Chinese toward the Japanese in Manchuria changed noticeably. Up to then, whenever a Chinese met a Japanese soldier on the streets of Anshan, the Chinese would give the soldier a snappy salute and show him the utmost respect. After that day, however, no

Chinese saluted a Japanese soldier. In fact, many showed open contempt toward Japanese soldiers, spitting on the street as they passed or purposely stepping on a soldier's foot on a bus.

The Japanese civilians in Manchuria, who had been fed constant propaganda regarding Japan's successes against her enemies and had come to believe in the invincibility of the Kwantung Army, suddenly became apprehensive. While most Japanese civilians had good relationships with ordinary Chinese in their daily lives, there were more than a few Japanese who had treated native Manchurians and Chinese as second-class citizens even in their own country. Many Chinese saw the Japanese simply as hostile occupiers, and the tables were about to turn on the unwelcome guests.

The Soviet Invasion of Manchuria

As Japan's army and navy began losing battle after battle to Allied forces in the Pacific in little-known places like the Gilbert and Marshall Islands, Saipan, Iwo Jima, and Okinawa, much of their military resources, both men and matériel, were diverted from the Kwantung Army in Manchuria to assist in those engagements. On the night of March 9, 1945, Allied B-29s burned and flattened Tokyo, killing more than 100,000 citizens in a single night.[1] With the unconditional surrender of Germany on May 7, 1945, the United States and her allies were now able to concentrate their efforts on defeating Japan.

Three months later, on August 6, a new weapon called an "atomic bomb" was dropped on the city of Hiroshima, completely destroying the city and obliterating the life of between 130,000 to 140,000 people in a flash. Three days later, a second atomic bomb was dropped on the city of Nagasaki. Finally, Japan had had enough, and Emperor Hirohito made an unprecedented announcement on the radio at noon on August 15, 1945, and called upon his subjects to "endure the unendurable" and accept defeat in order to "pave the way for a grand peace for all the future generations to come."[2] With that, Japan surrendered unconditionally to the Allied forces.

One week before the Japanese emperor's appeal to his subjects to fight no more, the Soviet Union invaded Manchuria shortly after midnight of August 8 with a massive force of more than one million soldiers, tanks, artillery, and planes after declaring war on Japan a few hours previously. Japan and the Soviet Union had signed a Soviet–Japanese Neutrality Pact on April 13, 1941, that pledged nonaggression against each other, and the pact was still in force when the Soviet Union formally declared war on Japan. The history of the Soviet Union, then and in countless later instances, has shown that they are a country that does not let treaties, promises, pacts, and ethics get in the way of ambition (to cite a few examples, witness the invasion into Hungary with one thousand tanks, brutally suppressing the Hungarian Revolution in November 1956; the invasion and internal meddling of Czechoslovakia in August 1968; or the Russian invasion of the Republic of Georgia on the eve of the opening ceremony of the 2008 Beijing Olympics). There was a good reason (at least to the Soviets) for this hasty attack on the Japanese in Manchuria and for declaring war on a country that was already in its death throes.

As the tide was taking an obvious turn for the worse for both Germany and Japan, the leaders of the "Big Three" nations, namely the United States, Great Britain, and the Soviet Union, met in a picturesque Crimean city on the Black Sea called Yalta in February 1945. U.S. President Franklin Roosevelt, British Prime Minister Winston Churchill, and Soviet Premier Josef Stalin met in what is known as the Yalta Conference to discuss plans for the future, on the assumption that Germany and Japan would soon fall. Much of what the three agreed to was kept secret at that time for political or military reasons and, in fact, was not fully disclosed until after 1947.

The Soviet Union had been amassing resounding military victories on European fronts in recent months, which gave

Stalin an influential voice in the agreements reached. One of the agreements was that the Soviet Union would enter the war against Japan within three months after Germany surrendered. In return, Stalin was promised that the Kuril Islands, the southern part of Sakhalin, and the railway rights in Manchuria would return to Soviet control. Another provision promised that the port at Dalian would be internationalized and that Port Arthur would be restored as a Russian naval base as it had been before the Russo–Japanese War of 1904–1905. (It should be noted that one party who was not consulted on these promises, made primarily by Roosevelt to Stalin, was China's Chiang Kai-shek. In fact, much of the territory and property that Roosevelt was bartering away at Yalta belonged to Chiang Kai-shek's China.[3])

In the months before the Soviet invasion of Manchuria, there was a flurry of contacts between Japan (through her ambassador to Moscow, Naotake Sato) and the Soviet Union to request the Soviet Union to intervene as mediator to bring about the end of the war with terms that would not be completely disastrous to Japan. In meetings and other communications with Soviet Foreign Minister Vyacheslav Molotov, the Soviet Union appeared never to seriously take into consideration Sato's appeals and offers, which originated from Japanese Foreign Minister Shigenori Togo. On April 5, 1945, the Soviets announced the abrogation of the neutrality treaty; when Sato met with Molotov on the matter, Molotov initially implied that the pact was no longer in effect, but later admitted that it was good for one more year. In any case, Japan was fully aware that the Soviet Union might enter the war against Japan at any time, at any place, but the Japanese military did nothing to prepare for that eventuality.[4] The Soviet Union, according to Maruyama's assessment, ignored all moral principles, breached an international treaty, and commenced war unilaterally.[5]

As Japanese soldiers in eastern Manchuria huddled against the falling rain on the evening of August 8, done with their duties for the day and content to keep dry, the massive Soviet attack began. Code-named "August Storm" and under the command of Marshal Aleksandr Mikhailovich Vasilevsky who commanded more than 1.5 million men, 3,704 tanks, and 1,852 self-propelled guns, the invasion began simultaneously from the east, west, and northwest of Manchuria. The Japanese Kwantung Army, under the command of General Otozo Yamada, theoretically numbered 713,000 men with an additional 280,000 men in southern Korea, Sakhalin, and the Kurils. An additional 170,000 men of the Manchukuoan Army supplemented the Kwantung Army. However, those Japanese numbers were completely misleading, since the bulk of its forces had been redeployed to various Pacific fronts during 1942–1945. In fact, the Kwantung Army was a mere shell of its former self. Tokyo, which had been aware of the possibility of imminent attack in Manchuria by the Soviets after the abrogation of the neutrality pact, alerted the Kwantung Army of only the "slight possibility of attack." The Japanese were taken completely by surprise, resulting in an almost complete rout by the Soviets in every sector.[6]

From the moment the Soviet Union declared war on Japan, the Japanese and Chinese in Manchuria, whether civilians or soldiers, were in mortal danger. Those Japanese living in Manchuria near the borders with the Soviet Union came under particularly heavy and deadly threat of Soviet gunfire. A belated order for mandatory evacuation was issued by the Kwantung Army to those Japanese residing in threatened areas. Families had no choice but to hastily pack what they could carry. With no reliable transport available, they sought refuge by making their way south, often on foot, with no definite destination in mind. They made their way toward southern Manchuria and North Korea, hoping to find regions populated by Japanese. Without adequate food, shelter, transportation, and knowledge of where they were headed, many of these refugees stumbled on until they perished from hunger, disease, cold, or fatigue before they could reach a destination. Many refugee groups were attacked by gangs of bandits and thugs and robbed of everything they owned, including the clothes on their backs. Women, in particular, were vulnerable to attacks by these bandits. Those suffering the most were infants and children whose parents could not console or feed them as they trekked in search of a refuge.

Because almost all men, particularly the young, had been hastily conscripted into the Kwantung Army in the waning days of the war, these groups of wandering refugees were almost exclusively composed of women, children, and the elderly. The Kwantung Army, which ordered the mass evacuation, was nowhere to be found to assist or guide the streaming Japanese refugees. The misery, hardship, pain, suffering, and deaths that often befall the innocent and the non-combatants during times of war were just beginning for the Japanese civilians in Manchuria. This was happening as the emperor announced Japan's unconditional surrender and the long war finally came to an end.

The First Encounter with the Invaders

Maruyama was, as always, working at the head office of Showa Steel Manufacturing in Anshan when the war ended. His immediate thought was the welfare of his family. What was the best strategy for getting them out of Manchuria, where the future was completely unknown and frightening to contemplate? His family consisted then of his wife Mary and four young boys, Robert (eight years old), Joseph (six), Paul (four), and Xavier (one), and a young female helper named Toki who had accompanied the Maruyamas from Japan and was like a member of the family.

On August 17, he departed Anshan by train for Shenyang and Changchun, the major cities of Manchuria north of Anshan on the South Manchurian Railway line, to scout out the best means of returning to Japan with his family. Upon reaching

Shenyang, which was about fifty miles north of Anshan, he had to purchase a new ticket to travel on to Changchun and await the next train, which was not scheduled to depart until the following day. After finding lodging at a hotel near Shenyang Station, he returned the next day about noon to the station to verify the departure time for the Changchun bound train. To his surprise, a large hand-made poster declaring "Train operation has ceased!" was posted at the entrance of the station. Much to his dismay, there were also about ten Soviet soldiers with guns standing guard at various points of the station.

These were the first invaders from the Soviet Union that Maruyama had seen, and he was shocked at their appearance. The uniforms of the soldiers were in terrible condition, hardly recognizable as uniforms. In fact, some did not even wear uniforms; they wore ragged shirts and trousers. Those in uniforms were in no better condition; tears and rips were visible everywhere. To Maruyama, they looked like gutter rats who had just crawled up from the ditches. Even after many years, when Maruyama reflected back to the days when he encountered his first Soviet soldiers, he always remembered the shabby and ragged-looking soldiers of the Soviet Union, many wearing unmatched pairs of shoes.

However, in two or three days, those same soldiers transformed themselves dramatically into elegant and stylish-looking gentlemen with new shirts and trousers and shoes that matched. Except for the guns they carried, one would not have known they were soldiers, since most were no longer in uniform. They had obviously raided Japanese and Manchurian private homes and helped themselves to whatever clothing they fancied. This was a phenomenon that happened everywhere throughout Manchuria.

Maruyama had to give up the idea of going to Changchun. At about 5:00 PM that day, there was a repeated radio announcement that declared, "Tomorrow morning, Soviet soldiers led by Major General Bitler will be advancing into Shenyang. All automobiles and trucks within the city must completely cease operation." It was obvious from the tone of the announcement that the Soviets would not harbor any disobedience to their directives. All hopes that Maruyama had of catching a train in any direction were completely dashed. Not only was safe passage to Japan a thing of the past, but traveling by train anywhere seemed impossible. Only a short time ago, he had been naively thinking that he would depart with his family for Dalian by train and try to find a ship bound for Japan from Port Arthur or else take the train from Shenyang east toward Andong, then cross the Yalu River into North Korea and find passage to Japan.

Realizing how naive he had been, Maruyama knew that if he wasted any more time in Shenyang, he would simply be bottled up and might not even be able to return home to Anshan. Fortunately his company had a branch office in Shenyang, and he immediately made contact to request a truck be made available for his return to Anshan. With ten other company employees who also urgently needed to go to Anshan, Maruyama boarded a truck that night to be driven back to Anshan. The ten passengers and the driver rode in silence, fearful of what awaited them in the night.

When they came to a bridge over a canal that crossed into Anshan, they saw Soviet soldiers with guns who appeared to be patrolling strategic points of the bridge. The soldier who was guarding the entry point that the truck had to drive through was sitting down on the bank and appeared to be taking a nap. Luckily, the soldier did not even challenge the truck. On the other side of the bridge was another lone Soviet soldier who appeared ready to stop them, but perhaps because he was alone and was reluctant to confront the truck by himself, he did not make any threatening gesture as the truck passed.

Though it was only a few minutes of tension, the passengers on the truck were extremely nervous and held their breath as the truck made its way across the bridge. Everyone was waiting for a shot to ring out. Fortunately, the truck safely reached

Anshan the next day at daybreak. Maruyama's family had been anxiously waiting for his return, since the news of General Bitler's arrival into Shenyang had been announced even in Anshan.

Shortly after Maruyama's safe return to Anshan, the city was effectively occupied by the advancing Soviet army and the Chinese Communist Army, which was called the Eighth Route Army. (In 1937, the Chinese Red Army was designated as the Eighth Route Army and had been nominally placed under Chiang Kai-shek's Nationalist command. However, in reality, the Eighth Route Army remained the Red Army under Mao Zedong, then engaged in a civil war against Chiang Kai-shek and his Nationalist government.[7])

Public Order is a Thing of the Past

With the presence of Soviet soldiers throughout Anshan, public safety became a critical issue, particularly for Japanese residents of the city. No woman dared walk out alone, day or night. Rape, even during daylight, became an almost common occurrence. Even men had to use extreme caution and made every effort to avoid running into Soviet soldiers who often hid around street corners looking for those they might hold up and rob of their possessions. They would point their guns at victims and demand everything in their pockets.

Female victims were lucky if they were merely robbed of their rings, purses, or ornamental hairpins. "The violence against Japanese women by Soviet soldiers," wrote Yasuo Wakatsuki in his well-documented book *The Record of Repatriation after the War*, "was, in one word, horrendous. Whether [the victim] was a girl of twelve or thirteen or an elderly grandmother nearing seventy, it mattered not whether the attack took place in front of other people or in broad daylight, or whether it took place in the snow. Women tried to disguise themselves as men by shaving their heads and rubbing black brush ink on their faces in their attempts to evade attacks; however, [the Soviet soldiers] would feel the breasts of each person and pull out those they determined were women."[8]

According to Wakatsuki, rapes by soldiers in the early days of the Soviet invasion of Manchuria could be divided into two categories: "unlawful rape" and "open rape." Both were rampant. In the first category, a lone Soviet soldier or perhaps a few soldiers would accost the unlucky victim in a relatively deserted place or by invading a home, avoiding detection by their comrades or superiors, aware that some kind of punishment or reprimand could befall them if they were caught in the act of rape. The victim might have the opportunity to prevent the rape, perhaps by screaming for help or running to a safe haven; in either case, the victim had the police and other authorities on her side to report the incident and perhaps seek justice.

In the second category, the attacks on women were carried out in public and open places, often in broad daylight, often by groups of soldiers, with absolutely no fear of any consequence, knowing that their actions were considered the rightful reward of their victory. No one, not even the police, could prevent the rape; anyone intervening was simply shot by the perpetrator. And there was absolutely no escape or recourse for the victim, except perhaps one: suicide. There is no record to show how many Japanese women took their own lives by consuming potassium cyanide (which most carried at all times) or by biting their own tongues, either during or immediately following the attack, but certainly there were many.[9]

Soviet soldiers seemed to particularly delight in wristwatches. A Soviet soldier wearing five or six wristwatches on his arm was not an uncommon sight, and some even wore ten or more, showing them off to their comrades and playing with them as if they were toys. Maruyama himself was accosted on two occasions and was robbed at gunpoint of his wallet and a watch.

At the time the Soviet Union launched its massive invasion against the Japanese in Manchuria, much of the country's labor and military resources were still engaged in various cleanup operations on the western front in the war against Germany. Thus, uneducated and untrained peasants, including common criminals from Russian prisons, were hastily drafted into the army for the eastern front assault on Manchuria. Discipline among the occupying Soviet forces, therefore, was severely lacking. There were several stories about soldiers who thought the second hands which moved unceasingly in the wristwatches were some kind of insects. Because they did not know watches had to be wound, soldiers would often throw them away in disgust (and sometimes even shoot at them with their semiautomatic weapons) when the second hands stopped moving.

Discipline among the ragtag Chinese Communist soldiers was often no better at first. Since they too had been suddenly dispatched throughout Manchuria (wherever the Soviet army appeared, the Chinese Communist army was right behind them), untrained farmers, miners, laborers, and other peasants were forcibly rounded up, given guns, and hastily drafted into the Eighth Route Army. While none were released prisoners, these *coolies* (common workers, laborers, miners, etc.), who came mostly from the very low end of the social status, saw themselves suddenly placed in positions of power over the Japanese who had been their lords and masters throughout China and Manchuria; given the chance, they treated the now-humbled Japanese accordingly.

Anshan and other cities throughout Manchuria that came to be occupied by Soviet and Eighth Route Army soldiers suddenly became very dangerous places for all Japanese. There was an endless succession of armed robberies, pillaging, rapes, and other scandalous incidences perpetrated not only against the Japanese civilians but against ordinary Chinese as well. No house was safe from marauding Soviet and Eighth Route Army soldiers who invaded homes without warning as if by inherent right, taking away whatever caught their fancy. On two occasions, Soviet soldiers barged in on the Maruyama home when Kunio was away, demanding food on the first occasion and cooking utensils the second time. Mary Maruyama's top priority was to protect her children, and she calmly acceded to their demands without resistance, but she was never able to erase her resentment toward the Soviet Union from those days of Manchurian occupation.

The misery that descended on the Japanese civilians in Manchuria could not have been imagined just a few days previously. Not only was there physical danger; now another kind of unimaginable hardship descended on all Japanese: economic terror. All Japanese employment, except in those endeavors deemed necessary for Soviet benefit, was suddenly terminated. All financial institutions, schools, hospitals, cultural centers, post offices, and government institutions were permanently closed. All means of communication were terminated, and there was no way to receive or send letters, dispatch telegrams, or make telephone calls to or from Japan. Radios were confiscated and banned, and newspapers were shut down so that the Japanese in Manchuria were effectively and completely cut off from the outside world. Finally, all bank accounts of Japanese citizens were frozen so that money could no longer be withdrawn from personal accounts. One might have a savings account worth a million yen that had been meticulously accumulated over years or decades of painstaking labor, but that bankbook suddenly had no more value than a scrap of paper. Since all means of earning an income had been eliminated, the Japanese were in a desperate situation financially.

Chapter 4

Aftermath of Soviet Invasion

Forced to Assist in Mass Looting

At the Yalta Conference in February 1945, the Soviet Union had been promised certain rewards for joining in the war against Japan, including possession of the Kuril Islands and southern Sakhalin and railway rights in Manchuria. However, the Soviets had a broader interpretation of what was promised to them. Their definition of entitlement included the right to various "spoils of war."

They immediately began dismantling industrial facilities and hauling them off to the Soviet Union. Factories, mining components, assembly complexes, furnaces, laboratories, steel mills—virtually all vital facilities associated with industrial work were targeted that would be useful for building up the Soviet Union which had been so massively destroyed during World War II. The dismantled industrial components were placed on rail cars and transported to Port Arthur or through North Korea to the port at Vladivostok, and then shipped to the Soviet Union. Labor for the work was provided by Japanese and Chinese who had formerly worked for the same facilities that were being dismantled.

Kazusada Hara was a mechanical engineer who was employed by Showa Steel Manufacturing, the same company that employed Maruyama. He had also helplessly watched as the American B-29s destroyed much of the company's capacity on July 29, 1944, during the first air raid. Hara continued working at the factory even after the Soviet occupation. In mid-September, an order was handed down by the Soviet military to commence dismantling all machine facilities. More than ten thousand Japanese and Manchurians were forced to work day and night until over 70 percent of all machines and facilities were dismantled and loaded onto rail cars for shipment to the Soviet Union in less than two months. Later, Hara would shudder when he thought about the punishment that would have been meted out had the work not been completed according to Soviet schedule or if there had been any resistance by those forced to work. In less than two months, twenty-five factories and more than sixty million tons of machinery were dismantled and readied for shipment. Often, supervisors who were unable to meet the quota of work expected during a specified period were threatened with court-martial and subsequent death by the Soviet overseers.

Hara was assigned to take charge of dismantling in twenty days four sets of German-made boilers associated with power generators. Dismantling the boilers so quickly was not much different from destroying them. When the task was completed on time, Hara expected the worst from the Soviet overseers for the rough and careless way the work was completed; instead, however, he was congratulated for completing the work according to schedule. The quality of the work was immaterial, it seemed. To Hara, the dismantled boilers were scrap that probably could never be put back together again.

On November 12, 1945, most of the Soviet overseers disappeared, together with the dismantled steelmaking company. Those small units of Soviet soldiers who still remained went around confiscating leftover valuables of the company, furniture, and other salvageable items, and they were also shipped back to the Soviet Union. (Hara was not able to return to Japan for another eight years, until 1953, since his talents were "required" by the Communist Chinese who took control of Manchuria after the Soviets departed.[1])

The Plight of the Settlers

Those suffering the worst ordeal in their effort to flee the invading Soviet army were undoubtedly the volunteer Japanese immigrants who came as pioneers to tame and till the harsh but fertile land of northeastern Manchuria, often at the urging of the Japanese government. Living in isolated villages and enclaves, they were the first to suffer the full impact from the violent attacks by Soviet artillery, tanks, and manpower. Carrying only what they could on their backs, including suckling infants and toddlers, they fled by foot southward, seeking to find refuge in areas where other Japanese resided.

In 1936, the Japanese government introduced a twenty-year settlement plan to turn the northeastern regions of Manchuria into an agricultural Japanese settlement. The plan, referred to as the National Immigration Policy, called for 100,000 Japanese pioneer families to settle and cultivate land in the first five years, then 200,000 in the second five years, 300,000 in the third, and 400,000 in the fourth five years. The span of the ambitious plan was to be from 1937 to 1956. Each pioneer family was to be given a plot of land equivalent to one hectare (about two and a half acres) to cultivate, raise livestock, and turn into farmland that would contribute food for the homeland.

One program, called the Volunteer Youth Corps Pioneer Group, targeted young people between sixteen and nineteen years of age. These volunteer youths were given two to three months of training in Japan before they were sent overseas to military-like camps in northeastern Manchuria where they were trained for three more years before they were sent to farmlands as pioneer farmers. Each youth corps numbered around three hundred, and the youth came from villages and cities throughout Japan. They dreamed of great adventure and promise of success in the land they had been hearing about so much and felt it was the patriotic thing to do to join a pioneer group to contribute to Japan's ambitious military aspirations.

There were other efforts such as the *Bunson, Bunkyo* program (Removed Village, Removed Native Home) that called for a particular village in Japan to send part of its population to set up a counterpart "removed village" in Manchuria; the village in Japan would remain the "main village" while the counterpart in Manchuria would be its "sister village." In this way, it was the government's intention to make the puppet regime of Manchuria a truly Japanese state, populated and farmed by Japanese. By the end of the war in 1945, it was estimated that more than 220,000 Japanese settlers and about 100,000 volunteer youth pioneers resided in northeastern Manchuria.[2]

As they fled the invading Soviet army in August and September 1945, these settlers had no idea where they were headed. Many died of hunger, cold, or sickness as they trekked southward, and those who were lucky enough to reach areas populated by Japanese set up makeshift camps or sought refuge in schools and parks, doing their best to survive from day to day.

Tales of Tragedy

Maruyama was on a train bound for Dalian one day in November 1945, when he happened to sit next to a man in his forties. As they struck up a conversation, the man slowly revealed that he was one Kenzo Tajima from Changchun. When the war ended, he had been one of the settlers in the Shengdongnin District of Mudanjiang and had been lucky to make his escape to far-away Changchun. There were thirteen members, all men, in the group that had escaped from Shengdongnin, but by the time they arrived in Changchun, only five were left. What happened to the other eight, no one knew; they just could not keep up with the main body and never rejoined the group.

Three of the five survivors had no money at all, but because they had had some canned foods to eat during their journey, they were able to survive. After consuming the food, they retained those cans. When they became unbearably hungry, they would knock on the door of some Manchurian villager and beg for food, sticking out their empty cans as containers. By eating the food that was given to them in their empty cans, they were able to survive and make their way to Changchun. With visible moisture in his eyes, Tajima quietly whispered that without those empty cans, they would surely have perished from starvation, becoming carrion for the birds.

After a little pause to collect his thoughts, Tajima continued with his narration. An acquaintance of his had left Hulin Prefecture, also of Mudanjiang region, with his wife and infant child to seek refuge in Changchun. In their haste to depart before they were captured (or worse) by the invading Soviets, they had no food for their journey, and the heat had become unbearable. As things got desperate, the couple came to the conclusion that there was no hope that they would survive if they continued on. Overcome by despair, perhaps even losing their senses, the couple did the unthinkable: they abandoned their infant child under the shade of a tree and continued on. When they finally reached their place of refuge and regained their composure and sanity, they suddenly realized what they had done. In a state of partial insanity, the couple broke down hopelessly, unable to stop crying for their abandoned child, unable to comprehend their own action.

Maruyama heard many such stories of desperate mothers, fathers, and couples abandoning their own children while fleeing and trekking hundreds of painful miles over mountains, across rivers, and through unforgiving terrain in search of refuge. Countless Japanese children were given away, or kindly Chinese families adopted them. In some cases, a mother was forced to stifle her child's cry or worse, to prevent Soviet soldiers from discovering the whereabouts of a group of refugees in hiding; in such cases, perhaps, the mother's obligation for the safety of the group overrode the love for her own child.

At a later date, Maruyama was in Liaoyang near the train station when he spotted an emaciated Japanese man in his thirties or early forties, wearing tennis shoes and the typical brownish khaki clothing that resembled a military uniform that most civilian men wore in those days. His ragged clothing and worn shoes were barely holding together; there was barely any color in his face, and he looked to Maruyama like a living corpse. He seemed to be wandering aimlessly, without a bit of strength, in a state of complete oblivion, and he was constantly talking to himself in a low voice, saying something about a child. Maruyama put his hand on the man's shoulder and asked, "Is something the matter?" but the man seemed not to have even noticed Maruyama's touch on the shoulder or his question. The man simply continued to wander lifelessly and aimlessly near the station. As the man walked away, Maruyama thought that this man also, like the half-crazed couple who fled from Hulin and who placed their own child beneath a tree and abandoned it, must have lost a loving child or a wife while fleeing for safety.

More Tragic Tales

In the waning days of the war, the seemingly invincible Imperial Army began losing battle after battle. They began resorting even to Japanese airmen sacrificing their lives strapped to suicide kamikaze ("divine wind") planes by diving into enemy targets with a last shout of *"banzai"* to the emperor. Personnel from the Kwantung Army was rapidly and increasingly shifted to other fronts to reinforce the losses to the Japanese army.

No longer could the Kwantung Army expect fresh and well-trained soldiers from the homeland. It became necessary to conscript Japanese civilian males living and working in Manchuria into the Kwantung Army. By the end of the war, almost every able-bodied male who had come as part of the various pioneer corps to tame, colonize, and cultivate the northern parts of Manchuria had been drafted into the Kwantung Army so that only the elderly, the women, and the children were left in the various settlements and villages.

Shortly after he had listened to the story of how a few empty cans had saved the lives of Tajima and his companions on the train, Maruyama heard another story from one survivor of a group that had fled a settlement village in Beian Province in northern Manchuria. When the sixty-four-year-old leader of the village, Eikichi Matsumoto, heard reports of the imminent arrival of advancing Soviet soldiers, he decided it was time to lead an evacuation and seek refuge for the forty residents of his village, all women, children, and elderly. As they were about to depart on foot with what few valuables they could carry, he gathered the villagers together to issue grave advice.

"As we depart our farms and village which we so lovingly built and cultivated for so many years, I cannot predict what awful hardship or disaster we might encounter. We must all help each other, no matter what, and as quickly as possible we must find some safe place where there are Japanese. If, however, we encounter any Soviet soldiers or are set on by a mob, and if any of you ladies are in danger of meeting with violence, I ask you to uphold your pride as a Japanese, even if it means dying. Just in case of such an eventuality, I have obtained a little amount of potassium cyanide for your use which I will now divide up among you. With the exception of children, I ask each of you ladies to carry it in your possession at all times and use it when it becomes necessary. If by remote chance it becomes necessary for you to take your own life, I want you to somehow let me know. If it is impossible for you to let me know yourself, you must do your utmost to have someone else nearby let me know." He then gave each woman in the group a small amount of the deadly poison.

Most of the women in the group cut off all their hair, wore men's clothing, and rubbed dirt and charcoal on their faces, all in an effort to make themselves look like men. Some even scratched and cut up their faces to purposefully make themselves look unattractive as they prepared to start on their journey. In normal times, the group might have looked like a parade of comical characters, but they had disguised themselves for a deadly serious reason. Fortunately, Matsumoto's group arrived safely in Shenyang without losing a single member, but many other groups were not so lucky. Countless refugees were attacked, raped, or killed by Soviet soldiers, mobs, and angry Manchurian villagers who sought revenge on the former occupiers of their land. There were many tragic instances of Japanese women who took their own lives by consuming potassium cyanide or killed themselves by biting off their own tongues.[3]

Famous Photographer Preserves Evidence

Tatsuo Iiyama was a well-known Japanese photographer who spent his life traveling to unknown parts of the world. His striking photographs made known hidden natural beauties, such as unclimbed mountains in North Korea and parts of mainland China into which even the Chinese had never ventured. He gained great fame after he spent several years on photographic expeditions in the Gobi Desert.

When the war ended, and the horrors of the Japanese experience in Manchuria began to be told with the start of repatriation in mid-1946, he went there to see with his own eyes the conditions he had heard and read about; his aim was to accumulate and preserve photographic evidence of what had happened in Manchuria after the Soviet invasion and make it available to the Japanese government and the Allied Powers. Iiyama later compiled his photos in an album entitled *Defeat in War: The Lamentation of Repatriation* that was published in 1979. Iiyama shared many of the photos that appeared in the album with his friend, Maruyama. Maruyama included many of the photos in his 1970 book *Why Was Koroto Opened.*

In addition to photographs, *Defeat in War* included stories and personal observations of the author to convey the raw horrors of the Manchurian experience. (*One of the lengthier articles that appeared in Iiyama's photo album was Maruyama's speech presented to the Japanese public at Tokyo's Hibiya Public Hall in April 1946, when he appealed to the Japanese government and to General Headquarters (GHQ) of the Allied Powers and its supreme commander, General Douglas MacArthur, to dispatch rescue ships as quickly as possible to Manchuria. The entire speech was included verbatim in the album.* See Chapter 23.)

Fleeing the Soviet Invasion

In 1954, while memories were still fresh, Tatsuo Iiyama interviewed two sisters from Nagano Prefecture (the same prefecture that was Maruyama's birthplace) who left Japan in the late 1930s with their parents and other relatives and in-laws, as a pioneer family, to settle in Ochiai village in Beian province in northern Manchuria. They were part of the *Bunson, Bunkyo* (Removed Village, Removed Native Home) program discussed earlier in this chapter. Life at Ochiai village for the two sisters, Kaneyo Miyashita (the elder sister, who had an infant child) and Harue Kitahara, and for their family was better than it was in Japan. Food was plentiful, nothing was rationed, bandits were not a concern as they were in other villages, and in spite of the brutally cold winters, the weather was pleasant overall. Crops, including soybeans, wheat, potatoes, and feed crops for animals, grew in abundance in the rich soil.

Kaneyo and Harue had no idea that the Soviet army had invaded Manchuria on August 9, 1945, but learned about Japan's surrender on August 15 following the emperor's broadcast. On August 23, they had their first taste of trouble when they were attacked by bandits who charged the settlement unannounced with guns blazing. The entire village fled into the local school or hid in the wheat fields. The bandits broke into homes and took what they wanted. A second attack came the next day, this time by local Manchurians. The attackers removed whatever had not been taken the day before by the bandits, and several villagers were shot and killed.

While Kaneyo was hiding in the fields with her child during the attacks, the baby began to cry. Other villagers, trembling in fear that they would be discovered, whispered to her, "Choke the baby to death!"

Kaneyo answered back, "I couldn't do that unless I was insane! If you can kill my baby, you do it!" Fortunately, there were no volunteers.[4]

Realizing they could not remain there, the entire village fled together, carrying only what they had when they ran out of their homes. Some did not even have shoes. It took them three days to walk twenty-five miles to the next settlement, which was a larger city that used to be the prefectural capital and was home to many Japanese. During the trek, they were constantly bitten by large mosquitoes; they had no food; they drank water that had collected in the tracks of horse-drawn wagons; everyone, particularly children, suffered greatly from the cold nights; and if an infant cried, the mother was severely scolded to keep her child quiet. Fortunately, everyone made it safely to shelter in the next settlement.

A few days later, in early September, the Soviet army came in and occupied the city. Life became precarious, especially for women. Whenever a Soviet soldier approached, women hid wherever they could. Sometimes Soviet soldiers appeared at their shelter in midday and demanded that young girls come and greet them. Any girl who was unfortunate enough to be caught was taken to a nearby warehouse where she was assaulted by the soldiers. Some who were taken away never returned; the fate of two girls from Kaneyo and Harue's group who were caught and carried away by Soviet soldiers was never learned. In shame, the villagers hardly ever talked about the disappearance of the two missing girls.[5]

After the villagers from Ochiai had been at the shelter for about a month, the local Japanese association issued an order directing them to go to Beian to get on a train. Their destination was to be Shenyang. After a stop-and-go journey of several days without any food, they were allowed to disembark at Harbin where they spent a few days in a school. The only food they obtained was from begging and sometimes from local Japanese families who still had money and compassion. Kaneyo noticed the many White Russians living in Harbin, and she was struck by the beauty of their young women. Apparently, they, unlike Japanese women, remained unmolested by the Russian soldiers. Kaneyo also noted that, although most Soviet soldiers had no qualms about plundering others' possessions, a few of the Soviet soldiers bought bread from Manchurian peddlers at the station and gave it to some of the starving children in her group. Not all Soviet soldiers, she mused, were evil.

When they finally reached Shenyang, the villagers were temporarily placed in a school until they were moved to a temple for the rest of their stay. "In Shenyang, many died. They died in droves," recalled Harue. Most died from typhoid fever brought on by malnutrition. Harue shuddered to think about the masses of white lice that collected on open wounds of the dying brought on by typhus fever.[6]

Many of the pioneers who came to northern Manchuria were young women who married in Japan and became pregnant just before setting off to the continent around 1943 and 1944. Thus, many of the young wives had given birth in just the past year or two. When they fled, they carried their babies on their backs, but from around October of 1945, those babies began to die. Kaneyo does not know anyone in her group who was able to take a surviving infant back to Japan. Kaneyo, whose body could no longer produce milk for her nursing baby, struggled daily to feed her child. At times, some Japanese housewives, who went into the business of selling dumplings and other foods to survive, took pity and gave Kaneyo some of their wares for her baby, saying, "I really feel badly for you pioneer groups."

Hope of Returning to Japan is the Only Incentive for Survival

In Shenyang, Japanese refugees from the various northern settlements died like flies. It seemed more young people than older Japanese, particularly those around nineteen and twenty, succumbed to death. They designated a small room in the temple as the mourning room where the dead were brought for prayers before burial. However, so many people died that the room was not large enough to accommodate the recently deceased. The dead were loaded like logs onto a hand-pulled wagon and taken to be buried in a large hole nearby. Because of the bitter cold, all the bodies froze, and since the hole dug in the frozen dirt was not deep, the bodies were exposed when spring came. Then dogs would finish unearthing them.

The one thing that kept Kaneyo and Harue alive was their desire to someday return home, to once more see their mother and father in Japan. Of course, because all news to their homeland had been terminated, the parents had no idea how their loved ones were faring and could only hope and pray that their children would someday return home. Daily, they prayed to Buddha and burned incense in hopes that they would someday be reunited.

There was one almost sure way that a Japanese girl could survive in Manchuria. That was to marry a Manchurian. (*Author's note: The terms "Manchurian" and "Chinese" are used interchangeably to mean native residents of Manchuria, which is northern China.*) Many entered such a marriage purely to survive. Marriage to a Manchurian assured there would be food to eat, and in most cases, a Japanese girl could have the Manchurian husband of her choice. Some gave away their child to a Manchurian family so that the child would be able to eat and survive. But the desire to return to Japan prevented most from marrying a Manchurian or giving their children away. A girl who became a Manchurian wife or a child who was adopted by a Manchurian lost all hope of returning to Japan.

A few days before the New Year (1946), Harue realized that Kaneyo's malnourished three-year-old was steadily losing her battle for life. Harue felt an overwhelming sadness and a misery that words could not describe as she stared at her sister's child, a little girl who had suffered so much to get to this place, now awaiting sure death. But the child was oblivious to the impending end as she chewed on some roasted, hard soybeans, savoring each nugget as she crunched them in her mouth, her eyes shriveled up in a state of malnutrition, obviously enjoying the juicy taste of the beans. That was to be her last meal. Harue could not hold back her tears as she watched her niece enjoying something so much that even death was not able to take away the joy of the moment from the innocent child. Harue later recalled that moment, saying, "I cried and cried and cried. I had never cried so much before, and I have never cried so much since."[7]

Desperate Times Bring Out the Worst in People

The Japanese, who were then and still are probably among the most disciplined people in the world, had only one thing on their mind: to survive until the day they could return to their homeland. Survival was not easy, and even they sometimes broke the rules of discipline to survive. It was common for things to be stolen in a flash. If one left clothes or diapers out to dry, they disappeared. If one was cooking at the community stove and left the cooking for even a moment to grab an ingredient from one's room, the food would be gone by the time one returned. If shoes were left outside the room while one slept, they would be gone by the next morning.

In desperate times, the only people one could trust were family members. While Ochiai villagers were still together, there was trust among them. But in the temple in Shenyang, they were with strangers they did not trust, who did not trust them. Several families shared the same room in the temple, and if one family ate white rice while the other family had nothing to eat, the family with the rice did not share with the starving roommates. If someone died, there was a race among the living to see who would get the dead person's coat, shoes, pants, and other items. Among those fortunate enough to flee their settlement with money, there was never any thought of sharing the money with the less fortunate who had fled with no money at all. Extreme hardship, it seemed, made everyone self-centered with the attitude that people should look out for themselves.

Harue and Kaneyo and their group departed Shenyang via unroofed trains for Koroto on July 17, 1946, to board a repatriation ship for their journey home. They arrived at Hakata in Kyushu (Japan's southernmost main island) on August 19, home at last. All in all, Harue and Kaneyo were extremely thankful that they were able to return to Japan. In fact, no one from their village of Ochiai who survived was left behind in Manchuria. No child was given away or abandoned to become a Manchurian, and no girl stayed behind to be a Manchurian housewife.[8]

Chapter 5

Desperate Times

Surviving from Day to Day

Because most Japanese lost their jobs with the arrival of the Soviet army and the Chinese Eighth Route Army, and since bank accounts had been frozen and Japanese could not withdraw money from their savings, most Japanese survived from day to day by selling what few possessions they had. There is a Japanese saying for that kind of life: bamboo shoot living (*takenoko seikatsu*). Bamboo shoot, a common and tasty vegetable in the Japanese diet, consists simply of tasty layers upon layers. Once all the layers are peeled away, there is nothing left. Similarly, as desperate Japanese slowly sold their possessions, eventually there was nothing left to sell.

On city streets all over Manchuria there soon appeared shopping markets, made up of dozens of hastily built stalls, selling foods like sushi, dumplings, cookies, rice cakes, crackers, pastries—anything the proprietor could make at home. Others sold cigarettes, candies, and sundry goods which they bought in a Manchurian store then resold. Others opened up simple outdoor eating establishments. These Japanese businesses operated in an atmosphere of great insecurity, always wary of gangs and delinquents as well as armed robbers who could set upon them at any time.

In the city of Shenyang, a great number of stalls cropped up at the once bustling Japanese shopping district of Kasugamachi Avenue. Two rows of stalls appeared on the left walkway, then two more rows in the car lane, then another two rows were set up on the left walkway; in all, there were six rows of stalls with shouting peddlers hawking their goods to passersby.

Suffering and Bravery of Innocent Children Bring Tears

Whenever Maruyama went by the market, the sight that brought a lump to his throat was the little children doing their best to draw customers. Until recently, these little children had been helped to put their clothes on in the morning by their mothers or perhaps by their older sisters. After eating a warm breakfast, they fumbled to put on and tie their own shoes. As they waved good-bye to go off to school, their mothers handed them their freshly packed *bento* (boxed lunches).

These same helpless children were now standing on the icy streets of Kasugamachi as the temperature barely reached thirty degrees below zero, noses running, shouting to passersby, "Sir, please buy one of these," or "Lady, won't you buy these delicious dumplings?" Some did not even have boots on, and all had to keep stamping the ground because if they stood still, their feet would freeze. Many were pitifully dressed against the freezing weather. If they thought they had a possible sale, they would follow potential customers, pestering them with tearful pleas.

Maruyama thought back to the time a few years ago when, after he had finished his studies in the United States and was on his European journey, he was walking through a poor district of London, and he was followed by a group of five to seven children, all holding empty cans or dishes, all calling, "Give me a penny, sir!" Back then, Maruyama found the experience rather whimsical as the children followed him for some distance. But the persistent children in Manchuria, calling out desperately to pedestrians as they stood in the severe cold, were anything but whimsical. Their plight pulled at the heartstrings of almost everyone who passed by. Maruyama had several occasions to pass through Kasugamachi Avenue as he checked on the living conditions of fellow countrymen before his departure to Japan, and on each visit, he could not hold back tears at the sight of those freezing children, doing what they could to help their families survive another day.

Some of the children, particularly the older ones, worked the stalls by themselves because their mother or father was too ill to get up and come out to run the business. Many children did not know the whereabouts of their fathers because they had been drafted just before the end of the war and never came back. There were many children, especially from the northern settlements, whose parents had been killed by gangs, mobs, and Soviet soldiers. They had been taken in by kindly Japanese families but still had to go out and earn their keep, because many of those families could not feed even one more child.

There was something valiant and courageous about the sight of these children. They showed no self-pity and carried on as best they could. Sometimes, as Maruyama bought and paid for an item, he would ask, "Where are your mother and father?" The children always replied innocently and truthfully, and their tragic answers always brought a lump to Maruyama's throat and made him turn away so they would not see the tears in his eyes. Even many years after he returned to Japan, he could not erase from his memories the images of those pitiful children, some as young as three years old, shaking in the cold, calling out to strangers to buy their wares. How many of those children, he always wondered, made it back to Japan?

"Don't Kill or Abandon"

One day, Maruyama saw an unimaginably painful sight when he passed by the school playground of Chunri Primary School in Shenyang. The school was turned into a shelter, as was every other school, temple, and suitable facility in the city which might provide sleeping space for the refugees who poured in. At the school, many people died daily due to hunger, cold, or illness; the dead were wrapped up in wool blankets or hemp bags and thrown into the many air-raid trenches that had been dug in the schoolyard. Because the frozen ground was so hard and dry, just enough dirt was thrown on the corpses to hide them from sight. When the wind blew hard as it often did in Manchuria, the head, shoulder, hands, and feet of the corpses would be exposed as the dry dirt blew off. It was almost impossible, of course, to tell whether the corpse was that of a man, woman, or child, but anyone who passed by and got a glimpse wondered how anyone could have come to such an end and how God could permit such a ghastly and tragic sight. Even Manchurians who passed by, and who were not always sympathetic to the plight of the Japanese, were visibly moved to pity; many would quickly move away, hanging their heads and averting their eyes. It was a sight that Maruyama would not have thought was possible in this world.

On another occasion, Maruyama visited the National School of Shenyang, which was also a shelter for refugees. As he entered the school's single building, he noticed that every window was broken, so the refugees had to endure the bitter cold wind that blew in completely unhindered. Most of the residents there had a torn woolen blanket or an ordinary hemp bag (the kind of bag that was used to contain beans or potatoes) as their sole bedding. There were some who lay on futons, all with stuffing poking through holes; most slept on the bare floor. A few lucky refugees had pillows for their heads. It was obvious several were sick and were simply suffering in silence, quietly lying between wooden boards. There were a few who were dying, patiently awaiting the end.

On the wall of the hallway of the school building, someone had scrawled graffiti in large characters in pencil. The writing stated, "Don't Kill, Don't Abandon; Just Give Away or Sell." Among residents there, some had become so desperate, or perhaps had gone insane, that they had killed their own children or abandoned them. The slogan was an admonishment to all that they should not kill or abandon their own children but instead ask a Manchurian to care for them. It even encouraged selling children rather than killing them.

In fact, the number of desperate refugees who sold their own children was not small; it was said that girls could command a relatively handsome price. A well-known local charitable organization (Dozendo) that took in and cared for abandoned children had recently ceased accepting any more since the number of abandoned children brought in had overwhelmed its capacity. Many of the abandoned or sold children were given loving care by their Manchurian families and grew up as good Chinese citizens. [*In recent years, many of these sold or adopted children, now in their sixties and seventies, have journeyed to Japan seeking to reunite with their natural Japanese families. Some have been successful. Sadly, others have not been able to this day to locate relatives they parted with over six decades ago.*]

The "Hemp Bag Corps"

Maruyama had to make visits to Shenyang quite often in late 1945 and early 1946 to confirm the present state and condition of the Japanese as well as to obtain information from the Japanese association officials prior to his escape to Japan. Whenever Maruyama conducted his intelligence-gathering activities, he always wore the typical clothing of a Manchurian laborer and consumed a great deal of garlic so that he might smell like the typical Manchurian peasant, all in a ploy not to attract attention. He wore a hood that he pulled down to obscure his face and stood up his collars so that only his eyes were visible in his heavy winter jacket.

On one of his excursions, he ran into a very odd sight, the famous groups of refugees who came to be called the "Hemp Bag Corps." Just as he came around a corner in the city, several people came his way, walking in groups of two and three. Most in the group were elderly women with a few younger girls; there were a few children as well. All their men had been drafted into the Japanese army and had been sent to the front; not one word had been heard about them since they left. The group was a pitiful sight. These people derived their name from what they wore: hemp bags.

This particular group of refugees had come from Harbin, Mudanjiang, Liaoyang, Siping, and other northern settlements and had undergone a horrendous ordeal before arriving in Shenyang. First, they were violently treated by Soviet soldiers who molested several of the women; then the Chinese Communist Eighth Route Army robbed them of all their possessions so that they had nothing when they arrived in Shenyang, and their clothing was in tatters. Without any money to replace their clothing, they had no choice but to pick up or beg for hemp bags that they used as replacement clothing. They cut a large hole in the middle of the bag at the bottom for their heads and an armhole on either side, and they pulled them on over their heads. Hemp bags were coarse but relatively sturdy since they were made to normally hold beans, chestnuts, and potatoes.

It was estimated that the "Hemp Bag Corps" numbered some two hundred. As Maruyama and other Manchurian pedestrians quietly watched the pitiful sight, there were some who ran into their homes, then returned with towels, clothing, and used shoes that they offered to the hemp bag members. Maruyama watched with wonderment at the sight and gradually became deeply saddened. Tempted to say some words of encouragement or sympathy to them, he stayed quiet as he loosened the strings of his hood so that he could wipe away the tears that were beginning to flow down his cheeks. They had found shelter at the Shenyang International Transportation Company's warehouse where they spent their nights, not knowing, like all other Japanese trapped in Manchuria, whether or when they might be able to return to their homeland.

Chapter 6

Belling the Cat

Only One Topic of Conversation: How to Escape

Every Japanese throughout Manchuria was touched by the mood of fear, depression, helplessness, and despair. Each lived from one day to the next as if treading on thin ice; the ice might crack with the next step, and death could come at any moment. As they looked up at the sky, their only thought was to return to their homeland that lay to the east under that very same sky.

The feeling of despair was magnified by the thought that no one in Japan, even their own anxious families, knew the terrible conditions that had befallen them since the Soviet invasion. All communication with families and friends in Japan had been totally severed. Telephones, telegrams, letters, newspapers, and radios were things of the past. Even worse, the strict security of the occupying Soviet army and the Communist Chinese Eighth Route Army made sure that no Japanese could escape, and no one from Japan could come into Manchuria.

In those days, whenever a group of Japanese got together, the conversation inevitably became a debate on the subject of the best way to return to Japan. Many ideas were discussed, some sensible and some ridiculous, but all were infeasible. No one had yet ever attempted putting any of the ideas to the test, since every idea involved risking one's life. Risking one's life was one thing, but if the attempt ended in failure, the lives of one's entire family and community could be jeopardized if the escapee's identity was discovered.

Maruyama too racked his brain as he thought about escape. As he contemplated the situation from his perspective in Anshan, he was made aware that Port Arthur in Dalian to the south, the most important and largest seaport in Manchuria, was completely closed up. Likewise, the route from east Andong via the Yalu River to North Korea was so heavily guarded that even a mouse could not have escaped undetected. The same was true for Yingkou to the west. Even if one miraculously found a ship and tried to escape via Korea Bay, the Soviet ships and guns that guarded against such foolhardy attempts were so efficient that the attempt would be akin to carelessly throwing one's life away. There was one port on the Bohai Bay called Koroto (Huludao in Chinese), which was firmly under the control of Chiang Kai-shek's Nationalist army, but as far as Maruyama knew, it was thought improbable that ships would be able to put out from there.

Maruyama was reminded at that time of the story of a group of mice who gathered together because they lived in daily fear of a certain cat. As they discussed the situation, one wise mouse said, "If we put a bell around the cat's neck, the bell will warn us of the cat's whereabouts, and we will always be able to escape danger." All the mice agreed that that was an excellent suggestion, but when the discussion turned to who would actually bell the cat, the bright idea was abandoned as utterly useless.

Escaping from Manchuria and appealing for help to the Supreme Commander for Allied Powers, General Douglas MacArthur, was also stymied by the question of belling the cat. Someone was needed to carry out the task, and the plan had to be 100 percent successful; it could not fail. If someone would do that, the lives of 1.7 million Japanese countrymen could be saved.

(Author's note: The number of Japanese stranded in Manchuria following the Soviet invasion in August 1945 has been stated several times already in this narrative as 1.7 million. While that figure is only approximate and is the number used by Kunio Maruyama in his book Why Was Koroto Opened, *as well as in Masamichi Musashi's book* The Dawning of Asia: Crossing the Lines of Death, *other documents substantiate that the number is essentially accurate. For example, in a November 8, 1945, SCAP memo, the approximate number of Japanese nationals in Manchuria that was in a "To Be Evacuated" category was estimated at 1,900,000.[1] In a similar SCAP memo dated January 16, 1946, the number "To Be Evacuated" was estimated at 1,703,000.[2] In a February 13, 1946 memo similar to the January 16 memo, the number was estimated at 1,603,000,[3] although not one Japanese would be evacuated from Manchuria until May of that year. Thus, the number used by both Maruyama and Musashi, 1.7 million, is about as accurate a number as anyone could estimate in those turbulent days. Prior to their escape, Maruyama, Musashi, and Shinpo collected the most up-to-date information about the status of Japanese in Manchuria, including the total number of Japanese civilians living in Manchuria, in order that they would be able to convey to SCAP and the Japanese government the most accurate intelligence possible about Manchuria. The best estimate from their intelligence gathering was 1.7 million.)*

According to the best estimate made by Japanese associations throughout Manchuria where the Japanese lived, almost 2,500 lives were being lost each day to hunger, cold, diseases, neglect, murder (at the hands of mobs, Soviet soldiers, Chinese Communist soldiers, and ordinary Manchurians intent on taking revenge), and suicide.[4] One month of delay in repatriation meant an end to nearly 75,000 lives. As time passed, Maruyama estimated, these deaths would accelerate dramatically. Maruyama had planned to return with his family to Japan immediately upon Japan's surrender on August 15, but when he went to Shenyang on August 17, he realized any thoughts of leaving Manchuria for the time being were naive and out of the question, as he saw soldiers of the Soviet Union everywhere. From that day on, however, he continued to look for an escape route, and he was determined to escape as soon as possible when the opportunity presented itself. Quietly but seriously, he asked himself, why should he not be the one to hang the bell around the neck of the fearsome cat?

A Quick Meeting with the Chairman

In early November 1945, when signs of early winter were casting an even gloomier feeling than usual everywhere, Maruyama decided to take his first decisive step in his plan to bell the cat. He determined that it was necessary to seek out the thoughts of a man who was probably the most respected of all Japanese in Anshan. Though Maruyama told absolutely no one (except his wife, Mary) about the scheme he was beginning to formulate in his mind, he sought a meeting with Ayao Kishimoto, the chairman of the board of directors of Maruyama's own company, Showa Steel Manufacturing Company.

Kishimoto held a PhD in civil engineering, was a retired four-star general in the Japanese Army, was the former president of Shibaura College of Engineering, and was mayor of Tokyo before taking on the helm of Showa Steel Manufacturing. In normal times, there would have been no problem for Maruyama to meet with his own company's chairman, but these were not normal times. Chairman Kishimoto, then sixty-eight, and his wife had been arrested by the Soviet army soon after they occupied Anshan and imprisoned in an unknown location.

The Soviet army had set most of Showa Steel Manufacturing's employees to the task of dismantling vital facilities, machinery, and factories of their own company and wanted Chairman Kishimoto, who had great influence in the community, kept out of the way during that process.

A meeting with Kishimoto, even if Maruyama knew his whereabouts, seemed unlikely and even impossible. If it were ever discovered that Maruyama, who had been in charge of public information for his company, was seen meeting with the incarcerated chairman, both Kishimoto's and Maruyama's safety would be gravely jeopardized. The Soviets would have no qualms about dispatching Maruyama with a single bullet and throwing his body in the nearest hole.

As luck would have it, however, the English-speaking Maruyama had been placed in a vital position as the liaison between the Soviet army and the company employees dismantling the assets of the company for transshipment. His main Soviet contact was a Major Babalkin, the only English-speaking Soviet officer among the group with whom Maruyama dealt frequently. In his liaison work, Maruyama had been meeting with Major Babalkin on a daily basis and had naturally established a mutually cordial relationship, to the point that he could ask favors of the Soviet officer that went beyond normal business. However, since one had to constantly be wary of spies, Maruyama needed to still use extreme caution, no matter how cordial their relationship had become.

One night, when he had a meeting with the major on a variety of issues in the company's reception hall, Maruyama decided to take the risk and laid the following request before the major: "I wish to see my company's chairman on a strictly personal matter. Can you make arrangements so that I can see him, even if it is for only three minutes?" Major Babalkin considered the request with a grave frown, but in the end he acceded to the request and assured Maruyama that he would make certain no one else would be able to observe the meeting.

On the appointed day and time, Maruyama went to the place designated by Major Babalkin, who awaited him in a Soviet staff car. The major apologetically blindfolded Maruyama, sat him in the back of the car, then got into the passenger seat in the front and ordered the driver to proceed to where Chairman Kishimoto was incarcerated. As promised, Maruyama was given three minutes with Kishimoto and had to dispense with all formalities as he hurriedly explained, "I want to leave Manchuria to return to Japan as soon as I can. My intention is to appeal to General MacArthur and the appropriate agencies in Japan to make them aware of the miserable situation of the Japanese stranded here so that the Americans will devise a means to rescue them. Obviously, I will not be able to carry out this plan by myself, and I will need help. My main purpose in coming to see you today is to ask if you know an appropriate person who can help me with my plan."

At once, as if Kishimoto had been expecting such a request, he replied, "Go and see Hachiro Shinpo in Anshan City, and discuss your plan with him."

Since the allotted minutes were up, Maruyama suddenly felt a deep pang of regret in having to part with his company's chairman who had had such a distinguished career but was now utterly helpless. "Please take care of yourself by all means, Mr. Kishimoto. I pray for your health and well-being." With that, and seeing Major Babalkin gesturing that it was time to go, Maruyama took his leave. Although the meeting lasted a mere three minutes, it was truly an emotional one. This was the last time Maruyama would see the chairman.

Recruiting Fellow Conspirators Shinpo and Musashi

The name that Chairman Kishimoto suggested, Hachiro Shinpo, was not a name Maruyama had ever heard. In the next couple of days, he discreetly asked some trusted acquaintances about Shinpo. Taisuke Otsuka, a friend he had known in Tokyo before they came to Manchuria, had become a successful and influential businessman in Anshan and had even been elected to the Anshan City assembly. Maruyama went to see Otsuka at his home to inquire about Shinpo, never mentioning that he had met with Chairman Kishimoto. Otsuka knew Shinpo well and told Maruyama a great deal about the man Kishimoto had recommended. Otsuka revealed that Shinpo was the owner and president of an extremely successful architectural firm in Anshan City called Shinpo-gumi and gave Maruyama his address.

Encouraged that Shinpo might indeed be the man he needed in his bold plan, Maruyama went to see him the next evening at Shinpo's house. Meeting Shinpo for the first time, Maruyama decided to completely trust and confide in the pleasant and confident-looking man in front of him and hold back nothing. He related to Shinpo that he had gone to see Chairman Kishimoto in secret through help from a Soviet officer and had asked Kishimoto to recommend someone in Anshan who would be able to join Maruyama in an escape out of Manchuria. It turned out that Shinpo himself had also been thinking seriously about escaping to Japan so that the two connected at once, both emotionally and intellectually. After some discussion, the two acted as if they had known each other for a lifetime. Shortly thereafter, they grasped each other's hands and together swore an oath by saying, "Let us both take on this great responsibility, and let us together share our fate." The thirty-seven-year-old Maruyama and the thirty-one-year-old Shinpo then hugged each other tightly, an emotional gesture rarely shared by Japanese men, even in private.

Regaining his composure, Maruyama said, "This mission will surely be a grave one that is certain to involve many extremely complicated elements. I think it would be far better for us if we had a third person join us in our mission, someone to assist us, perhaps someone among your employees or someone you know, someone whom you completely trust. I would feel so much more confident of our success if we were a group of three rather than just the two of us. How do you feel about that?"

Shinpo thought hard about the suggestion and closed his eyes for a moment as if in deep thought. Then he looked at Maruyama and said, "Yes, I agree. There is a young man in my company named Masamichi Musashi. He is a most talented employee whom I have had the pleasure of training closely as his mentor. We will take Musashi along with us. I know that he will be a most valuable help to us. I will ask him tomorrow to accompany us." Maruyama had no doubt that if Shinpo was recommending this young man named Musashi (then twenty-three years old), he must be an exceptionally capable individual. Maruyama was even more resolved to undertake the mission.

Late the next day, Musashi recalls, he had been busily working since morning at the Manchurian Iron Manufacturing Company under the watchful eyes of Soviet soldiers when he was summoned to see his boss, Shinpo. He had been assigned to supervise the loading onto rail cars of various machinery from the factories for their eventual shipment to the Soviet Union. It was a thankless task, even a hateful one, as the Soviets forced Japanese like Musashi to participate in the dismantling and removal of critical former Japanese industrial machinery, precision instruments, power generators, chemical industry machinery, and much more from over fifty installations in Anshan, including Manchuria Sumitomo Metal Manufacturing, Ordnance Workshop, Showa Steel Manufacturing Company, and Manchuria Hitachi. Because winter was coming and transporting factory facilities would become impossible when the ocean froze, the Soviets intensified efforts in November. Musashi derived absolutely no satisfaction from aiding in these expropriations of the Soviet Union.

As Musashi was about to finish his work for the day, an elderly Manchurian employee of Shinpo-gumi that he knew by sight came to him and said, "Wuzang [Mr. Musashi], the company president asks that you stop at his house on your way home tonight." As the elderly man's figure disappeared into the darkening evening, Musashi wondered what his president and good friend, Shinpo, wanted.

Musashi first met Shinpo in the spring of 1940 in Shimonoseki in Kyushu, just before the Pacific War began. Shinpo had returned from Manchuria for a short visit to Japan and was again on his way back when he stopped at the inn where sixteen-year-old Musashi was employed. A hardworking man of unlimited talent, especially as an architect, Shinpo had crossed the sea to Manchuria after graduating from Tokyo's Shibaura College of Engineering (where Kishimoto was then the president) with a degree in construction. With great ambition and dreams of success, Shinpo achieved just that as he started his Shinpo-gumi architectural company in Anshan. His company soon surpassed other architectural companies in the area. He invited many of his colleagues who graduated with him to join him in Anshan City, and he formed a corporation that established a network of branch offices in key locations throughout Manchuria. His company soon had a hand in many key projects throughout the territory.

"Money Makes the Mare Go"

Maruyama wrote in his book that, were it not for the generous financial contribution of Shinpo, their mission would not have succeeded. "It's the same the world over, that no matter what one may want to do, there are things that cannot be done without money despite the loftiness of the goal. Sincerity, effort, courage, and knowledge were necessary ingredients for our plan, but funding to back up its execution was necessary.... Hachiro Shinpo volunteered to put forth the necessary funding," noted Maruyama in *Why Was Koroto Opened.*[5] When all the banks were about to be closed following the Soviet occupation and just before accounts of all Japanese were frozen, Shinpo was astute enough to foresee the future and took the precaution of withdrawing much of his money from the bank so it would be under his control. Even had he not done so, he had many other valuable possessions that he could easily sell to the Manchurians for considerable money. "In Japan, there is a saying that can be translated as 'Money makes the mare go,' and in the West, the saying is 'Money talks.' This is a universal principle. Shinpo's commitment of his personal wealth on behalf of our escape from Manchuria was certainly a major factor that led to the successful accomplishment of our vital mission," reflected Maruyama in 1970.[6]

During his brief stay at the inn at Shimonoseki, Shinpo told the bright-eyed young Musashi about all the possibilities for success in the new territory called Manchuria as long as one was willing to work hard. Musashi was immediately awestruck with Shinpo's descriptions and, on the spot, begged to be taken there. Seeing that the boy was serious, and impressed with his intelligence and diligence demonstrated even during their very brief encounter, Shinpo agreed, and the two crossed the Eastern Channel of the Korea Strait on a Kanpu ferry, which crossed between Pusan, Korea, and Shimonoseki. Musashi became an employee of Shinpo-gumi. Company President Shinpo took Musashi under his wing, and the boy soon became one of his most productive and valuable employees.

Musashi soon learned Chinese, and in spite of his youthful age, he earned the respect of the Chinese who worked for Shinpo-gumi because he treated everyone as an equal, ignoring barriers of nationality. In those days, many Japanese considered themselves superior to the Chinese and often treated them harshly and disrespectfully. Musashi found it enjoyable to work alongside them, preferring to be "where the action was" rather than to sit at his desk ordering others around. As a result, he taught himself almost everything he needed to know to succeed in the construction and architecture business.

One of Musashi's talents was in accounting; he even won the all-Manchuria *soroban* (Japanese abacus) calculation contest one year. Another of his talents was in the sport of judo; a third-degree black belt, he became good enough to teach policemen at the Anshan police headquarters. Shinpo noted with great satisfaction that the young boy he had brought to Manchuria had the disposition to work hard at any task until he became an expert at it. Thus, when Maruyama asked for a third person to join them on their daunting secret mission, Shinpo immediately proposed Musashi to be that person.

Is Escape from Manchuria Possible?

When Musashi announced his presence at his company president's house, the sliding front door was opened immediately by Shinpo as if his arrival had been anxiously anticipated. Taking his shoes off and entering the house at the urging of his employer, Musashi climbed the stairs to Shinpo's living room on the second floor. A stranger in the room looked up at him with a smile.

After introducing the stranger to Musashi as Kunio Maruyama, Shinpo assumed a sober bearing and said, "The reason I asked you to stop by is because there is a matter with which I want to ask your help." So saying, with Maruyama sitting next to him, he began his explanation.

"There is no need for me to repeat that Japan has lost the war, and the nation of Manchuria has collapsed. We have no control whatsoever over all that has happened. For all Japanese, there is nothing left to do but to hope we can return to Japan. However, in the present circumstance under the occupation of the Soviet army and the Communist Eighth Route Army, there is no way for anyone to predict when we might be able to return to Japan...." Shinpo lowered his voice. "As of now, we in Anshan can still say that we are in a fortunate circumstance. The plight of the pioneer settlers from the north who have lost homes and properties in a single night, as well as other Japanese who have come seeking refuge in Sinkiang, Shenyang, and Dalian from outlying districts, is indeed dire. Seeing their condition makes us disbelieve what we see. If things continue as they are and nothing is done, there will be many, many who will die here and never be able to return to their homeland. We are all Japanese, and we cannot close our eyes to the realities we see. Maruyama-san and I have been discussing that something must be done."

Musashi agreed that truer words were never spoken: with the end of the war and especially with the Soviet invasion, everyone in Manchuria, particularly the Japanese, were placed in a terrible situation. Then Maruyama, who had been silent up to now, said, "Things will just keep getting worse. There is but one solution. Repatriation must begin without one more day of delay; we need to have ships come to take Japanese back to Japan. To have that happen, someone must escape from Manchuria and return to Japan, and then make known to the Japanese nation as well as to the United States and to the world the actual conditions that exist in Manchuria. Shinpo-san and I are willing to take that risk and escape to Japan, but we feel it will be impossible for just the two of us to flee on our own. Shinpo-san has told me that if you were to join us, we might succeed. Musashi-san, would you be willing to join us?" With this, Maruyama bowed his head deeply to Musashi.

For an instant, Musashi was not sure what he had heard. *Escape from Manchuria? Is such a thing possible? Are these two men serious?* He knew, of course, that Shinpo was a most honorable man and was never frivolous in words or action. This Maruyama beside him seemed to be an honest and straightforward man. It was obvious that both men were dead serious as they awaited his response.

"I understand. I too am a Japanese man. I ask you to please let me join you in your mission." Both Maruyama and Shinpo relaxed their tense countenances at Musashi's answer and they exchanged nods of satisfaction. Musashi later admitted that he worried about the chances of their success, but he was greatly touched by the grave concerns that his boss and Maruyama had for all their fellow Japanese in Manchuria.

That night, the three men—Kunio Maruyama, Hachiro Shinpo, and Masamichi Musashi—had their first "official" meeting to discuss how to go about executing their mission to escape from Manchuria and bring about the rescue of all the Japanese living under Soviet oppression. Their discussion went on until dawn was breaking. Before they separated, they solemnly swore an oath to keep their plan completely secret and never to talk to anyone else about their plan until their escape was successful. Only Maruyama's and Shinpo's wives were aware of their plan. Musashi was not married. Exhausted but satisfied with their resolve, Maruyama left Shinpo's house to hail a *yancho* (a Manchurian rickshaw) to head home.

The three men met in complete secrecy almost every night from then on in the second-floor room of Shinpo's residence at North Sanjo-machi in Anshan City. They put their heads together and absorbed themselves in formulating a plan of escape, enthusiastically discussing a potentially feasible idea, only to find a flaw that momentarily dampened their enthusiasm. Between their evening meetings, they were busily gathering information during the day about current situations throughout Manchuria. In fact, they spent a considerable amount of money in that endeavor since they needed to stay on top of every development in the current situation. When the three considered the enormity of the responsibility that they were about to assume, they had no other option but to succeed. Whether the Japanese residents in Manchuria knew it or not, each was counting on the three men to carry out the plan to escape and then to entreat the responsible officials in Japan to send the ships to rescue them out of the hellhole that was Manchuria. The mission of belling the cat had been entrusted to three mice named Maruyama, Shinpo, and Musashi. They could not depend on luck or entrust everything to the heavens; they had to evaluate their every move coldly, calculatingly, and scientifically. The success of their mission depended on their collective knowledge, wisdom, and judgment, not on luck or guesswork.

Chapter 7

Searching for a Way Out

The Story of Abraham Lincoln and the Young Mother

As they met night after night, at times everything looked hopeless, grim, and impossible. On one such occasion, when the three were exhausted and took a break to sip some warm *sake*, Maruyama told his companions the following story. The story was about a young mother during the Civil War in the United States. President Abraham Lincoln had been busy at work in the White House and sought to cool his head and refresh himself by stepping outside to enjoy a little solitude in his favorite rose garden. As he walked around enjoying the smell of the roses, he heard the distinct cry of a baby coming from somewhere. As he walked toward the source of the crying, he saw a young woman wearing very shabby clothing, hugging her baby close to her and trying to soothe the infant. Taken by complete surprise, President Lincoln asked the young woman if something was wrong.

"Mr. President, I came to ask you a favor," said the young woman in a low voice as she lowered her head. President Lincoln led the young woman with the infant into his private office, sat her and the baby down in a comfortable chair, and proceeded to listen to her story.

The young woman was a resident of Philadelphia and had married a skilled carpenter. Soon after their wedding, however, the War Between the States erupted, and her husband was drafted into the Union Army, and then the baby was born. One day, as the young woman was nursing her baby, and simultaneously praying for the safe return of her husband as always, a message was delivered to her. It was terrible news. It was not that her husband had been killed on the battlefield. He had been assigned to sentry duty one night, and due to fatigue, he fell asleep; an officer caught him taking a nap. The terrible news was that her husband had been court-martialed and sentenced to be executed by a firing squad.

"Mr. President, I am fully aware that my husband committed a terrible offense by falling asleep while on duty, and while I am stricken with grief beyond words, there is not much that can be done about the sentence that was handed down. All I want is for my husband to be able to see his child, whom he has never seen, before he is executed. To seek that permission, I went to the Department of the Army yesterday to plead with them, but they flatly rejected my plea, saying that women and children are not allowed on the battlefield. In desperation, I have come to plead with you, the president of the United States." With that, the young woman collapsed in tears with her baby at the feet of President Lincoln.

The president gently took the young woman by the shoulders and said, "I fully understand your situation." He then turned to his desk to scribble a note. He handed it to the woman and said, "Here, take this to the Department of the Army. I am pardoning your husband, and they will forgive him for his crime." The surprised young woman, unsure whether she might be dreaming, fell to the floor again, this time in utter joy.

When Musashi recalled Maruyama's story in his book *The Dawning of Asia—Crossing the Lines of Death*, he remembered how moved he was by the anecdote. The moral of the story was that if the young woman had simply given up hope when the

Department of the Army denied her appeal rather than pressing on, her husband would most likely have been executed, never to have seen his loving wife and infant child. But since the woman persevered and appealed directly to the president himself, her sincerity moved the president.

"Maruyama-san, that story is what we Japanese say in our proverbs, 'Sincerity moves heaven.'"

"Musashi-san, I agree. If we take on the task at hand and persevere with sincerity, heaven will surely not abandon us. We will find success for sure." Maruyama, who was not at all a strong drinker, looked at his two companions with his face very red from the *sake*.

The Tragic Death of Kishimoto and His Wife

Around the time the three men began meeting nightly, Kishimoto, the former chairman of Showa Steel Manufacturing Company, the man who had been responsible for getting the three men together and who had been under arrest in the custody of the Soviet army, was transferred over to the custody of the Chinese Communist Eighth Route Army, now his jailers. (In the beginning, the Eighth Route Army which appeared everywhere along with the advancement of the Soviet army, was nothing more than a ragtag army that was hastily put together wherever the Soviet army advanced.) Kishimoto's only crime was that he had formerly been a general in the Imperial Army. When the Chinese Communists came to take custody of him, he was in bed, ill with a cold. As the Chinese began to drag him away, his wife stepped forward and pleaded, "Please take me also so I can act as his nurse." The husband and wife were taken to a jail that was set up at Anshan Junior High School.

When Musashi first came to Manchuria following Shinpo as a sixteen-year-old boy, he knew no one besides Shinpo in his new environment. However, the Kishimotos took the boy under their wing and looked after him as if he were their own son. Musashi came to regard them as his surrogate parents.

Musashi, who had Chinese friends and acquaintances in both the Eighth Route Army as well as the Nationalist army, heard that Chairman Kishimoto was now under custody of the Eighth Route Army. He contacted former Shinpo-gumi employees who had joined the Communist cause, some of them now in positions of considerable authority. He tried to convince his former workers that Kishimoto might have been a general in the past, but he now was a civilian, and depriving Japanese society of such a man would not do any good for the Eighth Route Army. The resourceful Musashi had access to provisions and other goods that had previously belonged to the Kwantung Army, and he offered them to the Eighth Route Army as a gesture of goodwill. Negotiations went smoothly, and a tacit agreement was reached to have the Kishimoto couple released. Unfortunately, just before their release, Chiang Kai-shek's Nationalist forces were threatening to come into Anshan, and the Eighth Route Army decided to retreat, taking the Kishimoto couple with them. A Chinese friend reported to Musashi later that Mrs. Kishimoto took her own life by swallowing potassium cyanide that she always carried, and Chairman Kishimoto was executed somewhere in the suburbs of Anshan.

Musashi was devastated by the news and spent the entire day alternating between sorrow and anger. He wondered for a long time if he could have done more during his negotiation with the Eighth Route Army to obtain their release.

The former general and former mayor of Tokyo had played a significant part in the lives of all three conspirators. For Shinpo, Kishimoto had been his teacher and the beloved president of his university. For Maruyama, Kishimoto had been the admired and respected chairman of his company. For Musashi, Kishimoto was someone he adored like a father.

Musashi made his way up a low-lying hill on the outskirts of Anshan where he believed the chairman had been executed by gunfire by the Chinese Communist Army. Snow was falling. "Mr. Chairman, Mrs. Kishimoto, I swear to you that we will carry through in returning to Japan for the sake of all the countrymen left here. Please always keep looking after us." That was Musashi's tearful oath as the wind whipped the snow into a blizzard.

An Escape Route Proves Elusive

Winter came early in 1945, and as the weather turned icy with the arrival of 1946, the spirit of all Japanese in Manchuria fell even lower. Death was everywhere, especially among the young. Infants, who knew nothing of war, suffered the most due to lack of food and warmth. In spite of all the deaths, daily increasing numbers of refugees flocked into Anshan and other major cities with large Japanese populations. They found shelter where they could, in schools, temples, former community centers, abandoned buildings—wherever they were able to ward off the bitter cold.

Maruyama, Shinpo, and Musashi continued to meet almost every evening at the home of Shinpo. During the day, they were immersed in the task of gathering intelligence from throughout Manchuria, and they discussed their findings in the evening while continuing their search for the best escape route. The Communist Eighth Route Army had temporarily evacuated from Anshan when rumors of Nationalist advances became rampant; however, when that advance was stalled, the Communist army returned. That made the three men take extra precaution in their activities. When they met in Shinpo's home, they talked in low voices, and they put up curtains on all the windows so no light could be seen from the outside.

The information the three had been gathering gave them a relatively clear picture of the obstacles that lay in any path they might choose for their escape. While they were more than ready to risk everything, including their lives, they knew that their escape absolutely had to succeed; there was no other choice. The course that was usually considered whenever anyone returned to Japan before the end of the war was to cross over east on the Japan Sea from the Korean Peninsula. The popular and much used Kanpu ferry was the easiest route; however, the Kanpu Ferry Ship no longer existed.

Just before the end of the war, Hachiro Shinpo had been hastily drafted into the Kwantung Army in July 1945 and had been sent into North Korea when the war came to an end. His unit surrendered to the Soviet army and they were transferred to Pyongyang, North Korea, in late August. While there, Shinpo and about thirty of his fellow prisoners-of-war escaped from Soviet confinement and crossed the Yalu River via Andong and made their way back west and reached Anshan on September 1. Had Shinpo and his companions not made their desperate escape, they would surely have been sent to Siberia where many Japanese soldiers died as forced laborers of the Soviet Union.

Thus, Shinpo had firsthand knowledge of the security situation in the surrounding area as the three continued their discussions of escape. "The border area between Korea and Manchuria is certain to have come under the strictest security, and escape in that direction will be extremely difficult, if not impossible. Besides, the situation in Korea has become perilous for Japanese since the end of the war." So saying, Shinpo opposed any course that would take the three through Korea.

Another route to consider was to go south to Dalian or west to Yingkou, then find a fishing vessel from ports nearby and attempt sailing to Japan. However, they all agreed that was too risky, and they would probably have no chance of avoiding Soviet or Communist Chinese patrols even if they found passage on a fishing boat. As their discussions went on night after night, gloominess often crept into their optimism, but they never harbored the idea of giving up.

Dispatching Secret Emissaries to Japan

The three men did not know it at the time, but another Japanese in Manchuria had hatched a plan to dispatch a secret mission to flee Manchuria, escape to Japan, and appeal to Japanese authorities to rescue the Japanese stranded in Manchuria. Toshio Hirashima, then the vice president of the South Manchurian Railway Company (later elected to Japanese Parliament as member of the House of Councilors), saw the world around him in exactly the same way as the three men. When Maruyama wrote his book in 1970, *Why Was Koroto Opened*, Hirashima wrote the following that was included in Maruyama's preface: "In those times, I felt that in my position of responsibility, I had to do something to open a path for the repatriation of Japanese in Manchuria as so many were becoming refugees. I felt with all my heart that there was the need to contact those in position of responsibility in Japan without another day of delay, so we selected several individuals with exceptional talent and courage and assigned them the role as secret envoys and came up with a plan that would take them to Japan. Numerous times, these men entered the Yalu River from North Korea and they were to take the route that was to allow them to break through the 38th parallel and head them toward Japan. In spite of superhuman efforts on the part of those men, they did not succeed because the security in the area was just too heavy for them to overcome."

Hirashima, of course, was not aware of the secret plotting of the three men in Anshan. The first time he learned about their successful escape was when he heard a radio broadcast from Japan made by Maruyama in mid-April 1946, that for the first time ever, described the present conditions in Manchuria. The broadcast appealed to the people of Japan to put pressure on the Japanese government and GHQ (MacArthur's General Headquarters) to dispatch ships as soon as possible to Manchuria to repatriate the stranded Japanese. Since no Japanese in Manchuria was allowed to own a radio in those days, the news of the broadcast from Japan was passed on by word of mouth by those very few who heard the broadcast on radios they had hidden away at the risk of their lives. The news of the broadcast spread like wildfire among the Japanese residents. When Hirashima learned that three men from Anshan had successfully escaped to Japan, he later wrote in the preface to Maruyama's book, "it was as if they had taken the place of our emissaries who had been unable to overcome the difficulties, and we were overjoyed as if we ourselves had succeeded."[1]

At the time Toshio Hirashima wrote the aforementioned letter in 1970, he was unaware that the secret emissaries he had dispatched in collaboration with the chairman of the All-Manchuria Japanese Association, Tatsunosuke Takasaki, had in fact succeeded in escaping to Japan. The letters they carried appealing for help from the Japanese government had been delivered to the Ministry of Foreign Affairs. The emissaries departed Manchuria around September 22, 1945, and reached Japan about October 10. The letters had been written by an expert Japanese craftsman in Manchuria who specialized in writing tiny characters about the size of half a grain of rice, and were sewn into the clothing of the emissaries during their escape. The letters are in the possession of a private museum in Japan and were recently shown on NHK [Japan Broadcasting Corporation] in a documentary produced by the production company, Asian Complex ["This Was How Repatriation Happened," aired on December 8, 2008]. In the chaotic days following the defeat of Japan, the Japanese government was utterly powerless to do anything to react to the appeal for help contained in the letters. The whereabouts of the courageous secret emissaries who returned to Japan at the risk of their lives is completely unknown (see chapter 31).[2]

In January 1946, in Anshan, Manchuria, the three men continued to huddle together nightly, determined to come up with a plan to escape. Musashi, the youngest of the three, counseled patience as he said, "I'm sure we will never be able to come up with an absolutely foolproof plan that will guarantee success. In the end, we will need to leave our fate in the hands of 'Heavenly Power.' Let's continue to be patient, and I'm sure we will come up with a plan soon that will have the greatest chance of succeeding." Agreeing to be wary of the danger of impatience, the men continued to rack their brains to find a path out of Manchuria.

Chapter 8

Planning the Escape

The Unbelievable Sighting of Western Correspondents

In early January of 1946, Maruyama traveled about eighty miles north by train to Shenyang (then called Mukden) in his now customary Manchurian "uniform" of a peasant laborer to observe and inspect with his own eyes how the Japanese were faring in that large city. Since so many refugees poured into large cities like Shenyang, the living conditions for the Japanese were changing constantly, always for the worse.

As he got off the train and stepped into the main street, Maruyama was greatly surprised to see a group of about ten Westerners walking by. Since he had seen no foreigners anywhere in Manchuria, except the invading Russians and the missionaries at Maryknoll in Dalian, he was completely shocked by the sight. Foreigners had come to Manchuria! In fact, Maruyama could tell by their clothing, actions, and confident attitude that they were Westerners.

He had a strong urge to get near and speak to them, no matter who they were—American, English, French, Spanish, or whatever; he wanted desperately to ask what route they had used to come here, and for what purpose they were here. Unfortunately, they were closely guarded by several well-armed Soviet soldiers who seemed to surround them to insure that no one came near them. Maruyama knew that if he were to approach closer, let alone try to whisper something to one of the foreigners, the Soviet soldiers would swarm him and probably execute him on the spot. The foreigners, who appeared to be scrutinizing everything they saw, seemed to want to talk to the people walking around the main street. Of course, the Soviet guards made sure that would not happen.

The Westerners were soon herded into a waiting bus and the bus drove away. As Maruyama watched the bus disappear, he could barely control his frustration. Although he had no choice in the mattter, he had let slip an opportunity to talk to them. He found out later that the foreigners were journalists from Allied and neutral nations, including the United States, Great Britain, France, Spain, and Portugal, who had been given permission by the Soviet Union to inspect Manchuria in the aftermath of the Soviet invasion. They were forbidden to take any pictures unless authorized by the Soviet guards and were strictly prohibited from talking to anyone except the security personnel.

However, the clever journalists had been able to fool the Soviet soldiers by taking photos of the results of systematic Soviet looting as well as gruesome photos of abandoned Japanese corpses, some that had been left on the streets for weeks and most eaten away by dogs. Those photos appeared several weeks later in newspapers and magazines in the journalists' own countries. Maruyama surmised that, since the Soviet soldiers escorting the journalists were the type of characters who were seeing wristwatches for the first time, they probably had no idea that the small boxes that the journalists carried in the palm of their hands were actually cameras. On their escape to Japan several weeks later, the three men purchased a copy of *Newsweek* magazine while transiting through Tianjin (Tientsin), China, that contained an article written by one of the journalists, which also included some of the clandestine photos.

What the Correspondents Reported to the World

This author was recently able to obtain copies of several of the news articles written by some in the group of journalists that Maruyama observed in Shenyang, and it is noteworthy to highlight some of the main points in the articles. Although rumors of rampage by Soviet soldiers upon the civilian population, the systematic looting and transporting of industrial facilities to Russia, the forced transporting of captured Japanese soldiers to Siberia, and the many atrocities committed against Japanese and Chinese alike in Manchuria abounded, this was the first time eyewitness accounts appeared in the press.

In the March 11, 1946, issue of *Newsweek*, an article entitled "Manchurian Pillage" begins with the following statement from the U.S. State Department press chief, Michael J. McDermott: "We have no agreement, secret or otherwise, with the Soviet government or any other government, in regards to war booty in Manchuria. This government [i.e., the government of the United States] does not accept any interpretation of war booty to include industrial enterprises ... such as Japanese industries ... in Manchuria.... Some time ago, we informed the Soviet government ... that it would be most inappropriate at this time to make any final disposition of Japanese external assets in Manchuria." The article went on to say, "In raising the issue [of Soviet looting] again, the American government publicly admitted for the first time what the world had known for months: The Russian Army had systematically stripped Manchuria of plants and machinery vital to the future of Chinese industry."

The *Newsweek* correspondent found that, out of nearly one thousand large plants that were operational in Mukden (Shenyang) at the end of the war, only twenty still operated, most of them engaged in making cigarettes, beer, vodka, or cosmetics to aid "Soviet soldiers' fraternizing." After witnessing the devastation in Mukden, many of the visiting correspondents confronted the Soviet commander, Major

General Andrei Kovtoun-Stankevich, a gruff and earthy man whose build resembled a sturdy beer barrel. When asked about the systematic stripping of factories and other industrial facilities, he coughed and replied, "[They] could not be left here ..." so they had been shipped out "according to a decision of The Big Three ... either at Yalta or Berlin, I'm not sure, offhand." Major General Kovtoun-Stankevich also admitted to correspondents that "Jap troops captured by the Russians in Mukden last summer had been sent to Siberia. He didn't know what happened to them beyond that and seemed surprised that anyone should care." The article, which was written as a result of the Western correspondents' survey of Manchuria in January 1946, went on to say that the Soviets planned to leave Manchuria soon. However, Chinese officers countered that it was absolutely false: the nearly six thousand Soviet troops in Mukden were being reinforced by forces from north Manchuria, and thirty to forty thousand Soviet soldiers had recently landed at Port Arthur. In fact, Russian billets were being fixed up, and officers were sending for their wives from Russia, all indicating a long stay.[1]

Life magazine had a four-page pictorial spread in its March 25, 1946, issue, starting with a smiling photo of the bemedaled (including a U.S. Legion of Merit and a Bronze Star Medal) Mukden commander, Major General Kovtoun-Stankevich. In the interview by the Western correspondents, *Life* noted that the general, though he received the journalists cordially, was often vague and forgetful in his replies. *Life* declared that "in stripping Manchuria (which started in September, 1945) the Russians went beyond their usual practice of taking things which could be useful in rebuilding the Soviet Union. In Manchuria, what they could not carry away with them was destroyed. Factory after factory, from which machinery had been removed, was then burned."[2]

Time magazine correspondent William Gray, another of the Western journalists in the group spotted by Maruyama in Shenyang (Mukden), reported in his article that appeared in the March 11, 1946, issue of *Time* that "the atmosphere of Mukden is charged with a degree of fear that Americans should never experience, and find hard to believe until it infects them also.... In one street, we came upon ten blackening Chinese or Japanese corpses, a fortnight old and partly gnawed by dogs. Grisly as this sight was, it was more easily forgotten than the sight of Mukden's ravished factories." Somehow, Gray and some colleagues evaded Soviet guards to talk to a young Japanese engineer who had witnessed the dismantling of Japanese-built Anshan Steel Works. "The Russians," the Japanese said, "took seventy percent to eighty percent of Anshan's equipment including foundry tools, machine shop, steel rolling and milling machines, chemical equipment, trucks, locomotives ... [T]he booty was sent by rail to Dairen [Dalian] and to Russian-occupied Korea for shipment to Russia." To assure the safety of the Japanese engineer who dared talk to Western correspondents, he was removed by Chinese officials to a place where there was some assurance of safety.

On the subject of conflict between the Nationalist and Communist Chinese, the *Time* article stated that "the Chinese Central Government (under Chiang Kai-shek) and the Chinese Communists are still warring. Confusion and local control are the order of the day. The Nationalist army commander says flatly that the Russians are aiding the Communists. The Russians contend that they cannot tell one Chinese from another; there could be some honest confusion, but the Russians are smart enough not to be confused if they want to know the truth."

The article ended with the following observation: "The Russians have taken what Japanese they wanted as a labor force. They have made efforts to befriend and propagandize Japanese technicians. Finally, they will be content to leave a Japanese residue in Manchuria as a confusing and weakening factor for China to cope with. The Russians are not just leaving

China with an empty house in Manchuria; they appear to want to leave it full of termites, too."[3]

In a wrap-up article in the March 18 edition of *Newsweek* entitled "Rape of Manchuria," *New York Post* correspondent Andrew A. Freeman commented on the reaction of two of the Western newsmen who were presumably in the group Maruyama saw in Shenyang. "One of them [i.e., a Western correspondent] ... said he had gone there willing to give the Russians every break.... He did not want to believe that the Russians were looting the country as rumored, or that they intended to remain in Manchuria." However, he now was "disgusted and disheartened." An Associated Press newsman in the group, Richard Cushing, wrote, "The industrial area looks worse than Tokyo ... as if it had been bombed steadily for months.... The systematic stripping ... is all but complete." A veteran Far East correspondent for the *New York Herald Tribune*, A. T. Steele, wrote, "The Chinese here told me the Russians are even more disliked than were the Japanese." In his article appearing in the *New York Post*, Robert P. Martin wrote: "This is an evil country.... It is in the attitude of the people, their undisguised fear, the sight of empty streets, the sound of echoing shots.... Chinese tell you that six months of Russian occupation has been worse than fourteen years of Jap occupation."[4]

Even an Ally is Fair Game to the Soviets

In order to keep the world from finding out what they were doing, in addition to severing all communications between Manchuria and the rest of the world, the Soviet army even fired on U.S. planes that violated Manchurian airspace. According to *Newsweek*, the U.S. Navy revealed two earlier incidents in which the Russians fired on two U.S. military aircraft over Manchuria. It need not be pointed out that the Soviet Union, along with the United States, Great Britain, and the Chinese Government, was an Allied Power member at that time.[5] (Apparently one of the firing incidents happened as early as November 15, 1945. A March 23, 1946, message from Washington to the Commander of U.S. Army Forces Pacific noted that Moscow had still not explained why the U.S. plane was attacked twenty-five miles from shore. The same message advised all U.S. surface vessels and aircraft to remain twelve miles from the shorelines of Russian-occupied territories.[6])

Chiang Kai-shek's Victory Speech

In a speech on the day the war ended (August 15, 1945), Generalissimo Chiang Kai-shek made a memorable radio broadcast (particularly for the people of Japan) to the people of China from his headquarter in Chungking (Chongqing). In that address, he said, "I am deeply moved when I think the teachings of Jesus Christ that we should do unto others as we would have them do unto us and love our enemies.... We have always said that the violent militarism of Japan is our enemy, not the people of Japan.... [W]e should not for a moment think of revenge or heap abuses upon the innocent people of Japan...."[7]

In January of 1946, the Nationalist (or Kuomintang) Army of Generalissimo Chiang Kai-shek gradually sent a surreptitious underground battalion via the Hozan Rail Line to filter into Shenyang to increase its forces in the city. In fact, Maruyama, Shinpo, and Musashi found that the Nationalist Kuomintang Army, even in the remotest units, heeded Chiang Kai-shek's instruction well and demonstrated overall generosity toward the Japanese people in general throughout Manchuria. The three men concluded that their plan would require the help of the Nationalist army, and the man who could make contact with the Kuomintang Army was Shinpo.

As the three Japanese men evaluated the ever-changing conditions around them, they finally began to formulate a definitive plan for their escape out of Manchuria. The architectural company that Shinpo had owned and operated until the Soviet invasion, Shinpo-gumi, had had many outstanding Chinese employees who had the greatest respect for their employer. Shinpo, unlike many other Japanese employers, had always treated all his employees with respect and consideration regardless of their nationality. Many of Shinpo's Chinese employees had immediately joined the Nationalist forces as soon as they entered into Manchuria and many by now were in a position of great importance in the Nationalist army. Shinpo was able to make contacts with some of his former employees now serving in the Kuomintang Army. These men, in turn, put the three men in contact with members of the headquarters command staff of the Nationalist army's underground forces in Shenyang. The plan that Maruyama, Shinpo, and Musashi came up with was to set out south from Shenyang on the Shenyang Railway, make a brief stop to check out the port at Koroto, then break through to Shanhaiguan where the Great Wall of China separated China from Manchuria, then continue south in China to Tianjin and find passage on a U.S. vessel bound for Japan. Once in Japan, they would immediately go to Tokyo.

The three men took the first step to carry out their bold plan on the very dark night of February 8, 1946. Wearing their camouflage Manchurian clothing and smelling strongly of garlic, the three rode the train from Anshan under cover of darkness and disembarked at Shenyang Station where they hailed a *yancho* (rickshaw) and headed in the direction they had earlier been instructed to take by their Nationalist contact. Soon, thanks to arrangements made earlier by Musashi, a Chinese officer (who they later learned was a division commander) quietly boarded the *yancho* with the three men. Much like a cloud sparrow (which never descends directly to its nest but descends into a grass field nearby, then crawls to its nest), the men got off the *yancho* near the location of the underground headquarters, and each entered the headquarters building separately so as to not attract attention.

The Conflict between the Nationalists and the Communists

It may be helpful at this point to summarize briefly the history of the conflict in China between the Communist forces and the Nationalist army in order to understand why they were fighting each other at the time of the Soviet occupation of Manchuria. After the death in 1925 of the man considered as the founder of modern China, Dr. Sun Yat-sen, two men eventually emerged as rivals to continue Dr. Sun's dream of presiding over a unified China. One, a Communist, was the son of a rich farmer who never acquired much formal education but remained self-righteous and steadfast in his belief that he was destined to rule over China. His name was Mao Zedong. The other was an honor student graduate of the Japanese Military Academy and the son of prosperous minor gentry. His name was Chiang Kai-shek, and he was equally stubborn and self-righteous and believed he was the rightful heir to Dr. Sun Yat-sen. Chiang Kai-shek had staunchly supported Sun Yat-sen from as early as during the revolution in 1911 that had propelled Dr. Sun to the presidency of the Republic of China, if only for a brief time.

In the beginning, the Communists and the Nationalists made a show of cooperating with each other with Russia supporting both sides, but by 1927, the two entities split and conflict between the two forces continued until Chiang Kai-shek withdrew his forces to Taiwan in 1950. During the more than two decades that the conflict between the Nationalists and Communists raged on, the Japanese took advantage of the confusing situation by dominating Manchuria and began gradually penetrating southward toward the Great Wall and beyond into China. While Mao and the Communists were genuinely concerned with the Japanese encroachment and resisted with irregulars and guerrillas against the Japanese, Chiang was more concerned with defeating the Communists and chose to appease the Japanese through negotiations and yielding territories, and thereby tried to preserve his manpower and resources for the real fight to come, the one against the Communists Party and their Red Army. The Communists, whose tactic was to win the peasants and the workers over to their side, played on the sentiment of the Chinese peasantry to fight against the Japanese.

The Communists made an offer to the Nationalists for a temporary truce to focus their attention on defeating the Japanese, and a partial truce was signed in 1937. For a time, the two forces actively fought against the Japanese. The cooperation between Chiang Kai-shek's Nationalists and Mao Zedong's Red Army was, however, merely a facade. The Communists were just as diligent to limit losses against the real war against the Nationalists. As Chiang's forces retreated before the Japanese army, the Communists stealthily infiltrated the areas behind the conventional front lines and gradually began controlling the peasantry in a large part of northeastern China. With the Japanese attack on Pearl Harbor on December 8, 1941 (December 7 in the United States), the United States was unavoidably forced to become involved in the Communist–Nationalist conflict. With the entry of the United States into World War II, the Nationalists and Communists were both confident that America would eventually dispose of the Japanese; thus, the two sides husbanded their strength from 1941 to 1945 for a postwar confrontation.

The man who was assigned to take charge of leading the Communist Chinese troops into Manchuria upon the surrender of Japan in August 1945 was a brilliant young (thirty-seven) general named Lin Biao. With the tacit support of the occupying Soviet forces in Manchuria, Lin Biao eventually consolidated his Communist forces in Manchuria and built up a formidable army that was eventually launched into China proper. Initially,

Lin Biao's troops numbered about 100,000 in 1945 as they embarked on a forced march from mainland China northward into Manchuria. Once in Manchuria, they took in recruits from the puppet state to increase their number to well over 200,000 to become the single most formidable military force in China. By acquiring captured arms and munitions from the surrendering Kwantung Army, Lin Biao's soldiers quickly became a well-armed and formidable force.

The Soviet Union, meanwhile, did not completely sever ties with the Nationalists but maintained diplomatic relations with Chiang Kai-shek. However, when Chiang requested permission from the commander of the Soviet forces occupying Manchuria to send troop ships to Dalian, he was rebuffed. Chiang then turned to the United States for help, and America complied. American ships and planes moved hundreds of thousands of Nationalist troops into Manchurian cities so that by October 1945, almost a half-million Nationalist soldiers had been transported into Manchuria and other parts of northern China. Thus, confusion and chaos reigned throughout Manchuria as the Nationalists consolidated control in many major cities while the Communists established control of many "liberated" rural areas.

United States' support for Chiang Kai-shek and his Nationalists was, however, very limited from the beginning. Washington was reluctant to become too deeply involved in the confusing situation, and there was great popular sentiment in the United States to "bring the (American) boys home." President Harry S. Truman appointed General George C. Marshall on November 27, 1945, to attempt to bring about peace in China between the Communists and the Nationalists. But after two years of frustration that almost broke the heart of the great American soldier and statesman, General Marshall could not overcome the jealousies, ambition, and bitterness between the two sides.[8]

The Secret Meeting at the Underground Nationalist HQ

Such was the situation in Shenyang as Maruyama, Shinpo, and Musashi headed to their secret rendezvous on the evening of February 8, 1946, in a city that was dominated by Soviet occupation and by Chinese Communist presence, with the Nationalist army surreptitiously biding its time hiding in its underground headquarters. Upon entering the headquarters room, the three men were met by several Nationalist officers, including Guo Chang Shen, the commander, and exchanged cordial greetings in Chinese.

Then they sat at a table facing two men who were the principal officers the three would rely on for help: General Liu Wanquan, chief of staff, and the senior staff officer, Ye Huimin. (Ye's Japanese name was Torao Inaba. Inaba had been an Imperial Japanese army officer at the time of Japanese surrender and had quickly joined on the side of the Nationalists. This same Inaba later returned to Japan to become the capable secretary to a Japanese member of Parliament, Toshio Hirashima.) Early in their initial meeting, Chief of Staff Liu warmly informed the three men that he had had his life saved in the nick of time by a Japanese Imperial Army sergeant during the Sino-Japanese Incident (a battle that marked the start of the Sino-Japanese War, which erupted between Japanese Imperial forces and Nationalist Chinese in June 1937, near the Marco Polo Bridge not far from Beijing) and confided that he had quite an affection for the Japanese people.

During their friendly discussion, Maruyama learned that General Liu had been taught international law while at the military academy in Shanghai by the internationally famed Chinese diplomat, Wellington Koo, a graduate of Columbia University. Maruyama, whose last school in the United States was Columbia University, informed the general how much respect all international students at Columbia had for the famed Chinese diplomat, and this link with Koo played a large role in building trust among the three Japanese and the chief of staff, so that the three men were able to talk intimately and frankly. The presence of Ye Huimin (Inaba) was a major help in the discussion.

Chief of Staff Liu did not hesitate to promise full cooperation in aiding the escape plan of the three Japanese. He even offered his assistance in helping Maruyama's and Shinpo's families as well (Musashi was a bachelor at that time). While that offer was tempting, since Maruyama and Shinpo had been constantly concerned about the welfare of their families once they escaped, they informed Liu that they could not accept the generous offer. If the three men were able to successfully return to Japan with their families, when they reflected on what kind of impression that might make on the 1.7 million fellow Japanese countrymen still left behind to suffer in Manchuria, they did not hesitate to leave their own precious families behind along with everyone else. "We cannot find words to thank you for your kindness, but if something were to happen on the way, that would be an extremely grave matter, so we will leave our families behind entrusted to our acquaintances. Thus, we request that you help just the three of us to escape as quickly as possible," said Maruyama to General Liu.

Liu understood the position the three men were in, and he proceeded to take the steps that were essential for the three to make their escape. He provided them with all necessary papers and even assigned two young officers as escorts. One last document was specifically requested by Musashi. "If we safely return to Japan, it is possible that one or all of us may need to return to Manchuria again to assist in the repatriation of Japanese. Could we ask you to provide one more document, a document allowing reentry into Manchuria?" The look on Liu's face seemed to say, *Who would ever want to return to Manchuria once he has escaped?* Nevertheless, he readily provided Musashi the reentry documents.

The elation, gratitude, and emotion that the three felt as they thanked and bade farewell to General Liu Wanquan and Ye

Huimin were, Maruyama later admitted, indescribable. Months of agonizing, planning, and preparing for an escape out of Manchuria were finally about to end, and the actual escape was about to begin. Four months had passed since the three had come together in secret for the first time in Shinpo's house on October 15, 1945, and entered into a pact to carry out their bold plan. The three had been so careful and meticulous in their planning, not because they placed value on their own lives, but because they knew they absolutely must succeed in their escape. The lives of 1.7 million fellow Japanese rested on the successful accomplishment of their mission. Failure was not an option. As the three sat on the train on their way home, dressed in their Manchurian peasant clothes, they did not exchange any words for fear that they would be looked upon with suspicion. They could only look at each other eye to eye, full of deep emotion and understanding.

Upon returning home, Maruyama took his wife's hand and told her all that had happened during their meeting at the underground headquarters, but he told absolutely no one else.

Chapter 9

The Journey to Dalian

A Solution to Protect the Two Families

Maruyama, Shinpo, and Musashi decided that February 22, 1946, would be the day that their escape would commence. As the date approached, the three continued preparing for the secret journey. They went on gathering information about the latest conditions of the Japanese throughout Manchuria, movements of the Communist Eighth Route Army, the growing number of Japanese refugees, diseases and deaths of Japanese citizens, and other vital information that they knew that people and the government in Japan were completely unaware of. Both Musashi and Shinpo continued to communicate with the Nationalist army's underground headquarters through their Chinese contacts.

Preparations proceeded relatively smoothly under the circumstance, but one unresolved problem still required a solution. What could Maruyama and Shinpo do with their families to insure their safety? If it ever became known that three men had suddenly disappeared from Anshan, they had no doubt that the Soviet soldiers and the Chinese Communists would come to arrest the families of the disappeared men. It was necessary, therefore, to move the families out of Anshan, not an easy task in those days. But to where?

One day, as the day of escape neared, Maruyama mentioned to his companions that it would be a good idea to ask the Catholic bishop of Dalian to write some introductory letters to General MacArthur and to Catholic contacts in Japan. When they returned to Japan as three men with no official or distinct status except that they were crazy enough to escape the clutches of the Soviet occupation and Communist Chinese menace in Manchuria, an introductory letter from the head of the Catholic Church in Manchuria was certain to be taken seriously.

Maruyama, whose wife had strong connections to the Catholic Church from the time she taught Japanese at the Maryknoll School in Seattle as a college student, knew well the head of the Manchurian Catholic Mission, Maryknoll Bishop Raymond A. Lane. (Mary and her four sons were baptized as Catholics in Dalian in April 1946, shortly after Maruyama had made his escape to Japan.) In fact, Maruyama had visited the American bishop in Dalian on several occasions from about the fall of 1945 to seek the bishop's advice, counsel, and moral support on how to combat and lift the terrible gloom that had descended on both Japanese and Manchurians. Once the decision to escape was made, Maruyama even discussed plans for escape with Bishop Lane without going into full detail. He knew the bishop could be completely trusted to keep any and all conversations confidential.

When Maruyama asked his companions' opinion about obtaining introductory letters from Bishop Lane, they wholeheartedly agreed that it was a great idea. Musashi then asked, "Do you know this American bishop who is the head of Manchuria's Catholic Church well?"

"Yes, my wife and I know him well, and he is a man to be completely trusted," replied Maruyama.

"Then why not entrust your family and Shinpo-san's family to this Bishop Lane and request the church to shelter them while we make our way to Japan?" suggested Musashi.

"Musashi-san, I think you are reading my mind. That is the exact thought I have had for some time."

Shinpo was completely agreeable to the plan as well. He was obviously delighted and relieved that he, like Maruyama, could set off on their risky escape without having to constantly worry about the welfare of his family. The three gladly agreed to contact Bishop Lane immediately and to move the two families to Dalian.

Maryknoll Bishop Raymond Lane

In his book *Why Was Koroto Opened*, Maruyama paid special tribute to Maryknoll Bishop Raymond A. Lane and the Maryknoll Church of Dalian not only for sheltering his and Shinpo's families from the time of their escape to Japan (in February 1946) until they were reunited in Japan (in January 1947), but for all their unsung and unrecognized charitable works on behalf of both Japanese and Chinese who came to the church for help in those terrible times. The number of refugees who sought and received their help (food, clothing, and even money) would never be known. The following is excerpted from Maruyama's book:

> I must make special mention here of the incalculable help that we received in our escape from Manchuria, and in achieving our mission to return to our native land of Japan, from the Catholic Church in Manchuria. Foremost among them was the man who held the position as the head of all Catholic churches in Manchuria and who had his headquarters at the Dalian Catholic Church from where he continued his self-sacrificing rescue work on behalf of the refugees, the American Bishop Raymond Lane. Others were Father

Lebera (rector), Father Martelli, Father Schiffer, and the sisters of the convent of the Maryknoll Order, Sisters Sabina, Roseanne, Talita, Iriis, and Margaret (all are now doing their good work in Japan).

After the war, Bishop Lane returned to the United States and was until recently the U.S. head of the Maryknoll Order. During General MacArthur's tenure in Japan, he came to Japan twice to discuss various issues with MacArthur. When Bishop Lane came to the GHQ located in the Dai-ichi Sogo Building (in Tokyo), it was an often repeated story that MacArthur would always go down to the ground floor to await Bishop Lane. During World War II, Bishop Lane was placed under house arrest by the Japanese Kwantung Army in the Sichuan region, then was transferred to Fushun and then to Dalian at the end of the war. The economic sacrifices Bishop Lane and his nuns and priests paid in order to rebuild the Dalian Catholic Church and the efforts they put forth to save the lives of Japanese and Chinese refugees are all stories that truly bring tears to one's eyes. During all that time, they stood up risking their lives against the violence of the Soviet army and the Chinese Communist Eighth Route Army to take the necessary steps to protect the refugees and devoted themselves totally to secure peace throughout Dalian.

From about the fall of 1945, in spite of the danger, I sometimes visited Bishop Lane in Dalian to get his many thoughts and opinions on how changes could come about from the darkness that was in front of our eyes. Then, when we made our decision to undertake the escape plan, I went to discuss with him the many complications in carrying out the plan.

Bishop Lane always acted to me like an affectionate father and listened kindly to all my frank discussions.

In regards to our plans to escape from Manchuria in particular, he mediated for us by writing a letter of request to a priest with the United States Occupation Forces in Tianjin, which was on our escape route, to insure our swift departure to Japan. As a result, our flight from China unfolded very smoothly. Additionally, Bishop Lane wrote a very kind letter of introduction for us to Archbishop (Paul) Marella who was the official representative of the pope in Tokyo. We carried all these documents by sewing them into our Manchurian clothes. Finally, the bishop made many arrangements on our behalf through religious groups in Tokyo so that we would be able to efficiently accomplish the mission we needed to accomplish. Then, Bishop Lane said to me, "In Kyoto, I'm pretty sure that Father Patrick James Byrne is assigned there. Please be sure to go see him and explain to him what your mission is." Thus, when we returned to Japan, it was our desire to go and see Father Byrne as soon as we could....

The American Catholic church alone was immune from encroachment by the most violent Soviet soldiers or the most tyrannical Chinese Communist Eighth Route Army soldiers as its independence and safety continued to be protected throughout [the Soviet occupation]. The reason was that it was the lone stronghold in all of Manchuria that was guarded by the Stars and Stripes of the United States of America, the flag of a country that was a member of the victorious alliance. Of course, there was never an instance when the Catholic Church of Dalian raised the Stars and Stripes outside the church in order to prevent an invasion. The fact that he did not "advertise" the clout of his church to the outside demonstrates Bishop Lane's lofty ideals about his religious faith and love for fellow man; he repulsed injustice and violence silently despite the power that was available to him. There is no telling how much support was given by Bishop Lane and his Church, who possessed this great power, to the many Manchurians and Japanese who had lost all hopes in every aspect of their life's aspirations, particularly the Japanese refugees. Indeed, he was the light that brightened a very dark night and whose contributions were immeasurable.

When we had returned to Japan and were going about achieving the goals of our mission to repatriate Japanese from Manchuria, we heard comments many times from others who were aware of Bishop Lane's efforts on behalf of saving Japanese refugees in spite of the many threats he faced. The comments we heard expressed a fervent desire to properly thank the bishop: "Someday, somehow, a proper gesture must be demonstrated to Bishop Lane on behalf of Japan or on behalf of the citizens of Japan to show sincere gratitude for his truly great efforts," they said.... It is my fervent hope that we will soon organize such a ceremony that repays Bishop Lane for all he has done. I believe that we—as a nation which has for the most part regained the trust of other nations of the world, and as a people who pride ourselves in our ethical principles—have an intrinsic obligation to do this.

Thus wrote Kunio Maruyama in 1970 in his book *Why Was Koroto Opened*. Although Maruyama's wife Mary visited Bishop Lane at the Maryknoll Headquarters in Ossining, New York in the early 1950s, the bishop passed away in 1974 before the ceremony to honor him in Japan that Kunio had hoped for could take place. The bishop had served his God as a priest for more than fifty-four years.[1]

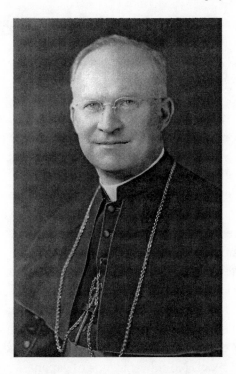

Maryknoll Bishop Raymond A. Lane was the bishop of the Maryknoll Catholic Church in Dalian, Manchuria. When the three men set off on their escape out of Manchuria in February 1946, they entrusted the families of Maruyama and Shinpo to the care of the bishop and his church. The many letters of introduction that the bishop wrote to key personnel in Japan played an indispensable role in opening doors that led to the commencement of repatriation. (Maryknoll Archives, Maryknoll, New York)

A Nerve-Racking Journey to Dalian

Maryknoll Bishop Raymond Lane readily agreed to have the Maruyama and Shinpo families live near the Dalian Catholic Church where he and his priests and sisters could keep an eye on them and lend help if the Soviets ever became suspicious of their identities. However, to move a large group of Japanese from Anshan to Dalian by train was no easy task; in fact, it was impossible under normal circumstances in those days.

However, thanks again to the influential connections that Shinpo and Musashi had in Anshan, they were able to get magnificent cooperation from the employees of the South Manchurian Railway Company.

In those days, the South Manchurian Railway was a vital organ to the occupying Soviet forces. The railway was necessary for transporting fresh Russian troops and supplies into Manchuria as well as for conveying to ports, such as Port Arthur in Dalian, the many factory components and machinery that the Soviets were removing to the Soviet Union. Executives and employees of the South Manchurian Railway Company were all extremely important assets to the Soviet Union because the Soviets could not have run the railroad without them; they could not suddenly have turned over operation of running the railway to Manchurian or Soviet soldiers; they had no choice but to depend on the Japanese who had been running the trains up to now. The Japanese who operated the South Manchurian Railway, therefore, were accorded special status and were treated with great respect. No other groups of Japanese in Manchuria were treated so well and given so much independence.

The deputy station manager of Anshan Station, Yoshiro Onari, took charge of providing passage on the train for Maruyama and the group, which consisted of twelve members (six members of the Maruyama family plus the young girl Toki who was a family helper from Japan and a distant relative of Mary's; four members of the Shinpo family; and Masamichi Musashi); designated them as "employees of the South Manchurian Railway on an important company mission"; and provided them with all the appropriate permits. Authoritative identification and family passes were issued so that no one on the train or at any station would question their authenticity.

When the large group of men, women, and children boarded the train at Anshan Station, they were met with the surprise of their lives. The particular car that they boarded had been reserved for Russian officers! Except for the twelve seats set aside for them, all the other seats were occupied by Soviet army officers. *What a predicament!* thought Maruyama, but there was no turning back as the train was already picking up speed. They tried to make themselves as small and as inconspicuous as possible in their seats, but as the only civilians in the car, and obviously of a different race, they stood out like sore thumbs.

The children, however, were oblivious to the danger that the adults felt. In fact, they began arrogantly walking up and down the aisle and were soon the center of attention and the objects of amusement for the Soviet officers. They were soon picked up by some of the officers, who were probably reminded of their own children they had left behind in the Soviet Union, and were making themselves at home on the laps of the officers. One of Shinpo's sons was seen playfully pulling on the mustache of a Soviet officer, while one of the Maruyama boys tried to grab the pistol on the hip of another officer. Not a hint of concern was expressed by the Soviet officers at the five adults who were fearfully cowering in their corner of the cabin. Throughout the entire journey of several hours, the Soviet officers continued to play innocently with the children who were obviously enjoying all the attention. As a result, although the adults remained in a cold sweat worrying that the lack of manners of their children would eventually end in disaster for all of them, they arrived in Dalian after an unexpectedly pleasant journey.

They collected their children and bags in great haste and disembarked at Dalian Station, each thankful that the journey was over. But when they gathered together on the platform to wave good-bye to the Soviet officers who were waving to them as the train slowly began pulling away from the station, Mary Maruyama suddenly noticed that one of her children, Paul (this author!), was missing. Just as she was ready to shout that their third son was still on the departing train, a Russian soldier hastily opened the window of the car and literally threw Paul into Kunio Maruyama's arms. Fortunately, the train was still moving slowly, and Maruyama was close enough to the window that he was able to firmly and safely catch his son. Obviously, the Russian officer had been amusing Paul in his lap and had not realized the group had disembarked at Dalian until the train began to pull out. It was indeed fortunate that the officer reacted quickly and safely by tossing the boy out of the window into the arms of the boy's father. A potential disaster had been averted!

Chapter 10

The Escape

A Prayerful Departure

After making sure the families were settled in the care of the Dalian Catholic Church, the three men finally prepared to set out on their perilous and historic journey to Japan for the purpose of appealing for the rescue of 1.7 million Japanese abandoned in Manchuria. On the morning of February 22, 1946, Bishop Raymond Lane; Fathers Lebera, Martella, and Schiffer; and Sisters Sabina, Roseanne, Talita, Iriis, and Margaret all gathered in the church with the families of Maruyama and Shinpo to send Kunio Maruyama, Hachiro Shinpo, and Masamichi Musashi off with a prayerful farewell. Everyone in attendance, Catholics and non-Catholics alike, knelt in front of the altar, each praying fervently for the successful completion of the three men's journey. As the three stood up to go, several of the sisters placed a beautiful rosary around each man's neck. Maruyama took his wife's hand and silently bade her and his children farewell. As he turned to go, Sister Roseanne suddenly came running up to him and said, "I know that it will be an extra burden on you, but please hand this to Kazuko Aso, the daughter of Foreign Minister Shigeru Yoshida." Then she handed Maruyama a thick letter.

That letter joined other vital documents from General Liu Wanquan of the Nationalist underground headquarters and from Bishop Lane that were sewn into the men's Manchurian peasant clothing.

As they stepped outside into the still pitch-dark and cold morning, what the men feared most was that someone, perhaps even a Japanese sympathetic to the Soviet side, might discover their escape plan and leak it to the Soviet occupiers or to the soldiers of the Communist Eighth Route Army. If their plan was discovered, there was not the slightest doubt that, in addition to the three and their families, everyone who was involved with them would be shot or buried alive or would suffer some other means of brutal execution. If that happened, the earnest hopes of 1.7 million Japanese would be dashed. The three had taken utmost precautions to keep their every move secret, and they could only pray that their efforts at complete secrecy had been sufficient. Maruyama would never forget, as long as he lived, the kindness and the cooperation of Bishop Lane and the fathers and sisters of the Dalian Catholic Church who stood by, unseen and unheralded in the shadows, to give the three men indispensable help and assistance that ultimately led to the successful completion of their mission.

The Skeptical Chairman of the All-Manchuria Japanese Association

The three men quietly boarded the train at Dalian Station and headed north to make a detour to the capital city of Changchun. The purpose for the long detour was to meet in secret with the then chairman of the All-Manchuria Japanese Association, Tatsunosuke Takasaki, formerly the president of the major industrial corporation, Manchurian Heavy Industry. Takasaki had begun his career as an industrialist pioneering in the canning industry and had lived in Mexico and the United States before coming to Manchuria in 1939. As undoubtedly the best-known and most influential Japanese in all of Manchuria, he had the chairmanship of the general assembly of Japanese associations throughout Manchuria thrust upon him by Japanese desperate for a leader and spokesperson for all Japanese now trapped there on the mainland.

The three men, after informing the chairman of their intention to find a way out of Manchuria and back to Japan, asked him to write several letters of introduction to key government officials in Japan to authenticate that the three men were indeed from Manchuria. They also requested his ideas regarding the best method for repatriating Japanese from Manchuria and, in particular, what matters should be brought to the attention of the Japanese government regarding the rescue of the Japanese. From the outset, Takasaki seemed skeptical about the three men's undertaking and did not seem convinced about their plan to escape from Manchuria. In fact, he was initially incredulous and asked, "Do you really think it will be possible to escape from Manchuria at this time?" Later, after their escape plan had succeeded, Musashi remembered reminiscing to his companions with a chuckle, "Do you remember that Chairman Takasaki stared at the three of us with a look that said, 'These are complete idiots who have no concern at all for their lives!'"[1]

In spite of his skepticism, Takasaki did write the letters and documents the men desired, including letters of entreaty addressed to then Japanese Prime Minister Kijuro Shidehara; the prime minister's chief secretary, Wataru Narahashi; the president of the Bank of Japan, Sakae Araki; and other key government officials. These letters were also carefully folded and sewn into the Manchurian clothing of the three men along with the other documents. Maruyama remembered that, at this time, he and his companions felt a tremendous responsibility to succeed in their mission to rescue all Japanese in Manchuria from the long nightmare that had descended upon them more than eight months earlier. The three men had volunteered to bear a most heavy cross, and feeling the weight on their shoulders as they prepared to take the first step of their escape, they came together once again to swear an oath to carry out their mission.

First Detour on the Escape: Koroto

On the evening of February 26, 1946, the three Japanese men secretly rendezvoused at a prearranged place near Shenyang Station with the two Nationalist officers who had been assigned to act as their escorts. The two young officers, Lieutenant Zheng and Lieutenant Wang, were not in uniform but wore civilian clothes to disguise themselves as ordinary citizens. Lieutenant Zheng suggested that they should not board the train at Shenyang Station since it was well guarded, so the four men quietly boarded at the much smaller station just down the line at Kokoton (Huang Gu Tun).

The five men divided into two groups as they seated themselves to avoid drawing undue attention. Their final destination was Shanhaiguan at the border between Manchuria and China. However, they had decided that they would first make a detour.

Koroto was a relatively small and unknown port that had been constructed by the Japanese army before war began to serve as a supplement to the main entry port to Manchuria, the port of Dalian (known as Port Arthur). Koroto was located at about the midpoint between Shenyang and Shanhaiguan on the shores near Kin Prefecture.

The three men knew that when they returned to Japan to appeal for the dispatch of ships to rescue the Japanese out of Manchuria, they had to be able to recommend a navigable port from which to conduct the rescue. In those days, Port Arthur at Dalian, Yingkou, and the Yalu River in Korea were all under Soviet and Chinese Communist occupation and control so that a rescue operation in any of those locations was completely out of the question. During their secret meeting with General Liu Wanquan at the underground headquarters, he had mentioned to the three men that the only port along the coastline presently under complete control of the Nationalist army was Koroto. With that valuable intelligence, the three concluded that the repatriation of Japanese from Manchuria could take place only from Koroto.

When they returned to Japan, it was their intention to plead with the Supreme Commander for Allied Powers (SCAP), General Douglas MacArthur, to dispatch ships to Koroto for repatriation. It was necessary, therefore, for the three to have knowledge of Koroto and to see the port with their own eyes and determine whether ships could actually dock there.

When the five men got off the train at Koroto to assess the situation, they had to be very careful not to look suspicious since, although it was under Nationalist control, they were still in Manchuria and could easily be mistaken for Communist spies by the Nationalist soldiers in the area. They were, therefore, only able to take a casual look at the port. Compared to Port Arthur, Koroto was a small and all-but-deserted military port with very few people visible. The remnants of two small dismantled Japanese military vessels lay at the side of the port; the sad and lonely looking wreckage seemed to symbolize the defeat of Japan. As the three men visualized the day when repatriation ships would dock there to carry home their fellow Japanese countrymen, they gazed across the waters of Liaodong Bay with the thought that this very sea connected all the way to their native Japan.

Soon, they boarded a train again and headed south to Shanhaiguan.

The Great Wall of China

"Shanhaiguan, Shanhaiguan ..." It was about 5:00 PM, and over the public address system came the announcement that they had arrived at last at Shanhaiguan. The energetic voice sounded to the three men like a premonition of both happy days to come as well as the unknown anxieties that awaited them. The station, on the border between Manchuria and China, was swarming with passengers getting on and off. The three Japanese and their Chinese escort officers got off the train and sought out a remote corner of the station, remaining as inconspicuous as possible but always with their guard up. In those days, although Manchuria was occupied by the Soviet army, and the Communist Eighth Route Army and the Nationalist army were confronting each other in skirmishes, Shanhaiguan, just north of the Chinese border, was under the control of the Nationalists. However, it was still in Manchuria.

As they looked to the west, they could see clearly the Great Wall of China. They were moved by the magnificent view of the ancient and wondrous structure that told the history of two thousand years of the violent rise and fall of China. In silence and awe, they were unable to look away from the majestic wall, bathed in the setting sun, its shadow spreading over the land. Here was the border of the Manchukuo Empire, and in a very short while, the three men were about to leave this place and go into China.

Sadness and pathos engulfed all three men, each deep in his own thoughts. To the east, they were able to see Liaodong Bay glimmering in the setting sun, while to the west, they looked up at the majestic Great Wall. Maruyama could feel his eyes filling with warm wetness. *Manchuria, you devil!* he thought, *you are holding captive one million seven hundred thousand of my fellow countrymen, and I am now about to leave you!* Wiping away his tears as inconspicuously as possible with the sleeve of his Manchurian peasant clothing, he glanced at his companions in the darkening station yard. As their eyes met silently, each visibly overwhelmed with emotion, the three men wordlessly came close together and pulled out their arms from inside their Manchurian jackets and reached out to tightly clasp hands. Silently and wordlessly, their shared emotions made this a moment they would never forget.

As they set out on their journey of escape, Maruyama, Shinpo, and Musashi were well aware that if it was discovered anywhere along the route that they were Japanese, the consequence would almost certainly be fatal. They would be pulled out in front of the crowd and subjected to unspeakable punishment that would only end upon certain death. There were, of course, no Japanese on the trains, and there certainly should not have been any.

The two Nationalist Chinese officers who had been assigned as their escorts had kindly but severely warned them: "Until you have traveled beyond Shanhaiguan, you must not speak any Japanese, no matter what happens. You must never make any gestures that would make anyone suspicious that there was any close relationship between the three of you. You must always look like ordinary Manchurians taking a trip, and everyone around you must never suspect you are more than that. Remember that there are more than a few who harbor hatred and hostility toward the Japanese. If anyone were to suspect that you are Japanese, there is no telling what incident you will cause. If that happens, you will even put our lives in danger. Our journey will be relatively short, but please be wary and cautious at all times!"

After addressing all three of the men with those words of instruction, Lieutenant Zheng turned to Maruyama in particular and said, "Your residency in Manchuria has been the shortest, Mr. Maruyama, and since you are not very familiar with Manchurian customs and other habits and manners of the ordinary Manchurian, you must make sure you never speak. Wear your hat as low as possible so that no one can really see your face. You must never do anything genteel, such as to blow your nose with a handkerchief or a tissue, and if you can't help but blow your nose, use your bare hands. Then wipe your hands on your own clothes, and act as if that is the perfectly normal thing to do. We are not talking about a long time, so for the short period of our journey, you must be extremely careful and patient and act at all times as if you have always been a Manchurian."

As the three Japanese came silently and very briefly together to grasp each other's hands, they were completely conscious of the warning they had received from their Chinese escorts. As they saw the path for escape from Manchuria right in front of their eyes, both happiness and anxiety filled their hearts. Had they allowed the great emotion they felt at that time to be detected by anyone, a catastrophe could have descended on them. Had this been somewhere in Japan and not at Shanhaiguan, they would probably have cried out at the top of their lungs and hugged each other in utter joy.

Maruyama Disappears

There was about an hour's wait for the departure of the next train to Tianjin. Maintaining a low profile, the men continued to wait in the station yard, away from everyone. Suddenly, Lieutenant Wang whispered into Musashi's ear, "Wuzang, what happened to Mr. Maruyama?"

Completely surprised, Musashi looked around and said, "What, Maruyama-san?" Shinpo was still there, but Maruyama had disappeared without a trace. In panic, the four men looked for him, but he was nowhere in sight. If something had happened, he would surely have made some kind of noise to alert his companions, but they had heard nothing. The four men divided up and looked all over the station and around its vicinity, but he was nowhere to be found. The four came back together, all with grave countenances, silently shaking their heads to signal Maruyama had not been found. There was not much time left before the departure of their train, and the men could not help but begin to panic.

While awaiting the next train to Tianjin on the Hozan Line, Maruyama had decided to take a walk on his own. In actuality, he was looking for a restroom. As he wandered around the twilit station, a soldier wearing the uniform of the Nationalist army came out of the shadows and said, "*Shi shei* (who are you)?"

Momentarily caught off guard, Maruyama replied with his limited Manchurian vocabulary, "*Shi de* (yes)!"

The soldiers again asked, "*Shi shei?*"

This time Maruyama replied, "*Wo shi zhong guo dong bei lu ren jiao wang* (I am a Manchurian traveler named Wang)."

The soldier, obviously suspicious by now, said very rapidly with anger in his voice, "*Ni zai zuo shen me* (what are you doing)?"

Maruyama replied, "*Ce suo zai na li,*" which he hoped meant, "I was looking for a toilet."

The soldier was now completely on his guard, probably not understanding the strange man's words. He came up to Maruyama's side, and put his naked bayonet against his stomach, and said sharply, "*Zhe bian lai* (come this way)!" Knowing that a moment's hesitation would cause the soldier to thrust the bayonet deep into his stomach, Maruyama gave the Nationalist soldier his full attention and cooperation as the soldier guided him with his bayonet to the guardhouse, which was on the opposite side of the station.

Once inside the guardhouse, Maruyama was made to stand in front of an officer who obviously was the guard commander. Without asking permission or wasting a second, Maruyama tore into the sleeve of the Manchurian clothing he was wearing and retrieved the passport document that Chief of Staff Liu Wanquan had issued. Quickly, before the guard commander had time to react, Maruyama handed over the documents to him and said, "*Kan kan zhe* (please look at this)." The surprised guard commander looked at the documents under the electric light in the room and read the texts.

After reading them once, the guard commander reread the documents, this time with much more care. Then, suddenly, he came to attention and said something in a low voice to the soldier who had brought Maruyama to the guardhouse. The soldier also came to attention, then bowed his head and silently apologized to Maruyama. All Maruyama could say was "*Xie xie* (thank you)!" over and over again, relieved that the documents from General Liu Wanquan had actually saved his life. As Maruyama indicated to the soldiers that he simply wanted to be on his way, the guard commander summoned several more soldiers who came together around Maruyama and gave him a salute by raising their pistols. Maruyama took off his hat and responded to the salute by bowing deeply to the soldiers. As Maruyama once again indicated he merely wanted to be on his way, the commander himself and the soldier who initially arrested Maruyama insisted on escorting him back to the station.

"Look!" It was Lieutenant Wang who first saw Maruyama approaching and raised his voice to alert the others. The four men could see Maruyama coming toward them in the dark at a trot. They were completely surprised by the two soldiers, one a foot soldier and the other an officer, who were obviously escorting Maruyama.

Trying to appear as calm as possible, Maruyama said to his companions, "I am sorry for causing you to worry," and said nothing else as they climbed on the train that was set to depart in a few minutes. The guard commander and the soldier also climbed on the train and, ordering Manchurian travelers who were already seated to vacate their seats, sat all five men together in the now empty seats. Since the station attendants were announcing that the train was about to depart, the commander and the soldier disembarked from the train, came to attention on the station platform opposite where the five men were seated, and smartly saluted as the train began to pull away. Maruyama stood up and waved good-bye to the two Nationalist soldiers on the platform and repeated over and over again, *"Xie xie, zaijian, shenti jian kang* (Thank you, good-bye, see you again, take care)!" as the train began to pick up speed. Then he let out a great sigh of relief.

After the train had left Shanhaiguan behind and the three Japanese were certain that they were no longer in Manchuria, Maruyama related to his companions in a low voice all that had happened. Musashi and Shinpo could not believe such a major, life-threatening incident had happened in so brief a time. For some time, Maruyama was the target of scolding, criticism, and teasing, even from the two escort officers. "To go on a stroll in that semidarkness sure seems like an extremely dangerous thing to do! Until we are in Japan, you must never go for a stroll by yourself!" Maruyama replied that he merely wanted to take care of nature's call. To that, his companions replied, "Over here, there is no such thing as a designated toilet! You just take care of business wherever it suits you!"

As they talked and teased Maruyama, the scolding and teasing turned to humor and laughter as Shinpo and Musashi felt relief at the happy outcome of the episode. "If at that time I had been thirty seconds slower in showing the passport documents to the guard commander, I am certain that I would have been stabbed with that bayonet and would, at this time, have been laid out as a corpse at that guardhouse!" said Maruyama philosophically. The two escort officers, however, did not appear to share as much in the joy exhibited by the three Japanese and seemed quite displeased with this "Maruyama Incident."

Maruyama looked out the window for one last view of the breathtaking grandeur of the Great Wall of China to calm his nerves, but it was pitch dark outside, and the Great Wall was only barely visible. Still, knowing that they were well out of Shanhaiguan, the three men began to fully comprehend that their escape from Manchuria had succeeded. Tears of joy welled up in all three at the realization of that reality. Although they knew that they had overcome only one of the many obstacles that undoubtedly still awaited them in their quest to rescue their fellow countrymen, they knew they had conquered what was perhaps the most dangerous step in accomplishing their goal. As they began to wipe away tears, they found that they were unconsciously gripping each other's hands.

Chapter 11

Freedom of Speech Is Nonexistent
in a Defeated Nation

Passage Home on an American LST

As the train puffed southward, now in China, a mood of relief spread to all five men. In a short while, the train arrived at Qinhuangdao. Bishop Lane had informed the three before their departure from Dalian that the U.S. military was stationed at Qinhuangdao. "Let's pay the U.S. military a quick visit," suggested Maruyama. Although his companions were somewhat reluctant to make any stops that were not completely necessary, since their mission was to return to Japan as quickly as possible, Maruyama insisted on making the stop. "When we get back to Japan, we must make an appeal to the MacArthur Headquarters, and if we fail to convince them of the urgency, there will not be any ships dispatched for repatriation. I think it would greatly help our cause to explain our situation [to the U.S. military authorities in Qinhuangdao] and have them communicate [to MacArthur's staff] about us ahead of time," argued Maruyama. Shinpo and Musashi reluctantly agreed that he made a logical case.

When the three Japanese men (still in their Manchurian peasant clothing) and their Nationalist Chinese escorts presented themselves at the U.S. military base, their sudden appearance caused great suspicion, especially since one of them spoke English. They were promptly placed in custody and were forced to spend the night in confinement. "It turned out exactly as we feared," grumbled Lieutenant Wang to Maruyama, but what was done was done. The next morning, after listening to Maruyama's explanation in English, the American officer who interrogated them agreed to dispatch a message to MacArthur's GHQ in Tokyo, and the five were shortly thereafter released and were allowed to proceed on to Tianjin.

Tianjin, which was under the control of the Nationalist army, was quite different from all the Soviet-controlled Manchurian cities with which the three men had become familiar. There was a feeling of bustling liveliness in the air. What was most surprising was the presence of Japanese military personnel still in their uniforms and patrolling the city in an orderly manner. All Japanese soldiers were still wearing their ranks, and the officers wore their swordbelts.

The now defunct Japanese Imperial Army unit under the command of Lieutenant General Shiro Omoto had been assigned to protect the thousands of Japanese who had assembled in Tianjin from throughout China, waiting to be repatriated on U.S. vessels back to Japan. Repatriation of Japanese civilians from China had been ongoing for several months now, and General Omoto's troops were charged with insuring that the operation went smoothly. To the three men who had witnessed the cowardly actions of the fleeing Kwantung Army, which did nothing to protect the Japanese in Manchuria, particularly the pioneers in the north, from the encroaching Soviet army, it was an unbelievable sight. To this day, Masamichi Musashi believes that if the Kwantung Army had risked their lives to protect the Japanese living in Manchuria and had given them the time to return to Japan at the time of the Soviet invasion, the number of Japanese civilians sacrificed in Manchuria could have been greatly reduced.[1]

The three men received cordial help and cooperation from Lieutenant General Omoto and his aide, Captain Yamamoto, as well as from the U.S. military personnel engaged in the repatriation effort. A letter that Bishop Lane had written addressed to the U.S. Catholic chaplain with the Tianjin occupying force was a major factor in insuring full cooperation. Since so many Japanese had gathered in Tianjin from throughout China to be repatriated, if the three men had lined up to await their turn to return to Japan on the waiting ships, they would have had to wait at least a month to board. Thanks to the understanding by both the U.S. and Japanese military of the three men's urgency to return to Japan, they were given priority to board immediately. Shinpo and Musashi were ostensibly designated as crew members, while Maruyama was assigned as an interpreter.

As Maruyama, Shinpo, and Musashi prepared to board the U.S. Navy LST 586 from the Port of Tanggu on March 9, 1946, for their long-awaited escape to Japan, the three men bade fond farewell to the two young Chinese Nationalist army officers who had been so patient and protective of them. They had developed a feeling of true friendship with Lieutenant Wang and Lieutenant Zheng during their journey from Shenyang. Moisture was visible in everyone's eyes as they firmly grasped each other's hands. Then the three quickly walked up the gangplank into the landing craft.

Huddling on Board to Craft a Statement

The mood of all the Japanese on the ship seemed cheery, as if they had already forgotten all the sufferings of the past as they looked forward to returning to home and loved ones. But the three Japanese from Manchuria could not celebrate with the others on board. They had work to do; their crucial task had just begun. In a corner of the ship, they put their heads together and began composing a statement that they would announce upon their return to Japan. They also mapped out their plan of attack on what they must do from the moment of their arrival in Japan. It was certainly necessary to work with Japanese government agencies to bring about the repatriation of Japanese from Manchuria as quickly as possible, but the critical key was to obtain the cooperation of the U.S. military who occupied and governed Japan.

Although Japan was theoretically governed then by the Allied Powers, which included the United States, Great Britain, Australia, France, China, the Soviet Union, and others, it was none other than the Supreme Commander for Allied Powers (SCAP), General MacArthur himself, who had to approve and set into motion the repatriation of Japanese from Soviet-occupied Manchuria. Without the help of the American military, nothing was possible. Also, the men theorized, it was crucial to rouse Japanese public opinion to move GHQ to take action. To that end, they decided to widely inform the Japanese public regarding the present horrible situation of all Japanese in Manchuria. As soon as possible after landing in Japan, they planned to read the statement they were now preparing.

As each man contributed ideas and points for the statement, Maruyama organized them into a coherent, convincing, and factual announcement. On the day that the three were finally satisfied that their statement was what they wanted to tell the people of Japan, a loud cheer erupted from within the ship. Everyone was running up to the deck.

Along the horizon far across the ocean, the outline of mountains of their native land was slowly becoming visible. On the fifth day of their journey, on March 13, 1946, the United States naval vessel was quickly approaching Senzaki (now absorbed into the City of Nagato) in Yamaguchi Prefecture on the coast of the Sea of Japan. As they looked around at the tearful Japanese on the ship who were returning to the land of their fondest dreams, the three men could not help but reflect on the 1.7 million Japanese who were still stranded in Manchuria. Their collective emotion was not so much that of joy in returning to Japan, but rather a sense of determination to succeed in their mission as quickly as possible.

When the three men descended the steps to set foot on their native land, five newspaper reporters who seemed to be waiting for them approached and asked, "You are from Manchuria, right?" They were from the *Asahi* and the *Yomiuri* newspapers. Because the identities of the three men had been kept secret on board the ship and since they had been portrayed as American crew members and an interpreter, no one could have known they were from Manchuria.

"How did you know about us?" the three asked.

The reporters looked at each other with a knowing smile and said, "Well, we have our own sources..." and that was about all the answer the three received. Then the reporters asked them what their plan was now.

Maruyama replied, "We would like to go to Tokyo as soon as possible."

Then one of the reporters said, "May we make a suggestion? For tonight, we would very much like to have you spend the night at the head office of the western division of the *Asahi* newspaper in Kokura City. We would like to have you hold a joint press conference tonight with reporters from all the major newspapers in Kyushu joining us in attendance. We will make all the arrangements, and you can depart for Tokyo tomorrow morning after a comfortable rest here tonight."

The three huddled and decided that if they made an announcement in Kyushu that night about Manchuria, word about Manchuria would be announced to all of Japan one day earlier than if they held their first news conference in Tokyo the next day. The three accepted the invitation, and the first news conference on the situation in postwar Manchuria was set for that night in Kokura City (which today, along with four other cities, has become part of Kitakyushu City in Fukuoka Prefecture).

The First Press Conference

The press conference began at 10:00 PM. Some thirty reporters assembled in a conference room of the *Asahi* newspaper's western division headquarters to listen and report on the announcement from the three men from Manchuria who had prepared their statement on board the repatriation ship. Maruyama spoke on behalf of the three men as Shinpo and Musashi sat at either side of him. The text of the statement follows below in its entirety, as translated by this author:

> We, Kunio Maruyama, Hachiro Shinpo, and Masamichi Musashi, burdened with the most earnest desire of over 1.7 million Japanese countrymen left in Manchuria, and acting as their representative to rescue them, secretly fled from Manchuria into China, then boarded a landing craft of the United States of America at the Port of Tanggu that was already there engaged in repatriating Japanese from northern China, and we arrived at Senzaki in Yamaguchi Prefecture on March 13.
>
> There are 1.7 million Japanese living today in Manchuria, not counting Japanese military personnel. The distribution breakdown of that population according to a survey conducted this February by the Japanese Association of Changchun is as follows: 350,000 in the Shenyang area; 300,000 in the Dalian area; 320,000 in the Changchun area; 170,000 in the Harbin area; 90,000 in the Anshan area; 73,000 in the Andong area; 70,000 in the Jinzhou area; 50,000 in the Qiqihar area; 20,000 in the Jiamusi area; 45,000 in the Mudanjiang area; 32,000 in the Tonghua area; 35,000 in the Jilin area; 11,000 in the Baicheng area; 13,000 in the Fuxin area; 33,000 in the Jiandao area;

26,000 in the Beian area; 65,000 in the Siping area; and some others scattered throughout Manchuria. Additionally, when the invasion into Manchuria by the Soviet forces commenced just before the end of the war, some Japanese fled Manchuria to seek refuge in northern Korea with approximately 50,000 now in the eastern region and 40,000 in the western region. These Japanese in all areas, which total about 1.7 million are not allowed to take one step outside of Manchuria. Every day, they gaze at the skies to the east over Japan and long to return as they tremble from cold and hunger.

Just before the war ended, the Soviet army invaded into Manchuria from the north so that by the end of the war, the Soviet army occupied all of Manchuria. From the other side, the Eighth Route Army of the Chinese Communists invaded from the west to advance and station soldiers throughout Manchuria simultaneously so that almost all public facilities and other vital facilities have been confiscated. Transportation and communications networks are in a state of paralysis; financial institutions have been closed; banks and post offices have become completely useless; and all types of cultural facilities have been carted away from Manchuria following the end of the war. In Manchuria, unlike the situation in Japan, provisions such as rice, *koryan* (sorghum), soybean, soybean paste, soy sauce, and the like are quite plentiful and are sold everywhere so that, as long as one has money, there is no lack of things that are necessary to sustain life. In fact, one could live rather luxuriously.

Now would be the time when one would withdraw some of the money one had been earning so diligently and with great struggle, money that one had accumulated in a savings account. However, those savings accounts of the Japanese, which had grown to a substantial amount as a result of ten, twenty, and thirty years of painstaking labor—those bank accounts have been completely frozen, and all banks have tightly boarded up their doors so that, even if one had a bankbook showing one million yen in his account, or if one had a check for two million yen, they are equivalent to mere scraps of paper and can do nothing to help one's daily needs. Thus, people generally sell their own private possessions at first and try to get by with the classic "bamboo shoot living." Others set up outdoors stalls in towns and try to do business in an attempt to make ends meet.

In Manchuria, something that is often needed even more than food is fuel for heat, but fuel has been confiscated and is in short supply and has become dramatically scarce; in Shenyang, fuel that had been available for 1,000 yen a ton now costs from 6,000 to 8,000 yen. Not only is fuel hard to obtain; Japanese in general do not have the money to buy any so that, since the time the weather turned cold around November, the number of people dying from the freezing cold has risen dramatically.

One of the painful phenomena that has become obvious among the Japanese in Manchuria in recent times is that illnesses have increased dramatically. Especially among the refugees who live in groups throughout Manchuria, diseases due to unsanitary conditions and lack of nutrition have resulted in many cases of typhoid fever, respiratory diseases, skin diseases, malnutrition, and other diseases. According to the survey statistics of the Changchun Japanese Association, the death rate of Japanese among the 70,000 refugees in Changchun in the month of February was 0.3 percent or 210. And of those that died, 63 percent, or 132, were innocent babies and infants who have no idea what a war is. Statistics from other districts are not available, but we speculate that there is repetition of misery worse than in Changchun. To put it bluntly, it is no exaggeration to say that the majority of Japanese in Manchuria are gradually becoming refugees. According to the results of a survey conducted by the Changchun Japanese Association just before our departure, of the 1.7 million Japanese left in all of Manchuria, an astonishing 46 percent or almost eight hundred thousand are already homeless refugees or are about to become refugees.

In such grave and worsening situation, every Japanese in Manchuria wants to escape from the difficult predicament and wants only to return as soon as possible to the homeland that they miss so much, and they are burning with desire for that day to come. However, all means of returning to Japan have been blocked, and the situation for all Japanese in Manchuria is as if they are shut up in a can. If there were means of communication between Manchuria and Japan, there would be some feeling of optimism, but not only are they not able to exchange letters with families, relatives, and friends in Japan, they are not able to read even one newspaper. The Japanese in Manchuria are living in a very dark world and can only moan with little hope.

With the end of the war, our countrymen have been thrown out into the wilderness of Manchuria that has lost all semblance of culture. They are tormented every day by hunger and cold with their lives always under threat, passing each day meaninglessly, greeting the next day without any hope, bidding farewell to the many loved ones who are sacrificed to illness, yearningly looking up at the skies of their faraway native country while driven perpetually by insecurity and anxiety—they are waiting for a hand to stretch out from their native land, a hand that will rescue them. Those pitiful countrymen are as if they are on a shipwrecked vessel far out on the other side of the ocean, floating aimlessly like a leaf in the vicious waves, and if they are not rescued even another day sooner, their lives are placed in a precarious situation.

Since last fall, we three, Kunio Maruyama, Hachiro Shinpo, and Masamichi Musashi, took on separate assignments to inspect and investigate with our own eyes the actual living conditions of our fellow countrymen in Dalian, Yingkou, Anshan, Liaoyang, Shenyang, Changchun, Harbin, Qiqihar, and other remote areas of northern Manchuria. We put on Manchurian clothing and encountered many dangers, but we did manage to meet with various representatives of Japanese residents in those areas and discussed the need for the earliest possible rescue and repatriation of Japanese. As a result of their passionate pleas, we three swore an oath to each other to act as representatives to carry out the mission of delivering their prayerful petition to rescue our fellow Japanese living in Manchuria.

Thus, carrying on our shoulders the earnest pleas of 1.7 million Japanese in Manchuria, we departed from Shenyang on February 26 and proceeded to Jinzhou; then we stopped to conduct an inspection of Koroto (Huludao) where we determined that the most suitable port for repatriation vessels from Japan to dock is Koroto. Then, we headed to Shanhaiguan, and from there we fled into China to finally return to Japan. Just before we visited Koroto to inspect it, we got off the train at Jinxian where we met with a member of the Japanese association who represented the Japanese living there, and we told him in extreme secrecy about our mission before parting company. We had about fifteen minutes before our train was scheduled to depart, and in that short time, a small group of about seven to eight Japanese men and women gathered on the second floor of a house of a Japanese resident on the other side of the road near the station, and we could clearly see that they were clasping their hands as if in prayer, wiping away their tears from time to time, and on their faces were written desperate pleas as they gestured their farewell to us. We were deeply moved by the sight of the grave and impassioned wordless pleas; even now, that tearful image cannot be erased from our minds.

Since we took on this most important mission to escape from Manchuria to return to Japan with the greatest secrecy from beginning to end, we informed only a very few select people about our plan so that hardly a soul in Manchuria knows about our escape. We firmly believe that the earnest expressions on the faces of the small number of Japanese who saw us off from the distance in Jinxian represent the feeling and the yearning and the hope of all 1.7 million Japanese in Manchuria. We wish to go to Tokyo as soon as we possibly can and visit with Japanese governmental agencies as well as visit with concerned agencies at GHQ, beginning with General MacArthur, and report in detail the true conditions in Manchuria following the end of the war. It is our heartfelt intention to ask General MacArthur to make arrangements as quickly as possible for a solution to rescue the 1.7 million Japanese in Manchuria who have been left behind in a far-off land, who are being daily tortured by cold and hunger, and who presently are hovering at the brink of death. We intend to petition General MacArthur with all our might to plead that he not hesitate one more day to dispatch ships to return the Japanese home....

We are ready to sacrifice whatever is demanded of us in order to bring about as quickly as possible the joyful reunion between our fellow countrymen left behind on foreign soils and the families at home who have been painfully waiting for the return of their loved ones. We will work to make this cherished hope come true with our whole body and with our whole soul.

It is our deepest yearning to ask you, the people of Japan, to stir up the love you have for your countrymen, and we plead from the bottom of our hearts for your help and support, in whatever capacity you can contribute, to promote the rescue of our fellow countrymen living in a foreign land.[2]

At the conclusion of Maruyama's statement, there was a volley of questions from the assembled reporters, which the three men took turns answering. As the press conference came to an end, they emphatically reemphasized one crucial point: For each day that repatriation was delayed, that many more people would be sacrificed. Keeping in mind that the reporters had to have some time to write their reports to make the deadline for the next day's papers, the three men concluded the press conference with a plea to the reporters for their sincere cooperation.

That night, as the three got to their beds to rest, they continued to mumble to each other how fortunate they were that the truth about Manchuria would be conveyed to the people of Japan and to the world with tomorrow's newspapers. "Everything about postwar Manchuria has been blocked by an iron curtain so that nothing is known in Japan or in other countries. With tomorrow's newspaper, they will learn the truth. Won't everyone be surprised!" With those thoughts, no one was able to sleep much that night.

Nothing Is Reported in the Papers!

The following morning, many different newspapers were delivered and left outside their room. They eagerly gathered them up, brought them into the room, and scanned through them. As they searched for the press conference articles, they felt as if someone had played a dirty trick on them. Each paper contained a small item of five or six lines, to this effect: "Three men, Kunio Maruyama, Hachiro Shinpo, and Masamichi Musashi, returned to Japan as representatives to petition for the rescue of Japanese in Manchuria. They returned to Japan yesterday at Senzaki, and they plan to go to Tokyo today...." Not one word was written regarding the statement released at the joint press conference; nor was there any mention of the questions and answers that followed. The news about Manchuria had been completely suppressed!

When an *Asahi* newspaper reporter arrived for work, Shinpo asked, as if cross examining him, "Why do you think this happened?"

The reporter sadly shook his head and replied, "Because representatives of the Soviet Union are part of the Allied Powers Headquarters, my guess is that everything was censored since they did not want anyone to know about the situation in Manchuria." The reporter lowered his head as if apologizing to the three men. The three understood immediately, and Maruyama recalled the scene several weeks before when he happened on foreign correspondents on an inspection tour in Shenyang who were under heavy surveillance by Soviet soldiers. There was not a thing the three could do about the unbearably frustrating situation. Japan was a defeated nation and at the moment was under the rule of the Allied Powers, and freedom of speech was not one of the Japanese people's rights for the time being. The statement they had worked so hard to put together while on board the American landing craft was destined never to be conveyed to the people of Japan. They quickly concluded that it was absolutely necessary to go to

Tokyo as soon as possible and meet directly with the people and agencies concerned. As they hurried to Kokura Station to catch the first train to Tokyo, they tried their best to encourage each other.

As the train neared Tokyo late in the afternoon of March 15, stopping at Shinagawa Station just before its final destination, several reporters who had been awaiting the arrival of the three men boarded the train. The reporters began interviewing them as the train continued to its final stop in Tokyo. About thirty more reporters were waiting on the platform of Tokyo Station as the train came to a stop. After disembarking, the three men were surrounded by a mob of reporters who began asking questions.

However, Maruyama, Shinpo, and Musashi had their own thoughts. The thought that whatever these reporters zealously reported on the story of the three men would not see the light of day just as in Kokura City saddened them immensely. Still, the reporters' spirited questions could not be ignored. Fruitless as the effort might be, the three decided that the time had come for them to forcefully explain the tragedy in Manchuria. Perhaps some of the reporting might reach the general public. With that in mind, the three men from Manchuria responded to the questions in clear detail, and they asked for the media's complete cooperation to stimulate strong public opinion so that the authorities would dispatch ships as soon as possible for repatriation of all Japanese under Soviet control in Manchuria.

Chapter 12

The Campaign Begins

Maruyama's Home Survives

The three men's destination after concluding the impromptu press conference at Tokyo Station was Maruyama's house at Kugayama in Tokyo. In the summer of the year when World War II began, Maruyama had had a new house built on a plot of land that measured thirty *tsubo* (approximately 118 square yards). But since he had moved with his family to Anshan, Manchuria, during the war years, he had rented the house to Tokyo Steel Manufacturing Company executive Masato Murata. Because he had no way to stay in touch with Mr. Murata, Maruyama had no idea what the situation was at his house in Kugayama. His biggest fear was that the house had been bombed and burned down during one of the frequent U.S. air raids.

After getting off the train at Kugayama Station on the Inokashira Line, the three still had to walk about fifteen minutes to the house, climbing a relatively long hill along the way. Then, when Maruyama turned the corner where his house would be visible, he instinctively called out to his companions, "It's still there!" As they looked where Maruyama pointed, they could see a stylish two-storied house with a veranda.

They announced their arrival at the sliding front door, and Mrs. Murata answered and was taken by complete surprise to see Maruyama and his two companions standing at the entrance. The Muratas, of course, had had no idea what had happened to Maruyama since he and his family left for Manchuria, leaving the house in their care. But at the sight of Maruyama, the Muratas welcomed the three men in and immediately served hot tea to their guests. When Maruyama informed the Muratas that he planned to make the house the headquarters for the repatriation activities the three men would be involved in from now on, Masato Murata graciously accepted the situation and promised he and his family would immediately vacate the house to another residence. In those days, when so many homes in Tokyo had been destroyed by air raids, finding a residence was no easy task. However, the Muratas understood the importance of the work of the three men and did not hesitate in moving out. The house had been well cared for during Maruyama's absence.

Many military related factories had been constructed in nearby areas during the war, many of which had been bombed and burned to the ground, so that the surrounding scenery was not as pretty as Maruyama remembered. However, when he went upstairs and stepped out on the veranda to gaze toward the setting sun, he could clearly see Mount Fuji rising majestically above the clouds. He thought, *Thank goodness the former image is still there!* He called to his companions to come up to gaze at the beloved symbol of Japan. When Shinpo and Musashi came up to the second-floor room and saw the beauty of the highest peak in Japan, covered with snow, they were struck for the first time by the reality that they had returned to Japan. The three had been emotionally moved at the sight of the Great Wall of China from the train platform in Shanhaiguan, but this sight moved them ten times as much. For the moment, all three were able to forget the bitterness and disappointment they had experienced when their statement was not reported in the newspapers.

A Committee for "Saving Our Countrymen in Manchuria"

Although Maruyama's house in Kugayama would eventually be filled beyond capacity with many repatriates from Manchuria who would spend a night or two there before going on to their homes, the house was luxuriously spacious for the three men who for a while could each have their own private bedroom. They were able to spend their first night back in Tokyo sleeping in rooms with *tatami* (straw mats).

In the morning, without wasting any time, Maruyama, Shinpo, and Musashi embarked on their first step as they dedicated themselves to conducting activities to bring about the repatriation of Japanese from Manchuria: they named themselves the *Zaiman Douhou Kyuusai Chinjou Daihyou* (Representatives to Petition for Saving Our Countrymen Living in Manchuria). The three men enjoyed the simple luxury of wearing ordinary clothing (they chose to wear suits with ties wherever they went) and the freedom to visit any government office and boldly say anything they wished. The sudden taste of freedom was indescribably delicious. An agency involved in repatriation provided the men with armbands that read *Zaiman Douhou Kyuusai Chinjou Daihyou*, and the three men wore them on their arms wherever they went.

Their first stop was at the office of the prime minister's chief secretary, Wataru Narahashi, where they delivered to him the secret letters that had been entrusted to them by Tatsunosuke Takasaki, the chairman of the All-Manchuria Japanese Association. Takasaki, though seemingly skeptical that the three would succeed in their mission, had addressed documents to Prime Minister Kijuro Shidehara as well as to Chief Secretary Narahashi. The three briefed Narahashi about their escape from Manchuria and then went into detail about the true situation of all Japanese in the closed-off country under Soviet occupation. In conclusion, they pleaded with Narahashi to devise a method to rescue as soon as possible the Japanese in Manchuria whose lives were all in extremely dire straits.

At the end of their meeting, Narashashi said, "I wish to express my utmost respect to the three of you who overcame such great difficulties to fulfill your mission. I am amazed that you were able to escape from Manchuria!" Musashi recalled that the chief secretary's eyes were moist as his countenance showed how emotionally moved he was.[1] At the conclusion of their meeting, Narahashi led the three men to the prime minister's office to introduce them to Prime Minister Shidehara. In a cordial meeting, the three repeated the same request to the prime minister that they had conveyed to Narahashi before they concluded their meeting.

Narahashi Reflects on the First Meeting

In a letter he provided as a preface to Maruyama's 1970 book *Why Was Koroto Opened*, Narahashi reflected on that initial meeting in March 1946 with the three Japanese men who had just escaped from Manchuria. He recalled as follows:

In those days, I was struggling in my efforts both internally and externally in an atmosphere of despondency to assist Prime Minister Shidehara who had been designated to head the postwar administrative government. Among the prime minister's most important duties was the question of how to safely return to Japan the millions of Japanese left overseas, and we spent days and nights tackling that problem. It was in those times that three representatives who returned to Japan for the rescue of Japanese countrymen residing in Manchuria—Maruyama, Shinpo, and Musashi— handed to me a secret letter from Mr. Tatsunosuke Takasaki; he was the president of Manchurian Heavy

Industries and had become the chairman of the All-Manchurian Japanese Association after the war.

As I was reading this secret communication from Mr. Takasaki that had been written very compactly, I could not hold back the tears that welled up in my eyes. I was envisioning the heartrending suffering that was being related by Mr. Takasaki of the Japanese overseas pushed beyond their capacity and of the miserable plight of the Japanese suffering from starvation. I reread the letter as I felt the constriction in my chest from the emotion. The gist of Mr. Takasaki's letter was a plea stating that an issuance of a guarantee from the Japanese government was necessary in order to make it possible for some Japanese in Manchuria, who had substantial personal assets, to donate those assets on behalf of the effort to save the Japanese refugees. It seemed that if those wealthy countrymen would be willing to present those assets for the rescue effort, it would be a tremendous help, and Mr. Takasaki had written the letter to notify the Japanese government of the need for such a guarantee.

I immediately discussed this matter with Minister of Finance Shibusawa, and then reported our intention to the headquarters of General MacArthur, but they did not assent to this request for a long time. Therefore, in the effort to save the 1.7 million countrymen in Manchuria, a document agreeing to that intention was prepared and entrusted to Masamichi Musashi, one of the Representatives to Petition for Saving Our Countrymen Living in Manchuria, in the last part of April 1946, when the decision was reached to dispatch the first ship to Koroto (Huludao) to repatriate the Japanese. Musashi agreed to once again cross the ocean back to Koroto and into Manchuria to take on the critical mission to deliver the document.

Wataru Narahashi, chief secretary to the prime minister, concluded his letter as follows:

> Thus, it was due to the selfless efforts of the three representatives, Maruyama, Shinpo, and Musashi, that the early repatriation of 1.7 million Japanese living in Manchuria, their return to Japan, and the subsequent relief operation on their behalf, was successfully accomplished. The difficult and heroic achievement of the three men will forever remain in the history of the repatriation of Japanese from overseas that resulted from the defeat of our nation.[2]

The Pope's Representative Lends Support

On the following day, the three set out from their headquarters in Kugayama to meet with the official representative of Rome and of the pope, Archbishop Paul Marella, at his official delegation office in Tokyo. They handed the archbishop the letter of introduction that had been entrusted to them by Bishop Raymond Lane before their departure from Dalian. After Archbishop Marella read the letter, he turned to the three men seated around his table and expressed his thanks to God that the three had been able to return to Japan safely. The three gave a detailed report on the current situation in Manchuria. They emphasized that, in these days of peace in most of the world following the end of the war, tragedies worse than during wartime were being repeated daily in Manchuria and that this was a catastrophic humanitarian problem that other nations must not disregard. What was happening in Manchuria was not merely a problem for the Japanese, but it was an international one that required international action. Maruyama pleaded with the papal nuncio to inform the pope at the earliest opportunity and ask His Holiness to exert his influence to bring about an immediate end to the Soviet oppression and deplorable conditions.

Upon conclusion of the report, the archbishop said, "This is a problem of such magnitude that it cannot be ignored for the sake of humanity. I will immediately send a report to the papal office and will call for a rescue effort." So saying, while the three men were still sitting around his table, Archbishop Marella scribbled a telegram addressed to the Vatican reporting on what he had just heard from the three men. For the first time ever, the situation in Manchuria was being reported to the outside world. Undoubtedly, the very personal letter of introduction that had been written by the head of the Catholic Church in Manchuria, Bishop Lane of Dalian, had a tremendous impact on the papal nuncio in how much he trusted every word spoken by the three men.

After charging his assistant to dispatch the telegram promptly to the Vatican, Archbishop Marella turned to the three men and said, "In order to bring about the rescue of the Japanese in Manchuria, you will need the assistance of the Allied Powers Headquarters. You will need to meet with General MacArthur and his deputies. I will write a letter of introduction for you so that they will accord you courtesy and so that your request will receive top priority." Again, he sat down and wrote out a letter of introduction addressed to General MacArthur's aide-de-camp, Colonel H. B. Wheeler. The men had already planned to make a visit to SCAP GHQ at the earliest time possible, but having in hand a letter of introduction from the papal nuncio was sure to have a favorable impact in how they would be treated and how seriously their plea would be considered by GHQ. The key to accomplishing their mission of rescue depended almost completely on the reaction of the U.S. military at GHQ.

Maruyama, a Buddhist, was immensely impressed and thankful for the kindness shown by Archbishop Marella. Surely, he thought, this man acted so kindly and sincerely based on his faith and reverence in the God he believed in, and his actions were a manifestation of his character, which resulted from his exceptional humanism. If all people in the world who were in positions of leadership were anything like this papal envoy, Maruyama thought to himself, how much better the world would be! He thought about his favorite book, *Utopia* by Sir Thomas More, and recalled the characters described in the book. He felt that he had found the ideal human being, particularly the ideal leader, in the person of Archbishop Marella.

Upon their return home to their headquarters in Kugayama that evening, the three had difficulty suppressing the optimism and elation they felt. They were finally set to pay a visit to GHQ and begin pleading their case.

"At last, the moment of truth is upon us!"

"We will finally take our first major step to bring about repatriation!"

"Let's remain patient yet tenacious in our task, as we have been doing so far!"

Exchanging such comments, the three men from Manchuria sat around the kitchen table to map out their plans as they prepared for the first meeting with GHQ.

Maruyama subsequently visited Archbishop Marella at his official apostolic office on six or seven other occasions, leading groups of Japanese families whose loved ones still remained in Manchuria or had been shipped off to Siberia by the Soviet military. Each time he met with the archbishop, who encouraged the family members to stay brave as they prayed and waited for the return of their dear ones, Maruyama was emotionally moved by the compassion and kindness shown by the papal representative.

Members of a delegation promoting repatriation of Japanese civilians
and still unreturned POWs pose for this 1947 portrait with Archbishop
Paul Marella, the pope's official representative in Japan. Kunio sits
at the left of the archbishop, while Mary, who had recently returned
from Manchuria, kneels in the first row, third from the left. (Kunio
Maruyama Collection)

Chapter 13

"Where Is Koroto?"

First of Many Meetings with GHQ

Maruyama, Shinpo, and Musashi left the Kugayama residence early on March 20, 1946, wearing their now familiar armbands announcing that they were representatives petitioning to save the Japanese in Manchuria, and took the train toward Tokyo Station to visit the Allied Powers GHQ. GHQ was then located in what later became the Dai-ichi Seimei Building in front of the palace moat embankment in Hibiya. They presented themselves to the military policemen at the entrance of the building, asked to see Colonel H. B. Wheeler, and handed the letter of introduction from Archbishop Marella to one of the guards. As expected, the papal nuncio's letter did the trick, and General MacArthur's aide-de-camp, Colonel Wheeler, came down to greet the three men and led them in to his office.

Several other high-ranking U.S. Army officers (including a Japanese-American officer) were waiting there to hear what the three Japanese had to say. Maruyama did almost all the talking for the three men, since he was the only one fluent in English. He brought Colonel Wheeler and the other officers up to date regarding the present situation in Manchuria, described their escape from Manchuria through Tianjin, and reported on their activities since arriving in Japan. Then they answered some questions from the officers.

Maruyama concluded his briefing by requesting that Colonel Wheeler arrange for the three to meet with various personnel in GHQ tasked with the repatriation of Japanese from overseas. Maruyama also boldly requested that the three have the opportunity to meet with General MacArthur at the earliest opportunity. Colonel Wheeler responded to Maruyama's request by saying, "We greatly appreciate your report, and we clearly understand your request. I will do my best to set up a meeting for you with the supreme commander. But for today, I ask for your patience, and I would now like to have you meet with the personnel in the division responsible for dealing with repatriation."

With that, Colonel Wheeler led the men to the office of the G-3 Operations Section, which was the occupation division responsible for all repatriation issues. There were six or seven officers busily working in that section, but when Colonel Wheeler and the three men entered, the officers rose to be introduced to the visitors by the SCAP aide-de-camp. All were senior field grade officers (majors to colonels) and reported to Colonel J. F. Howell Jr. After the introductions, the three men bowed deeply to Colonel Wheeler, who was about to leave the men in the care of the operations section, and thanked him for his kindness. Then the three men took the colonel's hand and grasped it firmly in gratitude in the Western custom as they bade farewell.

At the invitation of Colonel Howell, Maruyama, Shinpo, and Musashi sat down around a table to begin discussion with the officers of the G-3 Operations Section. It is probably no exaggeration to say that the three men's mission might never have had a chance to succeed without the involvement of Maruyama, whose fluency in English not only speeded up negotiations but engendered immediate and lasting trust as the officers and men of GHQ treated him as if he were one of their own. Once again, Maruyama related briefly how the three men had escaped from Manchuria. He followed that with an extensive and detailed report on the conditions of present-day, postwar Manchuria. He told the officers how the Japanese in Manchuria were facing hunger, sickness, and the bitter cold and bluntly told them how death was taking hundreds of Japanese lives daily.

Then he concluded his report with the following words: "Although war has ended and peace is supposed to be reigning, while there may be the absence of bombs falling in Manchuria now, a tragedy worse than the worst times during the war has befallen Manchuria. The condition there is a major crime against humanity, and it cannot be ignored and left alone one day longer. Can you tell us who it is that we should be appealing to? We feel that there is no one else to appeal to and cry to but to you officers who are under the command of General MacArthur, who has been carrying out occupation policies since arriving in Japan. We feel we must appeal particularly to you, the very officers in GHQ who are members of the division supervising the repatriation of Japanese from overseas. We appeal to you with all our being to dispatch repatriation ships to Manchuria at the earliest date possible. Since all the ports in Manchuria where repatriation would be likely, beginning with Dalian, are under the strictest control of the Soviet army, repatriation would be a most difficult task. However, the Port of Koroto (Huludao) is the only port presently under the control of the Nationalist Chinese forces, and it is our feeling that if the Supreme Commander, General MacArthur, would arrive at an understanding with the Nationalists, we are certain that repatriation from there could commence immediately without any problems."[1]

The senior officers of G-3 Operations Section thanked the three men for providing them with so much current intelligence about Manchuria and asked many questions. On the subject of

Koroto, they expressed general agreement about using a port under Nationalist control if and when repatriation commenced. One of the officers immediately brought out three maps of Manchuria and China and spread them out on the table and asked, "Where is this Koroto?"

Koroto Is Nonexistent!

The three men looked at each map to point out Koroto, but it was not on any of them. They asked the officer who had brought them out, "Do you have any other maps?" The officer went out and came back shortly with ten more maps. This time all the officers of the operations section bent to the task to help search for Koroto. But Koroto was not on any of the maps! The three Japanese looked at each other and said, "This is so strange ..." It was as if it were a bad dream.

Shinpo asked Maruyama to inquire if the maps they were looking at were new. One of the officers responded, "Well, since they were made before the war, they are probably quite old."

Maruyama said to all the officers who had helped in the fruitless search and were now standing with questioning looks on their faces, "Koroto is not shown on any of these maps, but believe us, there is a Koroto! Before our return to Japan, each of us had a good look at it. Not only did we see it with our own eyes, we walked on the wharf with our own feet, so there is no mistake!" He went on, "When the Japanese military engaged in operations during the Sino-Japanese War to make a landing in Manchuria, they found that the Port of Dalian was not enough to meet their strategy, so the Japanese hastily built Koroto as a port dedicated strictly for military purposes. It is a relatively new port, so it is not very well known. Koroto is located about two hundred kilometers to the north of Dalian and is about three hundred kilometers southwest of Shenyang (Mukden) which is in the interior of Liaodong Bay in the northern part of Bohai. Today, there are the remains of two military ships that had been operational during the Sino-Japanese Incident there with all the armaments removed and looking rather pitiful, lying on their sides. Because it is a new port, we fear that it would not appear on any American map unless it was a new map."

An officer mumbled to himself, "But we will not be able to send any ships to a port that is not on any maps."

In the end, the three Japanese promised to scout all over Tokyo on their return home that day and find a map with Koroto on it without fail, then return tomorrow to continue the discussion. The three stood up and shook hands with Colonel Howell and each of his officers, thanking them for their patience. The meeting had been almost four hours long. During that time, the Americans had been very kind and hospitable, offering coffee and chocolates while the meeting progressed.

Scouring Tokyo for a Map

As they hurriedly walked from GHQ toward the train station, they exchanged comments about not finding Koroto.

"What an unexpected problem!" said Maruyama.

"If we had maps made in Japan, we should be able to find Koroto," said Musashi.

"Don't worry, Maruyama-san," said Shinpo. "We'll find a new map made in Japan in one of the bookstores or map stores in Tokyo, and we will take it to GHQ to reassure the officers."

The three men went immediately to the Jinbocho District in Tokyo, which had been known before the war for its many bookstores, and then to the Kudanshita District, which had several map stores. To their surprise and consternation, not one of those stores was selling maps! Apparently the Japanese military had issued an order before the end of the war banning the sale of maps and removing them from all stores. Since the three had firmly promised the American officers to return with a map showing Koroto, they were put in a position to completely lose face. The three decided to go separately to

142

different parts of Tokyo to look for stores selling maps and schools where they might be available, and meet at Kugayama when they had found a map or when all stores and schools had closed. When the three met late that night at Kugayama, none had been able to locate the desired map.

The three men were desperate, but finding a map as they had promised GHQ was just not possible. Finally, Shinpo, an expert at architectural drawing, sat down to draw a map of Koroto and surrounding areas, putting all his professional talent to use for the task. The finished product was quite excellent, and they decided that was what they would show the officers of the G-3 Operations Section.

The next day they again met the same officers at GHQ. After a courteous exchange of greetings, Maruyama again spoke for the three. Feeling sheepish, Maruyama explained as follows: "Yesterday, the three of us went to stores all over Tokyo that we thought carried maps, and we went also to schools looking for maps, but we were shocked to learn that maps have disappeared from all stores! The maps we found at schools were all old and did not show Koroto. So we drew a map of Koroto for you, and we beg that you will be satisfied with this." Then Shinpo took out and spread on the table the map he had meticulously drawn the night before. The officers all looked at the map, but since it was a hand-drawn map and not a published one, they looked skeptical. Maruyama, Shinpo, and Musashi looked on helplessly as the officers studied the map with frowns on their faces, obviously unconvinced.

"I Found Koro Island!"

After some time of continued and uncomfortable embarrassment, one of the officers came running into the room shouting, "I found Koro Island Harbor!" (Koroto-Ko, or the Port of Koroto, is written in Chinese characters as Koro Island, but is actually not an island. In Chinese, it is pronounced Huludao.)

He brought in a large American map and said, "This is it! This is it!" Laying the map on the table over Shinpo's hand-drawn map, the officer circled Koroto with a red colored pencil.

The three Japanese looked at the map and the circled port and jumped up and down with joy. Although none had expressed it, the three men had begun to feel dejected and had lost confidence overnight, but suddenly they again felt confident. The map was a newly published, large-scale military map and contained a great amount of detail. The American officers' skepticism and concern seemed to vanish as they studied the map. In fact, they were just as happy as the three and congratulated them.

Finding Koroto on the map, however, did not mean ships would be dispatched there. That would not happen until the Supreme Commander for Allied Forces (SCAP), General MacArthur, made the decision. Until then, they had plenty to plan for and consider. The rest of the meeting was spent in long discussions, mostly centered on details concerning Koroto, and the three again reiterated their plea for the earliest dispatch of ships for repatriation before they took leave of the U.S. Army officers for the day.

The first mention of Koroto as the likely port of evacuation of Japanese from Manchuria, so far as the author is aware, took place at a U.S.–Chinese conference, "Return of Japanese POWs and Civilian Residents," held in Shanghai on January 5, 1946. In a Japanese document obtained by the author, approximately fifteen senior U.S. officers and six Chinese officers discussed issues pertaining to repatriation of Japanese, mainly from China, using Liberty ships. At one point, the document reveals that a senior U.S. officer named Colonel Richard Wittman[2] stated that at least two ports would be necessary if and when repatriation from Manchuria commenced. One of the ports named was Koroto, and the other was Dalian, if permission could be obtained (obviously from the Soviet Union). Colonel Wittman went on to say that preparation for repatriation needed to start on or before April 1 and not later than May 1, 1946. To do so, he continued, sufficient reconnaissance and intelligence information needed to be gathered from Manchuria.[3]

Subsequently, Chief of Staff Liu Wanquan of the Nationalist army underground headquarters in Shenyang urged Maruyama, Shinpo, and Musashi during their clandestine meeting on February 8, 1946, that Koroto was the best port to use for repatriating Japanese civilians from Manchuria.

Several days following the Shanghai meeting of January 5, a conference on repatriation was held, this time in Tokyo, on January 15–17, 1946. This meeting, attended by senior representatives of all the major U.S. Army and naval commands in the Pacific region, established procedures and task responsibilities for repatriation of Japanese from all regions of the Pacific, including China, the Philippines, Korea, Ryukyu Islands, and other Pacific areas. In the top secret report issued after the conference, mention was made of plans to repatriate a total of 1.6 million personnel from Manchuria using the port at Huludao (Koroto). One of the attendees of the conference was Colonel J. F. Howell Jr. of SCAP GHQ, head of the G-3 Operations Section responsible for repatriation issues.[4]

Thus, G-3 Operations Section Commander Colonel Howell, who sat in on the meetings and discussions with Maruyama, Shinpo, and Musashi, and who even participated in the frantic search for Koroto on several maps, probably was already aware that Koroto was the most likely candidate port for repatriating Japanese from Manchuria. However, since all of Manchuria was an unknown region to the U.S. military because it had been completely off limits to the United States as well as to the rest of the world, Colonel Howell probably did not know where Koroto was even if he had heard that name at the repatriation conference in Tokyo he had attended in January. Additionally, the Americans may not have recognized Huludao's Japanese name, Koroto. That these three men brought back so much intelligence to SCAP about the unknown Manchuria must have been invaluable for SCAP GHQ personnel perparing to deal with repatriation issues.

The Three "Impudent" Japanese

For the next few weeks, it became routine for the three men wearing the armbands to visit GHQ every two or three days. When they arrived at GHQ and were led in to meet with the officers of the G-3 Operations Section, they always started with cordial greetings and began their discussions in a calm manner. However, as conversation progressed, there were many occasions when the three Japanese would become quite excited and emotional as they pointed out the tragedy in Manchuria and made their appeals for quick action.

At times they would blurt out, "To not do anything about this situation is gravely inhuman, and we could never ask for forgiveness from the Japanese in Manchuria!" On more than one occasion, one of the three men would uncharacteristically pound on the table to make a point. The three realized that the American officers must surely have thought them impudent. But this was no time for the three men to worry about how they may have come across; deadly earnest and knowing that time was not on their side, they pressed on. By the time their meeting ended, however, and they were ready to say good-bye and depart for the day, the Japanese would regain their composure. As perfect gentlemen, they would ask forgiveness for their impudence, bowing and shaking hands with each of the officers. This routine was repeated many times.

Looking back later, Maruyama was amazed that he could have acted so brusquely to the men from whom he so desperately sought help. Perhaps because the three men had made secret visits to Shenyang, Changchun, Harbin, and many other Soviet-occupied areas before they made their break out of Manchuria and had seen the masses of nearly starving Japanese refugees with no decent shelter, weakened by illness and cold, many dying daily—perhaps those recent images had slightly unbalanced them psychologically. The sights they had seen, such as a young mother, who could not produce milk since she had not eaten for days, trying to breastfeed her dying, or even dead, infant—such tragic scenes, which seemed not of this world, rendered the three somewhat deranged for a time. Maruyama could not erase from his mind the terrible vision of countless innocent infants lying beside their mothers, pitifully, painfully, and helplessly dying from lack of nutrition, their debilitated mothers helpless to do anything about it. Maruyama at times dreamed that some of the fellow Japanese were clinging to the feet of the three and refusing to let go.

The three men had returned to their native Japan bearing the prayers and hopes of 1.7 million Japanese stranded in Manchuria. Countless souls of Japanese who had reached either heaven or Buddhahood were now looking down on the three men to make sure they did not fail in their mission. Their frame of mind in those days was such that they felt no constraint to act in a normal and civilized manner, with customary hesitancy or modesty. Whether they met with a high-ranking American officer or a Japanese of ministerial rank, they felt no fear whatsoever. In fact, the higher the rank and influence of the person they met, the greater the boldness and courage the three displayed.

However, at no time did they abandon their politeness or cross the line to become rude. Often, as they made their appeals, they would come to attention, lower their heads in a bow, and make their point firmly, bluntly, with tears running down their cheeks, but always politely—and they never failed to express sincere gratitude at the end of their meetings.

Chapter 14

The Campaign Continues

The Relentless Campaign Continues

Between their frequent meetings at GHQ, Maruyama, Shinpo and Musashi visited Japanese agencies and civilian entities whose influence was important in drumming up support of the Japanese government and the public. They also participated in assemblies organized by various citizens' groups engaged in repatriation efforts.

On March 23, 1946, they met with Soichi Saito who headed the Japanese government agency administering repatriation of Japanese from the Pacific regions. After the three had given a detailed report of the situation in Manchuria (a report the three were to present over and over to different agencies and organizations), they discussed such details as who should be brought back to Japan first once repatriation began (it was agreed that those who were ill or disabled should be first on the list), what medical and other preparations should be readied by the Japanese government, and other issues. As the meeting came to a conclusion, Saito said to the three men, "In any case, until repatriation ships begin sailing, our hands are tied. But as soon as the decision is made [by SCAP] for the dispatch of ships, we want to take measures, such as sending a rescue mission." That day, Director Saito made arrangements for the three to meet soon with His Majesty, Prince Takamatsu, the younger brother of the emperor. In the days and months that followed, Saito was most helpful in the efforts of the three men.

A few days later, on March 26, the three visited the railroad ministry. The railroad was, and still is, the lifeline of Japan in many respects. When repatriation began from Manchuria and the Japanese returnees disembarked at various ports, they would then need to take the train to their homes in various parts of Japan. The then–vice minister of railroads, Takashi Hirayama, had a personal interest in the quick and successful repatriation of Japanese in Manchuria, since his brother, the former president of the Manchurian Electric Works Company in Changchun, was still trapped in Manchuria. Vice Minister Hirayama made arrangements to convene a meeting of all executives of the railroad ministry holding the rank of division chief and higher so that several dozen of the top Japanese railway officials assembled to hear the three men report on the situation in Manchuria. After the presentation, the three fielded many questions. Also in attendance at the assembly was the head of Japan's railroad ministry, Eisaku Sato.

The Help from Eisaku Sato

Eisaku Sato, who later became prime minister of Japan, was extremely cooperative and helpful to the three men. As an example, he issued a railway certificate to each of them that allowed them to ride any nationally owned train free of charge for a period of two years. Other privately owned railways followed Sato's kind gesture by issuing similar passes. Soon, other means of transportation including buses, subways, and streetcars followed suit so that the three were able to travel anywhere in Japan free of charge. The ability to travel anywhere at any time without paying a yen helped the men tremendously in pursuing their mission with vigor throughout Japan.

When Maruyama reflected many years later on all the help and kindness they received from the head of the railroad ministry, he remembered Eisaku Sato as a handsome and capable young man with large bright eyes. Never did he dream that this man would ascend twenty years later to the highest office as prime minister of Japan. However, when Maruyama recalled that Sato was a man who fully understood and recognized the importance of the three men's mission, he could appreciate how the then head of the railroad ministry who acted with such wisdom and decisiveness in 1946, and who hesitated not at all in assisting Maruyama and his companions in so many ways, always had the capacity to lead the Japanese nation. Eisaku Sato became the longest serving prime minister in Japanese history (1964–1972) and was later awarded the Nobel Peace Prize for leading Japan to participate in the Nuclear Non-Proliferation Treaty.

Upon leaving the railroad ministry, the three headed to a well-known Japanese restaurant in the Ueno District of Tokyo, the Ueno Seiyokan, to participate in a press conference. The large restaurant was renowned because it was one of the first restaurants in Japan to begin serving Western foods. An organization called the Association to Rescue Japanese in Mongolia and in Manchuria, had organized a joint press conference with reporters from the major newspapers in Tokyo. Although the three were fully aware that much of what they would say might not appear in print in the various newspapers, they realized that the more people they talked to, the more information would get out, eventually generating more interest and enthusiasm among the Japanese public. Their presentation was better organized with each speech the three men gave, so that they could say more in less time and still include important details. The three were encouraged, and their spirits were lifted by the enthusiasm of the reporters and listeners attending the joint press conference.

Visiting the Foreign Minister

Early the next day, the three men left their headquarters in Kugayama for an appointment to meet with then Foreign Minister Shigeru Yoshida. Maruyama had met Yoshida several years earlier in London, when Maruyama was making his around-the-world journey after completing his graduate studies at Columbia University. At that time, Yoshida was the Japanese ambassador to Great Britain. After a cordial reunion, the three men described their escape from Manchuria and apprised the foreign minister of the conditions in present-day Manchuria. They concluded by speaking bluntly to Yoshida: "In our view, the government of Japan, and in particular the Ministry of Foreign Affairs, has been very cool toward the grave problem regarding the Japanese stranded in Manchuria. With all due respect, we feel they are negligent, and we would appreciate greatly your thoughts on this matter."

For a moment Yoshida looked bitter, but then he said, "That isn't true. Japan does not have any diplomacy right now. The foreign ministry's diplomacy has been shelved for the time being. Our nation, which has been engaged with occupation policies since the installment of the Occupation Forces, does not have an independent government. But do not worry; since the object of whatever policies are enforced [by GHQ] is the nation of Japan, we need to stay in the shadows and cleverly handle them without being obvious and have them take courses that are advantageous to Japan. I say this in a respectful way, but in the end, we need to manipulate GHQ like a puppet on a string for our benefit." Foreign Minister Yoshida spoke with his characteristic ironic humor. The three men appreciated Yoshida's light touch, but it did not alleviate their lurking depression: they realized that the Japanese government was, in fact, quite helpless at the present time.

Then Maruyama took out a piece of paper that had obviously been crumpled and then somewhat smoothed out. "If I may change the subject, Mr. Yoshida, when we were ready to flee Manchuria, a sister at the Catholic Church in Dalian gave this to us to deliver. It is addressed to your daughter. Could you make sure she gets it?" Then he handed over the letter that Maryknoll Sister Roseanne had thrust into his hand just as they were departing the church. "The letter was sewn into the Manchurian clothing I was wearing at the time of our escape and is difficult to read, but please ask your daughter Kazuko Aso to use an iron to take out the wrinkles so she can read it."

Foreign Minister Yoshida took the letter and looked intently at it for some moments, and he unconsciously blinked his eyes twice. The he said, "I am so grateful for all your efforts. To make GHQ do things, the power of ordinary civilians is more effective than that of the government at this time. Now is the time for people's diplomacy. I ask you three to please invigorate public opinion for your cause."

With those words, the three men stood up and bade farewell to the foreign minister. They could clearly detect moisture glistening in both his eyes.[1]

Japan does not have any diplomacy right now ... Those were the words that had the most impact on the three men. As they walked out of the foreign ministry building and toward the train station, those painful words from deep within the heart of Shigeru Yoshida left the three speechless for some time.

Then, as they sat on a park bench at a corner of Hibiya Park to collect their thoughts, Musashi said, "Is now the age of people's diplomacy?"

"We must work to spread the news of Manchuria's condition ever wider," said Shinpo, staring intently into the eyes of his companions. "Let's increase the number of our presentations throughout the country. We must renew our efforts to convince General MacArthur's officers."

"Let's go and appeal to them again tomorrow," replied Maruyama as his companions nodded in complete agreement.

Maruyama reflected back to eight years earlier when he had first met Shigeru Yoshida in Great Britain as he made his post–graduate studies European journey. Actually, he had two occasions to visit Yoshida, then the Japanese ambassador to Great Britain, in the ambassador's suite in London and had been given a warm welcome on both occasions. Maruyama remembered how Yoshida talked to him about various interesting topics as the ambassador fed coals into his stove.

The episode Maruyama remembered best occurred during his first meeting with Yoshida. It just so happened that on the next day, Prime Minister Neville Chamberlain and Foreign Secretary Anthony Eden were scheduled to announce a major policy related to Japan on the floor of the British Parliament. When Maruyama mentioned to Yoshida that he would very much like to be in attendance during that announcement, the ambassador immediately called his secretary and instructed that a ticket for the gallery of the Parliament be given to Maruyama.

After expressing gratitude to the ambassador and pocketing the ticket that was given to him, Maruyama continued to enjoy Yoshida's views on various topics. However, after some minutes, the secretary came excitedly into Yoshida's office and said, "We just had a call from Paris, and there are five Japanese members of Parliament who are attending an assembly at the Paris World's Fair who plan to come to England tomorrow. They want to attend tomorrow's session of British Parliament also. They requested that you provide them with tickets to the gallery if at all possible. Since we are short one ticket, would it be possible to ask that the ticket just given to Mr. Maruyama be returned?"

Without hesitation, Yoshida replied, "That's idiotic! Mr. Maruyama also came here because he wants to hear the announcement. You can't do something as rude as to demand the return of something that was already given to someone! If there are not enough, then, too bad, there are not enough. There's nothing to be concerned about." The secretary departed hastily after an apology and a bow.

Although Maruyama also felt some irritation at the secretary who had thought of him as merely a student who could be treated with rudeness, he felt badly for the ambassador who would be unable to fulfill the wishes of the important visitors from Japan. "Please give them the gallery ticket you gave me," he said as he retrieved the ticket from inside his pocket.

The ambassador turned to Maruyama with a wave of his hand and said, "There is no need to give it back to me. Rather than have someone who doesn't understand the language in attendance, the ticket itself will be much happier to be used by someone like you in attendance to listen."

Deeply moved by the action of the ambassador whose heart would not allow him to discriminate, Maruyama immediately respected and admired Shigeru Yoshida's sense of justice, honesty, and humor.

His attitude toward the former ambassador was reinforced by today's meeting at the foreign ministry. During their initial chitchat before turning to the subject of Manchuria, Maruyama had mentioned to Yoshida their meeting in London eight years before and said, "Mr. Yoshida, if I may speak bluntly, the hair on your head may have thinned some since that time, but in all other respects, you have not changed a bit." The foreign minister chuckled and ran a hand through his head of hair to confirm that observation.

The Non-Stop Campaign Continues ...

The three men began receiving many requests to appear as speakers and lecturers at assemblies and meetings dealing with Japanese left behind overseas, including in Manchuria. Most of the events were sponsored by family groups whose loved ones had still not returned after the end of the war. Following up on their vow after their meeting with Shigeru Yoshida, the three men did their best to accommodate each of those requests. Initially, all three attended together at the events; soon, they divided the engagements among themselves to appear at as many as possible.

Always wearing their armbands, they used each opportunity to press the immediate necessity to dispatch repatriation ships to Koroto and roused public opinion to put pressure on GHQ and the Japanese government to take action without delay. At every meeting or assembly, the three met with families and relatives who still had precious family members and friends in Manchuria, answering questions long after the event had ended, feeling the pain of each family member or relative who asked personal questions regarding the welfare or whereabouts of their loved ones that the three were unable to answer.

Between March 30 and April 4, Maruyama returned to his native Nagano Prefecture to speak at several assemblies sponsored by the Prefectural Committee to Rescue Fellow Countrymen in Manchuria and Korea. The assemblies were held in the major cities of Nagano, including Nagano City, Ueda, Matsumoto, and Iida. Each meeting was filled beyond capacity. Maruyama repeated the accounts he had told many times by now. To those who had come to listen, everything Maruyama reported was new and in most cases confirmed what they had been fearing about the condition of their loved ones still in Manchuria. The question and answer sessions were, in most cases, longer than the presentations themselves.

Even after the meeting or assembly was over, there were always some people in the audience who would stop him on his way out with more personal questions. Some even came to the hotel where he stayed to inquire about their children, their husbands, their siblings, their fiancées, and other precious ones still in Manchuria. Since Maruyama was unable to provide specific information on particular individuals, all he could do was to let them know the situation where their loved ones were thought to be and come up with a response based on what he thought. Even when he went to the train station the next morning, families were waiting for him; he would continue to relay information about Manchuria right up until his train departed.

The earnestness, desperation, and tears of the relatives and family members inquiring about those they loved only strengthened the three men's resolve to work even harder to move GHQ to take action. When Maruyama returned to Tokyo and reunited with his companions (who had each been in different parts of Japan, also speaking at assemblies and experiencing the same response from desperate families), he told Shinpo and Musashi how frustrated he felt that he could not gauge the resolve of GHQ on the Manchurian repatriation issue. His companions were just as frustrated and upset. After they parted, whirling thoughts and emotions kept Maruyama up all night.

Chapter 15

Face to Face
with General MacArthur

A Request to a Nisei Officer Pays Off

The next morning, as the three headed to Kugayama Station to catch the train to visit GHQ yet again, they concluded that their patience had run out. They must somehow speak to General MacArthur himself as soon as possible. That was their determination as they arrived at GHQ on the morning of April 4, 1946.

Although the three had been meeting almost daily with the officers of the G-3 Operations Section, they were aware that the senior officer who would most likely be able to arrange for a meeting with SCAP was his aide-de-camp, Colonel Wheeler. When they asked at once to see Colonel Wheeler, they were informed that the colonel was away on temporary duty. They learned, however, that there was a young Nisei (Japanese-American) major on the SCAP staff, so the three requested to meet with him. (Maruyama did not identify this officer by name.)

The three met the officer and introduced themselves to him. Maruyama began by saying, "I studied for several years in the

157

United States, and while I was in graduate school at a university on the West Coast, I taught Japanese history, law, and culture to many young Americans of Japanese descent. I even wondered if perhaps I might have met you before as one of my students." The two had never met until that day, but they had a cordial initial conversation.

Then Maruyama explained to the young, handsome officer that the reason for their frequent visits to GHQ was to ask GHQ's help in the repatriation of Japanese from Manchuria. "We would like to have a direct meeting with General MacArthur. We want to explain personally to the Supreme Commander the true situation in Manchuria following the end of the war and appeal to him directly for the rescue of the Japanese and propose a method for the dispatch of ships for repatriation. Is there anything you can do to arrange an opportunity for us to meet with General MacArthur?" After making that request, Maruyama continued, "It is possible that Colonel Wheeler has already relayed our request to General MacArthur in the past few days, but since he is away on temporary duty, we decided to ask you to intercede on our behalf." Then the three handed the Nisei officer their *meishi* (business cards).

Without hesitating, the young American officer of Japanese descent said, "I will see what I can do. Please come back later to see if I have any news for you." Then they all stood up and exchanged handshakes and smiles, and the Nisei officer went back to his office. Maruyama, Shinpo, and Musashi decided they should leave for now and return later that afternoon.

They returned to GHQ a few hours later and asked to see the young Nisei aide again. He came out right away, smiling at the men he had met earlier that morning. Without fanfare, the Nisei officer said calmly, "The general has agreed to the meeting. He will meet with you tomorrow, April 5, at 4:00 PM, in the office of the Supreme Commander. Please come to me just before that time tomorrow." Needless to say, the three men were elated. Then, because the young aide was an American of Japanese blood, the three bowed their heads deeply and somberly in the Japanese style and expressed their deepest gratitude before they parted company. The young officer's response to the three men was simply a happy look, obviously pleased that he was able to have helped.

That evening at their headquarters in Kugayama, Maruyama, Shinpo, and Musashi sat around the dining room table to prepare for their meeting with the most important man in Japan. The general was extremely busy, so they could not take up a lot of his time as they had been doing so stubbornly with the other officers at GHQ. The three discussed how they would make their presentation in a straightforward manner. The burden was on Maruyama to speak clearly and eloquently so that the general would have no misunderstanding or confusion on the points they intended to make.

Briefing General MacArthur

At 3:30 PM on April 5, Maruyama, Shinpo, and Musashi presented themselves at GHQ and met once again with the Nisei officer of the day before. When it was almost 4:00, the aide led the men to the office of the Supreme Commander and lined them up in front of the general's large table. General MacArthur rose from the chair behind his desk and came around to the large table, shook hands with each of the visitors, and invited them to sit down. As General MacArthur was sitting down at the table, Maruyama whispered to the young Japanese-American aide who took a seat next to Maruyama, "Could you ask the general how much time he would allow for this meeting?" He replied that they could take up to thirty minutes.

The three Japanese began by introducing themselves, starting with Maruyama. Maruyama then thanked the general for granting them the opportunity to meet in spite of his extremely busy schedule. He then summarized their mission by explaining that they had escaped from Manchuria a few weeks before, bringing with them the desperate hopes of 1.7 million Japanese in Manchuria; how their escape took them to China, where they found passage on a U.S. naval vessel at Tanggu; and how they had been visiting GHQ repeatedly to appeal for the dispatch of ships for the purpose of repatriation. Then he continued with the following summary of the situation in Manchuria, describing the plight of Japanese left there and the sadness endured by the families of those whose loved ones were still trapped in Manchuria:

The turmoil in Manchuria began with the sudden invasion of Manchuria by the Soviet army on August 9 of last year. And from the moment following the end of the war on August 15, tragedies as if in a nightmare have been occurring one after the other. Immediately following the end of the war, the Soviet army advanced from the north and the Chinese Communist forces advanced from the west. Since then, all public facilities have been taken over, public order has fallen into disarray, public safety has worsened everywhere, and violence and pillaging are occurring everywhere. Japanese in Manchuria have lost their jobs so that their abilities to make a living have been completely denied, and there has been sudden and rampant inflation so that simply the ability to continue living has reached a critical level.

Just before we departed Manchuria in the early part of February, according to statistics compiled by the Changchun Japanese Association of the total estimated Japanese population of one million seven hundred thousand, 46 percent have become refugees. That is 810,000 Japanese. Moreover, each and every day nearly 2,500 are dying from hunger, cold, and illness; that amounts to about 17,000 Japanese dying each week.

Among many of these victims are newly born infants and innocent little children. These innocent children are victims of hunger, sickness, and cold, quietly dying in the arms of their mothers who themselves are barely able to survive as they are mere skin and bones. Today, war has ended in every country of the world, and peace has descended on all. However, while bombs are no longer falling in Manchuria where peace has also come, due to hunger, cold, and illness, and due also to pillaging, violence, and rape, there is tragedy occurring day after day that is even worse than during the war. Victims continue to fall, and tragic scenes of carnage are repeated over and over.

Although eight months have passed since the end of war, and today we are at peace, justice and humanity have been devastatingly uprooted in Manchuria so that only raw power backed by bayonets and tyranny has the upper hand, and gun shots can be heard at all times, night and day. Each day, Japanese must struggle in an uncertain world as if they were stepping on thin ice, barely connected to the world of the living. The common yearning of all those Japanese pushed against the wall in such tragic state is just one wish, and that is to return to their native land as soon as possible. Every day and every night, they look toward the eastern skies and await that day when you—the Supreme Commander for Allied Powers, General MacArthur, who has resided in Tokyo since the end of the war, with your understanding and sympathy—will make the firm decision to send forth ships that will come to repatriate them so that they can return to their native land. That is their desperate longing. The only hope left for the Japanese in Manchuria, sir, is to hope for your compassion and subsequent decision.

I believe that you have already received reports from your staff officers, but we visited with the Operations Section on the lower floor of this GHQ at the invitation of your assistant, Colonel Wheeler. We met with many of your officers involved in these issues, and we spent much time reporting on the true situation in Manchuria as it is today, and we implored them to dispatch a ship to Koroto (Huludao) as soon as they possibly could. We three stopped at Koroto to see the port with our own eyes. It is at present the only port under the control of the Nationalist forces. If you would send ships there, repatriation of Japanese from Manchuria can take place without any trouble. In fact, the purpose of our visit with you today is to appeal to you to dispatch ships to Koroto without one more day of delay. Today, our appeal to you to request that the Japanese in Manchuria be returned to their loved ones in Japan is not just the desperate yearning of those families that are directly involved, but it is indeed the common yearning of all eighty million people of the Japanese nation. Needless to say, this is a great issue that involves justice and humanity. Tragedies worse than those that occurred during the war are being repeated in Manchuria in these days of peace. Where is the justice and where is the humanity if this dilemma and irrationality are silently overlooked and no intervention takes place?

We appeal to you, General MacArthur, from the standpoint of insuring justice and humanity in the world, and for the sake of the many millions of parents and children, wives and husbands, brothers and sisters, friends and lovers who have been separated as some stayed in Japan while others went overseas, and who are daily shedding tears of sorrow. We appeal to you for your infinite sympathy to take into consideration this grave problem, and as a first step, we ask you to make arrangements for the dispatch of a repatriation ship to Koroto at the earliest time possible. While we perhaps may seem audacious, we are here on behalf of the 1.7 million Japanese still left in Manchuria, and we are here also on behalf of the twenty million family members in Japan who have been waiting beyond hope for the return of those who are so precious to them; on their behalf we appeal to you from the bottom of our hearts.

Such was their appeal to General MacArthur.[1]

The General's Response

Secretly, both Shinpo and Musashi thought that Maruyama's appeal, which had been presented in different variations many times since their return to Japan, was extremely eloquent. More than forty minutes had already passed, but the general did not seem to be concerned; he merely listened intently until Maruyama was finished. After Maruyama once again expressed their gratitude to General MacArthur for his kindness and patience in meeting with them, the general spoke.

"I now fully understand the feelings of all the Japanese left in Manchuria and of all the families in Japan who are awaiting their return. I have already received a report from my staff about the possibility of dispatching a ship to Koroto, which you just mentioned, and I have already ordered my staff to conduct research on that possibility. I fully respect all that you have said today, and it is my intention to do all I can as rapidly as possible to set a course that will fulfill as much as possible the action you are requesting." The general was very forceful in his comments.[2]

The three men could not have expected a more positive reply. Full of strange and wonderful emotion, the three stood up and once again expressed their gratitude to the Supreme Commander and left after exchanging firm handshakes with him. As they followed the Nisei aide out of the general's office, they could not hold back the warm tears of gratitude and happiness that welled up in their eyes. They profusely thanked the Japanese-American officer, and the three walked out of GHQ feeling lighter on their feet than usual, and the world around them seemed brighter and warmer.

It had become something of a custom now for them stop at Hibiya Park and sit on the bench to reflect on the day's happenings before catching the train to return home. On this day again, sitting on the same park bench, they discussed their meeting with General MacArthur. They agreed unanimously that the general had listened intently to all they had said. Based on his body language, facial expressions, and especially his final comments when he mentioned Koroto, they agreed that a decision would be made soon to dispatch ships there. With their spirits buoyed, and feeling more optimistic than ever since their return to Japan, the three again made a pledge to push on even harder to rouse public opinion.

General of the Army Douglas MacArthur, Supreme Commander for
Allied Powers (SCAP). In a face-to-face meeting with Maruyama,
Shinpo, and Musashi on April 5, 1946, MacArthur promised early action
on their request to initiate Japanese repatriation from Koroto, Manchuria.
(MacArthur Memorial Library)

Almost every day, requests from various groups and
organizations were mailed to Kugayama asking the three men
from Manchuria to come speak at meetings, assemblies, press
conferences, and rallies. A particularly active group was an
alliance of students who had family members in Manchuria.
Their representatives came to Kugayama to offer help, and the
three gladly accepted this cooperation, which enabled them to
combine efforts for a common cause. Under the sponsorship of
the student alliance, a large assembly of citizens of Kyoto was
held on April 7. On the following day, an assembly sponsored
by the Kyoto newspaper was held at the newspaper's assembly
hall. Two days later, an assembly for Osaka area citizens
sponsored by the Osaka *Asahi* newspaper was held at the Asahi

Hall. On April 12, Isamu Takino, president of the All-Nippon Pharmaceutical Company, Incorporated, organized a meeting at the company's Osaka assembly hall that brought together representatives of the pharmaceutical industry. At all these and many other meetings and assemblies, Maruyama, Shinpo, and Musashi each spoke eloquently and passionately about the conditions in Manchuria and the need to send repatriation ships to Koroto before more Japanese died. While the speeches of the three men had been given with slight variation many times by now, they never failed to realize that those listening were hearing their information and pleas for the first time.

Chapter 16

The Story of Bishop Patrick Byrne

Father Byrne, a Confidant to SCAP

Ever since the three men had returned to Japan, there was one visit that they, and Maruyama in particular, looked forward to, but the opportunity somehow eluded them until April 13. On that day, they took the train and went to Kyoto to the Maryknoll Church at Kawaramachi in the Chukyo Ward of the ancient capital. When the three met with Bishop Raymond Lane in Dalian, he had recommended that the men meet with Father (later Bishop) Patrick James Byrne. Father Byrne had lived in Japan throughout World War II, spending most of his time under house arrest as a prisoner of the Imperial Japanese Army; his crime was that he was as an enemy alien.

Although this was the first meeting between the three men and the future bishop, Father Byrne greeted them as if they were old friends. After bringing the priest up to date on conditions in Manchuria, they related how Bishop Lane's assistance had been indispensable in their escape and how Maruyama's and Shinpo's families were presently under the care of the Maryknoll Church in Dalian. Father Byrne was particularly grateful to hear news about his old friend Bishop Lane and all the sisters and fathers of the Maryknoll Church in Dalian, who were all well known to him. Forgetting the passage of time, the three conversed for quite a while.

When they realized how long they had talked, Maruyama apologized for taking up so much of the priest's time. Replying that he was grateful for the courageous action of the three men in escaping from Manchuria, and even more grateful that they were engaged in efforts to initiate repatriation, Father Byrne promised to help in any way he could. He promised he would encourage General MacArthur to take quick action in dispatching ships to Manchuria for repatriation.

The influence of Father Byrne on General MacArthur cannot be overstated. From shortly after the Japanese surrender, even before American forces landed in Japan to rule every aspect of Japanese life, Father Byrne, who had just been released from confinement, had a major impact on the smooth and successful occupation of the defeated nation. A close confidant of Father Byrne, the Supreme Commander often conferred with him on occupation matters. In a December 31, 1945, letter that the priest sent to his superior at the Maryknoll headquarters in Ossining, New York, he reported on his activities in Japan, including his meetings with General MacArthur, as follows: "I've had two conferences with MacArthur. He spoke with what I considered amazing frankness, and his attitude toward missioners was most encouraging. Catholics, and not Protestants, are what this country needs, said he. They've lost Shintoism, with its ceremonies; and Protestantism, without ceremonies, will not have for them the appeal that [we have with our] rich liturgical functions, [our] sacraments, etc. etc. 'The country is now a religious vacuum, and you have the biggest opportunity that has been offered in hundreds of years. The whole country is [yours], if you'll come and take it. Your missioners should come in by the carload.'"

Father Byrne continued in the same letter to his superior, "I saw MacA. alone, for forty-five minutes. He was most informal, kept the big pipe going, and handed out smokes. With [Archbishop Paul] Marella, who saw him previously, there went Father Bitter, the rector of the University. Bitter asked him if the four Jesuits now in California could come out [to Japan]. 'Four,' said MacArthur, 'you ought to have four hundred coming out.' I asked him if it would embarrass [sic] at all to be quoted. 'No embarrassment at all,' said he, 'quote me as much as you please.'"[1]

Father Byrne's Address to the Troops on Ships

In his book *Why Was Koroto Opened*, Maruyama devotes several pages to a particular contribution that then Father Byrne made at the time of the first landing of American soldiers in Japan on August 25, 1945. The contribution, which was in the form of a radio broadcast he made to the U.S. military personnel on board ships awaiting orders to land on Japanese soil, is narrated here because of its historic significance in helping bring about the most bloodless and successful occupation of a nation ever seen in the world. Never in history had the world witnessed such a smooth occupation of an entire nation; the Americans saw no resistance by a former enemy that had sworn to fight to the last man. The episode is also narrated here because the author knows that Maruyama wanted the world to know what kind of man Bishop Patrick James Byrne was, a priest who was so helpful in every way to influence General MacArthur to dispatch ships to Manchuria for repatriation of Japanese.

Born in Washington, DC, on October 26, 1888, Patrick Byrne first came to Japan as a Maryknoll father in 1933 and took up residence in Kyoto. As a missionary in Japan, he came to love the people of Japan and their culture. With the outbreak of World War II, he chose to stay in Kyoto, his "second home," and did his best to survive under house arrest and lack of proper nourishment during the war years, tending his garden and studying the Japanese language.

On August 15, 1945, Emperor Hirohito made his unprecedented radio announcement to all citizens of Japan that conceded that the people had endured enough, and World War II came to an end. The next step was for the first wave of military soldiers of the Allied Powers, from the United States Army, to make its landing to occupy Japan. The Japanese people, who had been told to fight to the bitter end and that there would be terrible reprisals on the citizens of Japan by the occupying American soldiers, were in a state of abject fear. No woman would be safe, they had been told, so many women carried on their person vials of poison that they could consume when threatened. Panic spread among the general populace.

Fearing that the situation was getting out of hand and sensing that terrible tragedy could ensue, bringing further misery and deaths to the Japanese people, a staff reporter of the *Asahi* newspaper approached the Japanese bishop of Tokyo, Archbishop Peter Tatsuo Doi (who later became the first Japanese cardinal of the Catholic Church), to find someone who could "save the day." The reporter proposed that someone completely trusted by the Japanese people should make a radio broadcast to the American troops who were on board ships off the coast of Japan, preparing to make their first landing. The purpose of the broadcast was to explain to the American troops the psychology and situation of the Japanese people. The troops needed to clearly and fully understand that they should make their landing with warm, friendly, and peaceful attitudes. That appropriate individual, whoever that might be, should call upon the U.S. soldiers to do nothing that would besmirch American pride as victors and to temper any overbearing actions so that the Japanese people would see the first arrival of the former deadly enemies as peaceful and friendly. The Japanese people had to be reassured that American soldiers were not evil killers and rapists, as the Japanese government had been telling them for so long.

The man who should make the broadcast should not be a Japanese. The reason was that, during the many years of war in which Imperial Japan was engaged, the Japanese people had been constantly misled by the leaders of Japan, and no one at the present time could trust the words of a Japanese. Archbishop Doi thought a man who fit the bill was still living in Kyoto. That man was Father Patrick Byrne.

According to a report found at the Maryknoll Mission archives in Ossining, New York, and written by a Brother Clemente on June 23, 1953, the reporter visited Japanese Monsignor Furuya in Kyoto to look for Father Byrne. Although badly weakened by malnutrition during solitary confinement (his only companions during most of his confinement were a parrot and a cat), Father Byrne did not hesitate in cooperating with the reporter's request. The reporter, Monsignor Furuya, and Father Byrne went into a huddle for three days preparing the radio message.

When it was time for Father Byrne to go to Tokyo to make his broadcast, the pandemonium of people fleeing the cities before the arrival of the American soldiers was so great that it was practically impossible to get on the train at Kyoto Station. Two policemen went to Osaka Station, where the Tokyo-bound train originated, and boarded the train to occupy two seats before the hordes of people could get on. When the train arrived at Kyoto Station, Father Byrne was pushed into the train through the window nearest the seats and occupied the precious space that had been saved by the policemen. For fifteen hours the American priest, who could have been attacked at any time by a vengeful Japanese, endured the crowded train and arrived in Tokyo, feeling much like a canned sardine, but fortunately unharmed.[2] He was immediately hurried to a central broadcasting station in Tokyo where his radio speech was recorded. For the next few days, Father Byrne's speech was broadcast several times, directed at both the Japanese people and the approaching U.S. military personnel. The first news of

Father Byrne's radio broadcast was reported to the American public in an Associated Press dispatch from New York dated August 25, 1945.[3]

The following is Father Byrne's historic broadcast that was printed in the Osaka *Asahi* newspaper (the original sponsor of his speech) and is taken from the book *Ambassador in Chains*, authored by Maryknoll Bishop Raymond Lane. After an announcer introduced the speaker as a Maryknoll missioner who had been living in Japan for more than eleven years, Father Byrne began his broadcast:

> The war is over. What can I say first of all to the Japanese people whom I have loved and who loved me as a brother for more than ten years? I shared their grief when the emperor spoke to them and told them that they had fought a good fight, but now he wanted them to give up the war and turn to peace. I, an American, speak to you Japanese in the name of those soldiers about to enter your land to assure you that you need have no fear. They are not coming to these shores as invaders, with tanks, bayonets, and bullets, but merely as representatives of their country, taking occupation of Japan to help you once more to reconstruct and build on the new foundation of democracy. The eyes of the world are on this occupying army. You may rest assured they come peaceably.
>
> What can I say to you, the soldiers of my native land, regarding these people? Their feelings will naturally be mixed with emotions as they look upon the victors entering their land, where their homes have been destroyed or burned, their sons and fathers of families killed or maimed and wounded. It is only natural that they look with anger, fear, mistrust, and frustration at your arrival. Should you add to their present feelings by any ruthless attacks upon the

women and young people in this land, I am afraid of what the consequences might be. So I urge you to cooperate with me as I assure the Japanese people that you will commit no degradations, that you will have goodwill and charity in trying to realize what these people, the real victims of the war, have suffered, and will not do anything to add to the pain they endure.

You are on trial before the eyes of the world. Any violence or immorality, any unjust or criminal act on your part will not only be a stain on your character but on that of the nation you represent.

I believe I may assure you people of Japan that the army chaplains will do everything they can to remind our soldiers of their moral responsibility. The Military Police, too, will carefully protect your interests and will arrest anyone found violating the law. If there seems to be any violations of this protection which is your due, I have been assured by the Archbishop of Tokyo that he will appeal to the Holy Father in Rome, who in turn will make known to the whole world by radio and the press any form of injustice. Freedom of the press in the United States will cooperate so that such news will not be suppressed.

I am not afraid because I know these Americans and trust them, but I can understand the fears of the Japanese people. Soldiers coming into Japan, I strongly urge you to come with kind hearts and be good friends of these people. You have fought hard and won a victory. I know you want to enjoy it and want to be proud of it, but please try to understand the distress of the Japanese and make your behavior calm and warm as representatives of a great nation. Perhaps after two or three months they will begin to understand you better, and then I think there will come an intimate friendship between you and them.[4]

Father (later Bishop) Patrick James Byrne was an adviser and confidant
to General MacArthur during the early days of the occupation.
Under house arrest in Kyoto throughout World War II, his influence
with MacArthur undoubtedly helped speed up the start of Japanese
repatriation from Manchuria. (Maryknoll Archives, Maryknoll,
New York)

Reaction to the Maryknoller's Address

The broadcast was greatly welcomed by the Japanese people
who, as a nation, had been sunk into deep despair. Initially
many, including Monsignor Furuya, feared for Father Byrne's
life in case the broad promises the Maryknoller had made
regarding the peaceful intent of the Americans toward the
Japanese were broken by the landing GIs. Fortunately, no
major incident occurred. (One incident was reported to Father
Byrne by the Japanese police, about a stolen watch and a girl

who had been molested; that was quickly resolved when, at the behest by Father Byrne to GHQ, additional Military Police were sent to the area.) As a whole, the people were reborn and felt as if they had been miraculously brought back to life. Father Byrne had become the spark of hope for the whole nation.

Among Americans, there were mixed reactions. Many wondered what was the motive behind Father Byrne's message. However, particularly among the soldiers who heard the broadcast on board ships as they made ready to land, negative or doubting attitudes toward the contents of the broadcast quickly changed when they realized the truth of what Father Byrne had said. For the most part, American soldiers heeded the advice relayed in the broadcast, and fear of the American GIs soon disappeared among the people of Japan. During the early part of the occupation, newspapers in the United States referred to Father Byrne as "Japan's Number Two American." "Number One" was, of course, General MacArthur.[5]

As General MacArthur pursued his occupation policies, he called upon Father Byrne on many occasions for advice and counsel in the treatment of the Japanese people so that a lasting foundation of democracy in a peaceful atmosphere could be established in the once feudal and imperial nation. "The vital role played by Bishop Byrne with his many firm and convincing suggestions based on his love for mankind must never be forgotten," wrote Maruyama in *Why Was Koroto Opened.*[6]

Father Byrne returned to the United States in June 1946, to recuperate from his ordeal as a prisoner of the Japanese Imperial Army during World War II and returned to Japan in the spring of 1947. Shortly thereafter, he was appointed by Rome as apostolic delegate to Korea and was elevated to monsignor, then to bishop. He became a prisoner of the Communist army of North Korea in 1950 where he underwent a terrible ordeal. For months, he, along with other missionaries, diplomats, and

American POWs, was forced to endure the infamous "Death March," where those who could not keep up were simply shot by their North Korean captors. Bishop Byrne eventually fell ill along the way and was sent to a "people's hospital," which was nothing more than a rickety shack where no one was expected to survive. As he lay dying, surrounded by other prisoners, many of them priests and brothers, he said, "After the privilege of my priesthood, I regard this privilege of having suffered for Christ with all of you as the greatest of my life." Lying on the freezing cold ground of the "hospital" with nothing but straw on the floor, he died on November 25, 1950, at a place called Ha Chang Ri, North Korea, and was interred in a simple grave dug by his fellow priests and brothers. No coffins were made available for the dead.[7]

Chapter 17

The Nationwide Radio Broadcast on NHK

Finally, an Opportunity to Inform the Japanese Nation

Returning to Tokyo after their visit to Father Byrne, the three men continued their hectic schedule of speaking at assemblies and meetings in the Tokyo area to groups involved in rousing public interest in the immediate repatriation of Japanese civilians, not only from Manchuria but also from other areas of Asia. In most cases, the groups' high interest and restlessness stemmed from the fact that some of their relatives and loved ones remained overseas after the end of the war. The numbers of Japanese still in Manchuria, China, and Southeast Asia in those days were anyone's guess, but the Japanese press often estimated the total to be in the neighborhood of seven million. (A GHQ G-3 memo of January 2, 1946, estimated Japanese nationals originally awaiting repatriation from around the world numbered 6,922,522.[1])

At the conclusion of one such assembly, the presidents of Shimizu Construction Group and Takenaka Construction Company donated 500,000 yen to help the three men continue with their work. Since they were not subsidized by any private or government agencies, they accepted these and other donations with sincere gratitude. (At the end of the war, the official yen-dollar conversion rate was 15 yen to one dollar. Thus, the 500,000 yen donation from the construction groups was officially equivalent to a little over $33,000 in 1946. On February 19, 1947, however, approval was granted by the State-War-Navy Coordinating Committee for the Far East to affix the conversion rate at 50 yen per one dollar.[2])

Around mid-April 1946, the three were contacted by NHK (*Nihon Hoso Kyokai* or Japan Broadcasting Corporation) and were invited to make a major broadcast about the Manchurian situation during prime time. The men jumped at the opportunity, since, no matter how vigorously they carried out their activities to kindle public concern about the plight of Japanese in Manchuria, it was impossible to carry their message to every part of Japan. Much as they did while on board the U.S. naval vessel that brought them out of China to Japan on their escape several weeks before, the three put their heads together in a second-story room of Maruyama's residence in Kugayama to hammer out a statement for the broadcast. Although the men wanted to be as forceful and truthful as possible in their appeal, they struggled to tone down their comments considerably to minimize deletions by the censors.

When the text was completed, Shinpo mumbled the question that had been in the minds of all of them: "But do you think we will actually be allowed to broadcast the entire script?" The text had to pass the scrutiny of the censors at GHQ. When the statement was submitted for approval the next day, a couple of sections were censored, but somehow the major part of the text was approved, much to the relief of the three men. Thus, NHK scheduled the broadcast, entitled "An Appeal Regarding the Conditions of Our Countrymen in Manchuria," for 7:00 PM on April 17, a time slot thought to be most favorable for the widest audience, just past dinnertime when families gathered to relax. The value and importance of the broadcast was, of course, the opportunity to inform every Japanese household about the plight of Japanese in Manchuria. However, as Musashi pointed out at that time, there was a possibility that the broadcast might be picked up in Manchuria, and who knew what impact it would have as a morale booster to the Japanese if it was heard there. Thus, much was riding on the success of the broadcast.

The statement was read by Maruyama, wearing his customary armband. The following is the text of the broadcast that was translated by this author from Maruyama's book *Why Was Koroto Opened.*

The Broadcast to the Nation

As representatives appealing for the rescue of our fellow Japanese in Manchuria, we three, Hachiro Shinpo, Masamichi Musashi, and I, Kunio Maruyama, departed from Shenyang on February 26 and escaped from Manchuria into China by way of Shanhaiguan. Upon reaching the Port of Tanggu, we were taken aboard a ship engaged in the repatriation of Japanese from northern China, and we arrived on March 15 in Tokyo. Not counting military personnel, it is estimated that there are one million seven hundred thousand Japanese civilians in Manchuria.

The general Japanese population has lost their jobs, and all means of making a living have been cut off for them. Moreover, the distribution of foods and other provisions necessary to sustain life has completely ceased while the cost of living has skyrocketed. Rice, which was distributed before the end of the war at about fifty sen [one-half yen] per pound jumped to about seven yen per pound, and it has continued to rise, so that by the time of our departure, it had risen to twelve or thirteen yen for a pound. Other prices rose correspondingly, so that the cost of living now is

179

about ten times what it was before the end of the war. However, Manchuria is quite rich in all the necessities of life starting with foods; therefore, if one has money, one can live quite a luxurious life.

In normal times, when a situation gets to this point, one would normally withdraw money from one's savings account held at the bank and apply that toward purchasing the necessities of life, but all savings accounts of the Japanese in Manchuria, which now may have grown to quite a vast amount through conscientiously toiling for ten, twenty, and even thirty years, have been frozen since the end of the war. Even if one has a million yen in the bank, it is of no use to the saver; even if one has a two million yen check, it is worth no more than a piece of scrap paper and is completely useless in helping one's livelihood. Therefore, the situation is that ordinary people are selling their personal possessions or have opened street stalls in order to earn barely enough to eat. But by now, most have run out of things to sell so that with each passing day, the ability to survive is reaching a critical stage. In Manchuria, moreover, a commodity just as vital as food is fuel to stay warm, but all fuels have been confiscated so that they have become dramatically scarce. In Shenyang, a ton of coal costs six to eight thousand yen, but even at that, it is hard to obtain, and the ordinary Japanese cannot buy any coal. With the weather turning cold from November on, the number of people who have died due to hunger and cold has risen greatly.

Another recent unfortunate phenomenon that is of great concern is the alarming outbreak of typhus, pneumonic plague, and malnourishment among infants; all these maladies are due to unsanitary conditions and lack of access to food. There are no medicines or facilities available to treat these conditions, so the reality is that many are falling victim to these diseases daily. If we look at the statistics in Changchun during the month of February as an example, of the 70,000 refugees there, an average of 0.3 percent are dying each day, which is 210 lives lost daily, and the trend is ever rising. A particular tragedy in Manchuria that needs special mention concerns the 200,000 Japanese volunteer land developers who were encouraged by the leadership of Japan to emigrate and settle in the northern reaches of Manchuria; another tragic group is the military personnel, civilians, and their families who are said to number about 700,000 at the time the war ended. A vast majority of these volunteer land developers, military personnel, and their families became refugees much earlier than did the general Japanese population.

In truth, it is by no means an exaggeration to state that the majority of Japanese in Manchuria are steadily becoming refugees. Based on the records compiled by the Japanese association in Changchun that we looked at just before we departed, of the total of 1.7 million Japanese countrymen remaining in Manchuria, a staggering 46 percent of them, or over 810,000, are counted as refugees. Each and every Japanese countryman living in Manchuria under these tragic conditions cannot wait one more day as they desperately yearn to return to their native land.

However, all roads that would return them to Japan have been completely cut off so that it is as if all Japanese are trapped in a can. There are not just a few Japanese in Manchuria who are beginning to harbor ill feelings toward Japan as they worry that their native country will simply abandon them and leave them all to die. To state the main point, the 1.7 million

Japanese in Manchuria have lost all culture since the end of the war and have been left to flounder in the vast wastelands of Manchuria, terrified daily for their very lives as they bid farewell to many victims around them who are dying from hunger, cold, and disease. All they can do is look to the skies over their faraway native land as they are driven by insecurity and frustration, and hope beyond hope for an outstretched hand that might come to rescue them. They are as if on a shipwrecked vessel, a most pitiful sight, adrift in the far-off turbulent sea, simply pitching with each wave, visible only in between the waves.

Stated in a straightforward way, I am not exaggerating at all when I say that the survival of our Japanese countrymen in Manchuria is simply a matter of time. No one can deny that by simply delaying their rescue for one more day, more lives are sacrificed, and the increase in these deaths accelerates with time. During the few minutes that I have been speaking to you here, several tens of our countrymen have died. In these days of peace when eight months have already passed since the war ended, while bombs may no longer be falling on the soil of Manchuria, one can hear the sound of gunshots daily, and many hundreds and thousands of our countrymen are turning to corpses as they lay their heads side by side on pillows, dying quietly from starvation, cold, and sickness. While these horrible tragedies worse than war itself are repeated daily right in front of our eyes, for us to do absolutely nothing to devise a means of rescue, to merely look away, and to simply abandon our countrymen, would be a terrible catastrophe that humanity will not tolerate.

Since my return to Japan, several kinds of governmental and private agencies have been organized to work for the rescue of Japanese left overseas. I know that many of my countrymen in various regions of Japan have been deeply concerned about this issue, and they have given us great encouragement. In particular, I attended several meetings by citizens involved in the rescue of Japanese in Manchuria that were held in Nagano at the beginning of this month, and I have been deeply moved by the tearful and enthusiastic zeal of the masses of citizens of that prefecture.

While many of those organizations in Tokyo and in various other cities that are working vigorously for the rescue of Japanese are emphasizing aid to those Japanese once they are returned back to Japan, and while that is of course a most important thing, I would like to particularly encourage placing greater emphasis first on all-out efforts to relieve the miserable plight of those who are still in foreign lands, including Manchuria, North Korea, Sakhalin, and other places, before we worry about what we can do for them after they have returned to Japan. Getting a doctor to run to the aid of a patient who has already passed away will not do any good. A water pump is no longer necessary after the fire has burned out. No matter what arrangements are being made to secure living accommodations for the returnees, and no matter how much warmth and kindness and food and luxurious clothing are being prepared to await them, if those returnees become corpses before they are repatriated, such preparations do no good if what they would really require are grave markers waiting for them.

The best means for rescuing our countrymen left in Manchuria is first to give them food to eat. I am not suggesting that there is a need for us to send food to them from Japan. Actually, there is plenty of food in Manchuria, and it is freely sold in the markets.

We should send money from Japan, and if that is distributed to the refugees, they will be able to easily obtain provisions so that they can avoid starvation.

Second, medical supplies must be sent there quickly to provide the means of cure. The many patients who now develop typhus and other contagious diseases would easily be cured if shots and medicines were available; however, since there is no medicine, all that can happen in present-day Manchuria is to sorrowfully watch the sick die without any means to help them. Since there are no materials available in Manchuria to produce pharmaceutical products, there is no solution but to send actual medical supplies from Japan.

Third, along with the other steps already mentioned, we must dispatch one or two ships and begin the immediate repatriation of refugees. Even if repatriation of a small number is initiated, all Japanese stranded in Manchuria, whose hopes have been sinking to the lowest depth, will again be able to grasp the bright hope that, finally, the path to return to Japan has been opened. That will once again renew courage in them so that they will somehow find the strength to survive until they can come back to Japan; the psychological strength that will be given to them will indeed be immense.

Therefore, if you ask me how these means of rescue can be put into action, I would like to stress to you here what we feel are the most plausible steps to take, based on our own observation of the situation in Manchuria since the end of February. Stating the specifics, Japanese in Manchuria should be directed to proceed from the Shenyang area to Jinzhou and then in a southwesterly direction to Koroto, which is located deep in Liaodong Bay. Ships should be sent to the Port of Koroto, where we believe they may embark with the least complication. Any relief supplies that are sent to them can be transported by reversing the route I just outlined.

Naturally, to make all this actually happen will require the help of the Headquarter Section of the Supreme Commander of Allied Powers which we must persuade, and we will naturally need to have them obtain the cooperation of the Chinese. In considering the latest developments in Manchuria, we are convinced that these means have the most potential to succeed. Since our return to Tokyo, we have met with and appealed to our government and to personnel at Allied Command General Headquarters in an effort to appeal to them with what little influence and ability we have to quickly mobilize the means to bring about a rescue.

We have reported to you the overall situation in Manchuria, and at the same time, we would like to take this opportunity to appeal for utmost effort by the relevant agencies to rescue the Japanese left in Manchuria at the earliest date possible. We also ask for the understanding and compassion of General Douglas MacArthur, in whom we have the greatest trust, and ask him with all our hearts to dispatch repatriation ships before another day passes. And we ask you, the people of Japan, for your utmost cooperation in our efforts.[3]

On the night of April 17, 1946, Maruyama made a nationwide, thirty-minute prime time broadcast on NHK (Japan Broadcasting Corporation) regarding the true situation in Manchuria. For the first time, the Japanese nation was informed about the terrible plight of their fellow countrymen stranded in Manchuria. (Kunio Maruyama Collection)

Reaction to the Broadcast

Beginning two or three days after the broadcast, letters and postcards from throughout Japan began pouring into the NHK office and to the "headquarters" at Kugayama. Day after day, five hundred to one thousand letters from families and relatives with loved ones overseas were delivered, most asking if the three might have information about a loved one in a particular part of Manchuria. It was impossible for just the three to read and respond to the letters, so volunteers from various groups involved in repatriation, particularly student groups, pitched in to read, sort, and respond to the letters. Those who read the many heart-wrenching letters could not help but be moved with emotion, often to the point of tears.

There was no way that the three could provide information about particular individuals still trapped overseas; they often had difficulty responding, since the last thing they wanted to do was cause any further pain to the sender of the letter. But they and their helpers made certain that each letter and postcard received a response.

Below are translations of two actual letters to illustrate the kind of letters they received; the first one was quoted in Masamichi Musashi's book *The Dawning of Asia—Crossing the Lines of Death*, and the second is from Kunio Maruyama's book *Why Was Koroto Opened*.

1. Letter from a mother whose son and family were in Shenyang:

Dear Sir:

I am sorry to be disturbing you, but I am sending you a letter without notice. I am sincerely thankful to you for having returned from Manchuria, and knowing you are working so very hard so that Japanese who have been left behind in Manchuria can come home as soon as possible.

My son, his wife, and our grandchildren are at this time in Shenyang, Manchuria, and we have no idea about the situation in Manchuria following the end of the war; letters that we have sent have been returned to us marked 'addressee unknown.' In the bitter cold of Manchuria, we are worried as to how they are surviving and whether they are safe or not. No matter where we have inquired about where they are or how they are doing, no one knows what the situation in Manchuria is.

The other day I heard your speech on the radio, and if you know anything about the situation in Shenyang after the war, or if you know anything about my son, his wife, and our grandchildren, I beg you

187

to let me know. I am sending this letter addressed to the broadcast station, not reflecting on how impolite I am being. My son is a teacher at the Shenyang Girls School of Commerce. [The writer then provided his address, family name, and age.] My daughter-in-law was expected to deliver in August of last year, but we are concerned whether she had a safe delivery, and whether she has recovered well after the childbirth.

I pray night and day to Buddha that the parents and children are all doing well, and that their return to Japan will not be delayed even one more day. I am sincerely sorry to be a bother to you and hope you will forgive me, but if you know the whereabouts of those I so dearly love, please let me know.[4]

2. Letter dated April 25, 1946, from the wife of a soldier who remained in the Soviet Union:

To Mr. Kunio Maruyama

Both plum blossoms and cherry blossoms are in their prime, blooming with pride, and spring has come to stay for a while in our city of Shinano.

The other day, I listened to your earnest talk on the radio and I am someone who has been greatly moved by it. I learned from your talk that the situation in Manchuria is even more critical than I had imagined, and for someone like me who has a loved one in that land, I am barely able to stay on my feet because of the way I feel....

My husband received orders to northern China at the end of January last year upon his graduation from Rikudai, and his whereabouts have become unknown since June of last year. To this day, as a result of much research with many sources, the information is that he went from northern Korea into Manchuria. During his absence, the two children who my husband left in my care have died one after the other, and I am at the lowest point of misery as a human being at this time. I beg you from the very bottom of my heart to plead with the Allied forces to make arrangements for the earliest return of also those military personnel who have been taken away to Siberia and Ukraine.

If by some chance you have any additional information concerning the military personnel, I implore you to send me even one letter, knowing that I am being troublesome to you.[5]

Public response in Japan from the NHK broadcast was indeed resounding. The issue of repatriation, particularly from the Soviet-occupied territories, seemed now to be in the forefront of Japanese consciousness: the three men were inundated with requests to appear at assemblies and meetings dealing with repatriation. But the three wondered, had any of the 1.7 million Japanese in Manchuria heard the radio broadcast, and had they come to realize that their miserable plight was now becoming known in their homeland, and that they were not forgotten and abandoned?

Chapter 18

Utopia Arrives at Last!

The Broadcast Was Heard in Manchuria

The April 17 radio broadcast from Tokyo's NHK station was heard in Manchuria. The Japanese in Manchuria were strictly forbidden to have radios, and being found with one was most likely grounds for execution at the hands of the Soviet army. In spite of the possible consequences, some Japanese had hidden away radios and had kept up with whatever news they could pick up from their homeland.

Masamichi Musashi shortly later returned to Manchuria with the first repatriation ship and met in Shenyang with the former vice president of the South Manchurian Railway Company, Toshio Hirashima. He learned from that gentleman that the broadcast was indeed heard by those few who had radios and that the news of the broadcast was spread by word of mouth throughout the Japanese community. Hirashima, referring to the attempted secret mission back to Japan related in chapter 7, said to Musashi, "In the midst of every member of our secret mission having completely failed in their attempt, we learned from the broadcast that you three had miraculously returned to Japan and that you were actively engaged in efforts to bring about repatriation. Suddenly a new hope was revived in all of us Japanese in Manchuria, and we all began praying for the earliest return to Japan!"[1]

A particular group of people in Manchuria who were overjoyed to hear about the radio broadcast were the families of Maruyama and Shinpo, who had been left in Dalian under the care of the Maryknoll Catholic Church. The broadcast told them that Maruyama, Shinpo, and Musashi had indeed safely escaped to Japan; for two months, they had not heard one word about what happened to the three men, and unable to even share their concern with anyone, they worried and agonized in private. Both the Shinpo family and Maruyama family were living under assumed names to avoid any suspicion by the Soviet army, who had spies everywhere. A Maryknoll sister heard the broadcast and relayed to Mary (who had resumed her maiden name, Mariko Takeda) the news that Maruyama had just made a radio speech in Japan detailing the situation in Manchuria. Overjoyed at the news, Mary hugged the sister and immediately informed her four sons and their helper Toki the eagerly awaited wonderful news: Their father was safe in Japan! Their prayers had been answered with a miracle! Now, Mary and her family needed to keep their spirits up and survive the best they could until ships arrived from Japan to take them back to their father, who awaited them in Japan. Little did they know that they would not return to Japan until the following year, among the last groups to be repatriated from Manchuria.

(Because Mary and her four sons were American citizens, they had one opportunity in June of 1946 to be evacuated from Manchuria aboard a U.S. naval ship that returned some U.S. diplomats and American missionaries back to the United States. However, because the ship would return to the United States and not to Japan where her husband was, and because their helper Toki would be left behind, Mary declined the offer and decided to await repatriation along with all the other Japanese. Toki was the daughter of a relative of Mary's in Yamaguchi Prefecture; it was not unusual in Japan for a young girl of marriageable age to become a "maid" of another family to learn skills, such as cooking, cleaning, sewing, and caring for children, desirable in a future bride. Thus, Toki was never considered by the Maruyama family as anyone but another member of the family.)

A Summons from GHQ

Back in Japan, the three men kept as busy as ever following the radio broadcast. On April 18, the three were the main speakers at a meeting of deputy directors of various government departments involved in the rescue of Japanese in Manchuria. The next day, a member of Parliament (Tadanori Nagayama, who later became Minister of Home Affairs) provided them with a car and driver; the same day, the chief of the Police Security Agency under the Ministry of Home Affairs, Noboru Tanikawa, made arrangements for them to be supplied with gasoline from the traffic section of the Metropolitan Police Department. Nagayama also offered the free use at any time of his office, conveniently located in the Ginza District in the heart of Tokyo. These and other developments made Maruyama, Shinpo, and Musashi feel day by day that public support for their self-proclaimed entity, the Representatives to Petition for Saving Our Countrymen Living in Manchuria, was rising steadily.

On April 20, they visited with Bank of Japan Chairmam Araki to discuss how the closure of bank accounts in Manchuria might be lifted. This was a vital issue to everyone in Manchuria without access to their own money in various banks, including the Bank of Japan. Araki made an appointment for the three to meet with key finance ministry personnel at a later date to discuss this all-important matter.

After their meeting at the Bank of Japan, the three returned home to Kugayama around 2:00 PM. Since they did not come home most days until late at night, it was a rare treat for them to sit down and catch up on the many things they had been planning to do but never had the time to fit into their busy schedule. As they settled down in the upstairs room in Maruyama's residence, their de facto headquarters office, to discuss the necessity to send letters of appeal to heads of various foreign countries, beginning with the president of the United States, there was an energetic banging on the front door followed by "*Gomen kudasai* (Is anyone home?)."

From the staircase on the second floor, Maruyama called back, "Who is it?"

"I am Patrolman Takikawa, and I need to speak to Mr. Maruyama as soon as possible." Maruyama ran downstairs and opened the sliding door to let the local police officer in. They knew him as the officer who manned the local police box near Kugayama Station, and they always exchanged friendly greetings as the three went to and fro from their headquarters. "Maruyama-san, there was a special summons for you from GHQ. They are requesting that you go to see a Colonel Howell as soon as you are able." As Maruyama looked questioningly at the police officer, he continued, "I have been requested to report back to them with your reply right away. When can you depart for GHQ?"

"Do you know what they want?" asked Maruyama.

Patrolman Takikawa responded, "No, I don't have a clue. I only know that this is a matter of great urgency."

By now, Shinpo and Musashi had come downstairs to listen in on the exchange between Maruyama and the patrolman. Looking at both his companions, Maruyama said to Patrolman Takikawa, "It is now just past 3:00 PM. Please let GHQ know that we will arrive for certain within an hour and a half." The patrolman gave a quick salute and rushed out the door to ride his bicycle back to his police box and telephone the response to GHQ. The three went to their respective bedrooms to retrieve the coats they had discarded and readied themselves to go back out.

Unfortunately, the car that had been put at their disposal by Member of Parliament Nagayama only a few days ago was not available. In those days, one did not simply call a cab when in a hurry; even telephones were scarce. They had no choice but to walk rapidly to Kugayama Station and take the train to GHQ. "Let's take the Inokashira Line to Shibuya, and if it seems like we are behind schedule for our meeting, let's just stop any passing car the way Hideki Tojo did and have the driver take us to GHQ. We must get there by our promised time of 4:30." So saying, the three hurried to the station, reminded of a famous episode about the wartime prime minister then on trial as a war criminal.

Colonel Howell was the head of the G-3 Operations Section, the group responsible for repatriation matters, with which they had had many meetings. As the train sped toward Shibuya, they speculated on the meaning of the urgent summons.

"I wonder if this has anything to do with repatriation ships?" asked Shinpo.

"I'm not sure," said Musashi. "Lately, we have been especially insistent in our appeals, and we may have been perceived to be rude. We may be in for a good scolding!" Seeing his companions' concern, he continued, "The day before yesterday, Maruyama-san never took a step back in his argument with them, so they may be calling us for a reprimand."

Maruyama defended himself: "That was not entirely my fault. You both urged me to go ahead and say it the way it was, so I just said it on your behalf!" When Musashi could not hide an impish grin, Maruyama realized he had taken the bait and looked a bit sheepish. Still worried, but with some of the tension relieved, the three looked at their watches as the train made many stops before reaching its destination.

"Today We Have Good News!"

They arrived at GHQ with four minutes to spare. Colonel Howell had been watching for their arrival. Three other senior officers, all familiar to the men, were with the colonel. As usual, they warmly shook hands and exchanged greetings, and the three were invited to sit down in the chairs set up around the conference table. Then, still standing, Colonel Howell broke into a happy smile as he began. "Today, we have good news for you! The decision has been made to dispatch repatriation ships very soon. General MacArthur issued an order this afternoon saying, 'By the last part of April, dispatch two ships to Huludao (Koroto) for the purpose of repatriation.' All the people of Japan will learn of this when they open their newspapers tomorrow. We have a press conference scheduled in about two hours to make this announcement. But before we went public with the announcement, we wanted to let you know in advance, which is why we asked you to hurry over here. Let me be the first to congratulate you!" Colonel Howell repeated "Congratulations!" several more times as he shook each man's hand with a very firm grip.

Maruyama, Shinpo, and Musashi were unable to speak, choked up with emotion. Did they actually hear correctly what the colonel had just said? They were unable to stop the tears of joy that slid down their cheeks. Setting aside any feeling of embarrassment, not caring how they might look to others, the three grabbed each others' hands and continued to cry. Totally unconcerned that they were in the presence of senior officers of the U.S. Army who were observing the spectacle with wonderment and smiles, the three Japanese men carried on, acting like a bunch of happy children. Since the first time they came together and made a pledge as they gripped each others' hands tightly in a room in Shinpo's house in Anshan City six months ago, this was the moment the three had thought about, dreamed of, hoped for; their every effort in all that time had been for this precious moment.

As they thought back, they realized how much had happened since the end of the war eight months ago. As they saw the total helplessness of the Japanese people in Manchuria under Russian occupation, as they witnessed the plight of so many Japanese becoming homeless and refugees, as they saw with their own eyes innocent children dying from hunger, cold, and disease in the arms of their helpless mothers, they had decided to be the ones to bell the cat. Carrying in their hearts the hope and crying appeal of 1.7 million Japanese who wanted merely to return to their native land as soon as possible, the three had fled Manchuria fearful for their lives at every step, experiencing life-threatening adventures in Shanhaiguan, and finally returning to Japan on a vessel of the United States of America. Upon reaching Japanese soil, the three had been explaining, appealing, begging, entreating, and crying nonstop to all sorts of people in Japan. The wonderful news they had just heard from the American army colonel had been the goal of all their effort.

After some time, when the three had regained their composure, they lined up in a straight line, came to attention, and bowed their heads to the officers. Then extending their hands once again to shake hands, all they could repeat over and over was, "Thank you! Thank you!" Then they took their leave and walked outside.

Dusk was just falling, and the three stopped at an outdoor stall near Shinbashi, ordered three glasses of sake, and raised a toast.

"Who was it that said we were in for a major scolding?"

"The person who seemed most worried was Maruyama-san!"

"Yes, it sure seemed like he was tense!"

Ribbing each other, the three savored their moment of joy. On reflection, it seemed amazing that, only a little more than a month after their return to Japan, General MacArthur had given the order to dispatch repatriation ships to Koroto. But it had been a month filled with many dramatic and memorable moments. Was it really possible, wondered all three men, that relief was about to arrive for the 1.7 million Japanese who had been living their lives in a hell on earth for over eight months in Manchuria? Was relief about to come to the millions of relatives and friends in Japan who had no idea whether those they loved were even still alive?

Maruyama, Shinpo, and Musashi realized they now must switch gears and prepare their defeated and devastated nation to welcome home the repatriates. Many would be sick, malnourished, and impoverished. Many would learn at last that their yearned-for loved one would not be there to greet them upon arrival in Japan because they had been killed in the Allied bombings or the resulting fires. Many would find out their homes had been burnt to the ground. Pressure now must be put on the public and the government to do all they could to welcome home the soon to be returned countrymen from Manchuria. Additionally, there was the immediate need to get the word out to all Japanese scattered throughout the vast Manchurian territory that they should proceed to Koroto in an orderly manner to be evacuated. The work had just begun for the three men; now was not yet the time to celebrate.

Documents on Repatriation Found at the National Archives

Documents found by this author at the National Archives at College Park, Maryland, as well as at MacArthur Memorial Library in Norfolk, Virginia, show that the United States had always intended to take on the responsibility of repatriating the Japanese who had been caught overseas at the end of World War II. The 1946 edition of *Foreign Relations of the United States* discusses President Truman's policy toward China (which included Manchuria) that was declared on December 16, 1946, in which the president "made clear that an important corollary of the basic United States policy of helping the growth of a 'strong, united, and democratic China' is the elimination of Japanese influence from China. Although the president indicated that this was to be done primarily by evacuation of Japanese troops from China, it is obvious that the elimination of Japanese influence from China also calls for the repatriation of those Japanese civilians whose presence in China would permit continued Japanese influence or would threaten the peace and security of China, and thus prove to be a threat to U.S. security and a detriment to U.S. interest." Repatriation of Japanese, therefore, as Truman saw it, was not a matter of humanitarian concerns but rather to rid China of any Japanese influence whatsoever.[2]

A top secret report by the Joint Chiefs of Staff dated March 20, 1946, on the subject, "Repatriation of Civilian Japanese from China," reiterated and clarified a December 11, 1945 proposal approved by the president to assist in the repatriation of Japanese from China and specifically mentioned the inclusion of Manchuria in the proposal. Paragraph 3 of the document reads, "The War and Navy Departments and the War Shipping Administration have issued instructions to the United States commander and representatives in the field to the extent that they understand the objective is the repatriation of all Japanese nationals, military and civilian, from China, including Manchuria, Formosa and French Indo-China north of 16 degrees North latitude. It is not known to what extent the Chinese authorities understand this is the United States objective."[3]

A top secret report of March 17, 1946, "Subj: Conference on Repatriation, 15–17 January 1946, Tokyo, Japan," that included plans to return Japanese from Huludao (Koroto), has already been mentioned in chapter 8.[4]

Research at the National Archives clearly showed that, until April 1946, documents referring to Huludao and repatriation from Manchuria were scarce indeed. However, from mid-April, numerous documents mentioning Huludao were found. Among significant ones were the following:

On April 18, 1946, the U.S. Commanding General of China sent an unclassified message to the U.S. Commanding General Nanking Headquarters Command stating that the Laoyao Repatriation Group would take initial charge of repatriation from Manchuria and would be redesignated as the Huludao Repatriation Team. The message requested SCAP shipping to be set up to initially repatriate three thousand Japanese per day beginning on or about April 27.[5] A Memo for Record that responded to this April 18 message stated that "15 LSTs [should be] allocated [for] the Huludao-Sasebo shuttle immediately." It further stated, "Our plan is sufficiently flexible, moreover, to meet any future rate of evacuation that may be requested by China in regard to Huludao, or other Manchurian ports yet to be designated."[6]

On April 23, 1946, SCAP sent a message to the U.S. Commanding General in China letting him know that a partial shipment of medical supplies was being sent from Sasebo, Japan, to Huludao on about that same date.[7]

A routine April 30, 1946 document from the Commanding General of China to SCAP discussed the situation of the medical team in Huludao that would be required once repatriation went into full swing. It reported, "Huludao Repat Team reports no Japanese Medical Establishment in Huludao except 1 aged Jap [sic] Doctor; nor English speaking Jap [sic] interpreter.... Cholera reported not prevalent in Huludao. Therefore request, if feasible, a fast ship with approximately 25 Medical Technicians and 5 English speaking Japanese be sent to Huludao from Japan...."[8]

While the above messages and memos clearly indicate that SCAP GHQ had been working on plans to initiate repatriation of Japanese from Koroto for several weeks, the three men were apparently not kept in the loop on GHQ's progress. Then, on April 20 when MacArthur gave the order to dispatch two ships to Koroto, Maruyama and his two companions were summoned to GHQ to be told about the order just before it was publicly announced. MacArthur's order of April 20, 1946, could not be found at either the National Archives or at the MacArthur Memorial Library; it is possible the order was issued orally and not in writing, given the sensitivity of such an order contrary to the plans of a key member of the Allied Powers, the Soviet Union. However, a handwritten top secret document that simply stated, "Memo for Col. Howell 'Repatriation from Manchuria' 2 May 46, G.E. White. Filed under Russia" was found at the National Archives among SCAP documents for the period, but the document itself could not be found.

Japanese from throughout Manchuria, many of them refugees, made
their way to Koroto (Huludao) riding flatcars and coal cars, enduring
the hot sun and cold rain in unroofed cars, often taking weeks to reach
their destination. Each trainload brought about three thousand people to
awaiting repatriation ships. (National Archives, Washington DC)

Repatriates march to inspection areas after disembarking from trains at Koroto, a final step prior to boarding ships that will take them home. (National Archives, Washington DC)

At the inspection areas, repatriates were doused with DDT prior to boarding ships. The dustings were carried out by Japanese nationals, presumably to lessen the embarrassment and humiliation. (National Archives, Washington DC)

The sheer joy of knowing that they would soon board ships bound for
Japan overcomes any sense of humiliation and degradation of being
fumigated. (National Archives, Washington DC)

A little girl carries all her belongings on her back as she awaits her turn to be dusted with DDT at the Port of Koroto. (National Archives, Washington DC)

Loaded almost to the breaking point as he carries everything he owns strapped to his back and hanging from the front, this repatriate and his children wait patiently for their turn to board a ship at Koroto. Each repatriate was allowed to take back to Japan only that which one could personally carry. (National Archives, Washington DC)

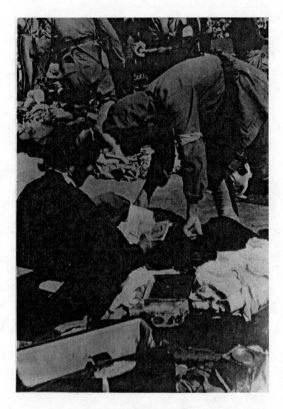

All possessions of the repatriates are carefully inspected for contraband
by Chinese soldiers before being allowed on board repatriation ships.
(National Archives, Washington DC)

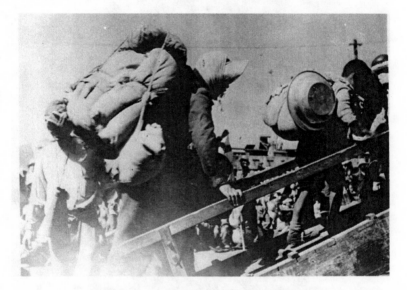

Repatriates struggle up the gangplank with their heavy load at Koroto. The crew of this U.S. Navy Liberty ship is all Japanese. (National Archives, Washington DC)

A Japanese boy stands at the dock waving farewell to a Liberty ship
taking a load of repatriates back to Japan from Koroto. The boy's turn to
be repatriated will come when his technician father, who is detained by
Chinese authorities, is released. (National Archives, Washington DC)

Chapter 19

Back to Manchuria

Musashi Volunteers to Return to Manchuria

The first American vessel to be dispatched to Koroto for the sole purpose of bringing home Japanese from Manchuria was scheduled to depart the Port of Sasebo on the southern Japanese island of Kyushu on April 25, 1946. Maruyama, Shinpo, and Musashi had planned from the outset to adhere to the following schedule: (1) escape from Manchuria and return to Japan; (2) report to the Japanese government, to the people of Japan, and to GHQ and General MacArthur the actual conditions in Manchuria; (3) appeal to promote rescue and repatriation; and (4) only then to return to Manchuria to help organize the repatriation effort. However, they realized it would not be possible for all three to return to Manchuria considering the mountain of tasks that had to be accomplished in their Tokyo office to prepare for the arrival of the repatriates.

The three discussed the present situation, surveyed all that had to happen in the future, and finally decided to have only one of them return to Manchuria while the other two would remain in Tokyo.

"There will be much work to carry on here in Japan to keep everyone's eye on the ball," remarked Shinpo. "The pressure must never be let up to insure continually sending repatriation ships. Relief supplies will need to be gathered and sent to Manchuria."

"Continual negotiations with GHQ and the Japanese government, as well as with various relief agencies, must be kept up," commented Maruyama.

Musashi said, "That is true. And only you, Maruyama-san, who speaks English, will be able to negotiate with GHQ. I believe Shinpo-san with his vast business acumen is essential to organize the gathering of relief supplies. As the youngest of the three of us and being fluent in Chinese, I believe I should be the one to return to Manchuria."

"We feel badly that we are entrusting to you, the youngest of us, perhaps the most difficult and perilous of all tasks," said Shinpo to his former employee and protégé, bowing his head and taking Musashi's hands in his. "If by any chance something happens to you, I promise that I will cross over to Manchuria and take over your tasks."

There was not a lot of time to have a prolonged discussion, but in the end, all three agreed to the decision to have Musashi return with the first repatriation ship bound for Koroto. They also agreed that if something should happen to Musashi, Shinpo would be dispatched to take his place. If anything then befell Shinpo, Maruyama would follow.

With this framework in place, the three helped Musashi devise his plan of action in Manchuria. He would contact Japanese associations wherever there was one and assist in the efforts to promote orderly repatriation operations, insure everything possible was done to help the hundred of thousands of Japanese refugees to be transported to Koroto, and support the relief operation of the many who were disabled, were helpless, or had contracted diseases.

Contact was made with the various repatriation and relief agencies in Japan the three had come to know in the past several weeks, and a variety of relief provisions was gathered together.

One major contributor of vital pharmaceutical supplies was the All-Nippon Pharmaceutical Company of Osaka. A large amount of medical supplies was also donated by Takegoro Nakanishi, chairman of the Japan Koshikai Pharmaceutical Industry. (One particularly noteworthy item included in the donation was a new home medicine that had recently become a big hit in Japan, "the cold medicine to be taken with tea.") Volunteer groups pitched in to help organize and sort the relief items. Unrestricted support was provided in transporting the items by train to the ship by the director of the railroad ministry, Eisaku Sato (who, as mentioned earlier, later became prime minister). They also received generous monetary donations from two major construction companies. One particular purpose for which money was necessary immediately was for transferring thousands of Japanese, mostly refugees, to Koroto without delay. Musashi entrusted those funds to various Japanese agencies while in Manchuria to assist in repatriation efforts.

As Musashi prepared for his departure, several government agencies and individuals entrusted him with letters and documents intended for various key individuals and Japanese associations in Manchuria. Among those asking him to carry messages and documents were Foreign Minister Shigeru Yoshida, Chief Secretary to the Prime Minister Wataru Narahashi, Health and Welfare Minister Ashida, Director of the Committee to Support Repatriation Saito, and Railroad Ministry Director Eisaku Sato. Additionally, several Japanese corporate headquarters with company and branch offices in Manchuria (and with whom they had had no contact since the end of the war) also asked Musashi to carry letters to their offices in Manchuria. Perhaps the most important document that was entrusted to Musashi was the one from Narahashi addressed to Tatsunosuke Takasaki, chairman of the All-Manchuria Japanese Association, the one person in Manchuria who represented all the Japanese there. Just as he did when escaping from Manchuria, Musashi carried the most important of the documents by sewing them into his outer clothing.

A final set of supplies was a large amount of newspaper articles intended for the news-hungry Japanese in Manchuria, which was donated by Nagasaki Prefecture Governor Sugiyama. In his additional capacity as chief of the Sasebo Bureau to Support Repatriates, the governor was well aware that even one sheet of newspaper was a precious commodity in Manchuria.

A final document that was handed to Musashi before his departure was his "marching orders." Maruyama and Shinpo explained that this was "an identification document for you while in Manchuria, and also itemizes the activities you will do while there. Please have it with you when you are in contact with Japanese people in various regions. We are confident it will prove useful on more than one occasion." The document was intended to protect Musashi and to make his efforts go smoothly. The document stated that all actions taken by Musashi were the responsibility of the Representatives to Petition for Saving Our Countrymen Living in Manchuria; that he had been entrusted by the same representatives to report on the situation in Manchuria (i.e., he was not a spy); and, most important, that if it became necessary for Musashi to borrow funds to carry on his activities, such funds would be strictly accounted for and would be repaid at a later date by the representatives.

With all the documents sewn into his clothing, Musashi looked much heavier than he actually was.

As April 25 approached, the representatives, as the three often came to be called, tried to convince GHQ to agree to allow a voluntary Japanese medical team to accompany Musashi to Manchuria. However, a glitch developed just before departure, and the medical team was not allowed to go. As a defeated nation, Japan was under many restrictions, including the free movement of its citizens abroad. The medical team would be allowed to enter Manchuria only if they formally obtained permission from the Chinese government, and there was not enough time to go through the process. As for Musashi entering Manchuria, that also was, in a strict sense, an illegal act. However, at the time of his escape, he had obtained a reentry permit letter from the chief of staff of the Nationalist army's Shenyang underground headquarters, General Liu Wanquan, and because of it, GHQ looked the other way and allowed passage to Musashi.

To Manchuria Once Again

At the Port of Sasebo on the morning of April 25, Musashi boarded the U.S. naval vessel *LST QIO58*, which was empty except for the Japanese crew. Just before boarding the vessel, he was briefed by a U.S. Army officer from GHQ who brought him up to date on the latest intelligence estimate that GHQ was aware of. Pitched battles and skirmishes between the Nationalist army (Chiang Kai-shek's troops) and the Communist Eighth Route Army (Mao Zedong's guerrilla army under the command of Lin Biao) had intensified in Manchuria. Although the Nationalists were in firm control of some areas, including Koroto, Shenyang, Yingkou, and others and were expected to advance into other cities including Changchun, Anshan, and Jilin during May, no one could predict the situation in Manchuria. The staff officer said, "Going to Manchuria at this time is like jumping into burning oil from water. We strongly recommend you not carry out your intention of returning there."

"Thank you for your concern," Musashi replied to the well-intentioned officer, "but that is the mission assigned to me."

A frown crossed the officer's face, but he immediately extended his hand, and shaking Musashi's hand tightly, he said, "Then, good luck to you!" Absolutely no formal diplomatic arrangements had been made for Musashi's entry and sojourn in Manchuria, but officers of the Allied Powers GHQ were well aware that, as long as ships were being dispatched to Koroto to repatriate Japanese residing in Manchuria, someone had to contact the Japanese there to help organize and keep the repatriation process on an orderly course.

For Musashi, this would be the third time he would cross the sea region north of Kyushu known romantically to the Japanese as *Genkai-nada* (roughly translated as the "mysterious high seas"). The first time had been when, at the age of sixteen, he accompanied his new employer, Hachiro Shinpo, with an ambitious dream in his heart to succeed in the land he had heard so much about. The second crossing was when he and Shinpo, along with a new companion named Maruyama, made their escape back to Japan, shouldering the mission to rescue their countrymen stranded in the now Soviet-occupied territory. And here he was now, this time all alone, once again crossing *Genkai-nada*, to a dark land of turmoil and tragedy.

As the U.S. LST departed from the Port of Sasebo, Musashi finally had time to contemplate the enormous task he had volunteered to take on. He was about to reenter the tiger's cage to help insure that more than a million and a half Japanese, many of them sick, starving, and penniless, safely returned to their homeland. His most important task was to deliver the many important documents that had been entrusted to him by Chief Secretary to the Prime Minister Narahashi and others to the chairman of the All-Manchuria Japanese Association, Tatsunosuke Takasaki, who lived in Shenyang. Takasaki was the one man in Manchuria who could communicate to all Japanese associations, which in turn would communicate to Japanese residents throughout Manchuria to begin the orderly exodus to Japan via Koroto. If he failed in this first, most important mission, repatriation would be delayed and could become extremely difficult. But with the present turmoil and confusion resulting from the fighting between the Nationalists and the Communist Eighth Route Army throughout the region, it had become difficult even for a Chinese to travel.

Musashi asked himself, *Should I disguise myself as a refugee or as a Manchurian?* But for him to go northward from the coast toward Shenyang was to go against the tide of Manchurians and Chinese who were fleeing southward to escape the fighting. He was sure to arouse suspicion, especially if he took the train. Walking would take days, and besides, he had no idea who controlled Shenyang at the present. When the ship arrived at the Port of Koroto, he still had not decided on his plan of action.

Quickly Devising a Strategy

Looking down at the pier from the deck of his ship, Musashi spotted a group of Nationalist soldiers patrolling the dock. After disembarking, he approached them and asked in Chinese, "Is Shenyang under Nationalist control yet?"

The soldiers looked at Musashi with suspicion, but his fluency in Chinese and his Manchurian peasant's clothing apparently allayed their suspicion. One of the soldiers replied, "The other day, the units under [Nationalist] Northeastern Commander Du Bi Min were reported to have completed their occupation."

"Xie xie," replied Musashi as he headed back to the repatriation ship again. Learning that Shenyang was under Nationalist control, Musashi knew what his next move should be: using the reentry permit that had been issued to him by General Liu Wanquan, he would go directly to the Nationalist army commander at Koroto and request assistance from them. In all honesty, there was no way of knowing how much clout Liu Wanquan had there, and Musashi was not 100 percent confident that the reentry permit would be honored as a valid document.

But he could not idly sit back and take no action. Harking back on a Japanese proverb that said, "Unless you go into the tiger's den, you will not catch the tiger's cub," Musashi entrusted his fate to the heavens and decided to take the gamble.

"I would like to meet with your commander," he told the security guard on duty at the entrance of the Nationalist headquarters near the entrance to the port area. The surprised guard looked at him and alertly raised his rifle. Musashi hurriedly thrust the reentry permit forward for the guard to read. At least recognizing that the document looked official, the guard called an officer who, in the end, took Musashi in for a meeting with the commander, He Shi Li. Musashi explained why he had just returned to Manchuria from Japan on an American vessel. "I am here to spread the news to the Japanese throughout Manchuria that, thanks to the cooperation of the Nationalist army and the U.S. military, ships are being dispatched to Koroto to repatriate them back to Japan. In order to bring about the earliest repatriation without disorder, I would like to meet again with General Liu Wanquan in Shenyang."

Commander He was polite during the meeting with Musashi, but at times he displayed a severe countenance. As Musashi talked, he later learned, He's security unit was conducting a security check on the Japanese who spoke like a Manchurian. The commander himself was carefully scrutinizing Musashi as the Japanese talked. He Shi Li, who at a later time was appointed as the Chinese representative to the Allied Powers Committee to administer Japan, was born of Dutch and Chinese parents and had prominent European features, a rarity among Nationalist officers. As Musashi concluded his explanation to the commander, he said, "In the very near future, there will be many, many Japanese coming and gathering at the Port of Koroto, and they will be indebted to your care. As one Japanese speaking on behalf of all Japanese, I would like to express my sincere gratitude to you and your men. As a small token of that appreciation, I would like to present this to you." So saying, Musashi handed a copy of *Time* magazine and a wristwatch he had brought from Japan to the commander.

The commander showed great interest in the American magazine, and it was obvious he understood English as he quickly scanned some of the articles. It is customary in the Eastern culture to smooth over relationships or negotiations with an appropriate present. Musashi, an astute young Japanese businessman, had also given small presents to the officers in the Nationalist underground headquarters in Shenyang before the three made their escape. He had even made a small donation to the Maryknoll Catholic Church in Manchuria to help with their reconstruction project after entrusting to their care the families of Maruyama and Shinpo. These presents, therefore, were never perceived as "bribes" by either side.

The commander excused himself to conduct discussions with his subordinates and returned after a short time. Sitting back down and looking straight into Musashi's eyes, he said, "There is no longer an individual, much less a general, named Liu Wanquan at the Shenyang headquarters. We are not able to confirm the information you have given us at this time, but we will escort you to the northeastern commander-in-chief's section in Shenyang. I will assign two soldiers to act as your escorts." Musashi at once accepted the offer (which he could not have refused in any case) and thanked the commander for his kindness.

He quickly made arrangements to leave all the medical and other donated supplies he had brought from Japan at Koroto to be used there by all the Japanese expected to pour in there soon. The two young Nationalist army soldiers, one a Second Lieutenant Sun and the other an ordinary soldier, were waiting to accompany Musashi as they headed for the train station. It was immediately obvious that the two soldiers' job was to keep a close watch on Musashi. Musashi was grateful that, at least, he was being allowed to go to Shenyang, and somehow, while there, he had to find the opportunity to deliver the documents to Tatsunosuke Takasaki. But how would he be able to do that with these two "escorts" watching his every move?

Cultivating Trust with the Escort Officers

After settling in their seats on the train headed north, Musashi began talking to his escorts in a friendly, causal manner. Initially, the two Chinese were on their guard, but after a while, an atmosphere of relaxation and less vigilance was displayed by the soldiers. Musashi explained to them, "Anshan is my second home. I've been working with the people there since I was a teenager."

As the train made its long trip toward Shenyang, the lieutenant asked, "Wuzang, are you really a Japanese? You seem more Manchurian than even a Manchurian! Why don't you stay and live in Manchuria? I'll even introduce you to a bride!" By the time they arrived at Shenyang, they were even exchanging jokes. When Musashi gave the men some souvenirs from Japan as presents, they became even closer friends.

They had been given strict orders to report to the Nationalist army's northeastern command headquarters upon arrival at Shenyang. Musashi feared that some kind of complication might occur at the headquarters that could result in delaying, or even preventing, him from getting the important documents to Takasaki. Of all the important documents that had been entrusted to Musashi by Chief Secretary to the Prime Minister Narahashi to deliver to Takasaki, the most important was a letter stating that any funds donated by Japanese countrymen in Manchuria to help in the repatriation effort would be repaid by the Japanese government upon the return of those donors to the homeland. With that guarantee, it opened the door for the Japanese in Manchuria who still had financial resources to help support the repatriation process.

Musashi had to visit Takasaki immediately upon arrival in Shenyang, before he did anything else. Taking a deep breath but still appearing to stay calm, he said to Lieutenant Sun, "Lieutenant, before we go to the command headquarters, there is one person I want to see just for a moment. All I need is ten minutes. Can you allow me that?"

"Someone you want to see? Who is it?"

"It is a girl. Actually, she is like a mother to me."

The lieutenant looked momentarily confused, but he soon wore a knowing smile on his face and said, "OK, but only for a brief time." Musashi's ploy on the train to develop rapport with his two escorts had paid off!

With Musashi leading the way to the main office of the All-Manchuria Japanese Association in the Heianza Building on Kasuga Avenue that he knew well, the two Nationalist soldiers even kindly divided up his bags and helped carry them. When they arrived at the Heianza Building, Lieutenant Sun said to Musashi, "We will wait right here, but please remember your promise that it will take only ten minutes." Nodding his agreement, Musashi ran into the building and headed directly for the Japanese association office.

Chairman Takasaki, unfortunately, was out at the moment. However, several staff members gathered around Musashi as he said, "My name is Musashi, and I just came from Japan on a repatriation ship." Apparently Takasaki had briefed all the staff members about the three men who had escaped to Japan, and they had probably heard the NHK radio broadcast from Japan, but they never expected one of the three to suddenly come running into their office. Totally surprised, they could only stare at Musashi momentarily.

Then one said, "My goodness, you are safe ... Thank you for all your efforts!"

Musashi immediately took off his jacket and began extracting all the important documents that had been sewn into it. He gathered up the documents and letters and handed them to one of the staff members, saying, "I don't have time to give you a detailed explanation. Please give these to Chairman Takasaki. The decision has been made to dispatch repatriation ships to Koroto. Please ask him to immediately take all necessary actions." With that, Musashi hurriedly ran out of the office, leaving the staff members in a daze. He ran to the two waiting Nationalist soldiers, and the three quickly headed for the northeastern command headquarters.

A Less Than Friendly Welcome

The command headquarters officers had been awaiting Musashi's arrival, not to welcome him, but to subject him to severe cross-examination. As Musashi later found out, the source of his trouble was the reentry permit signed by General Liu Wanquan.

Shortly after Maruyama, Shinpo, and Musashi departed on their journey out of Manchuria, a scandal involving the commander of the Shenyang underground headquarters, Guo Chang Shen, and his senior staff officers had been exposed, resulting in the reassignment and disgrace of all the senior officers. Thus, a Japanese possessing a document signed by the chief of staff of the disgraced command was naturally looked upon as a possible spy. Musashi was promptly arrested, incarcerated, and harshly interrogated for the next several days.

While he was not physically abused, Musashi was in dire straits. No one knew where he was or what had happened to him; he could expect absolutely no help from the outside.

One day, when the guards changed where Musashi was imprisoned, the new guard looked at him with a suspicious stare. After a while, the guard came to take a closer look at Musashi who feared the worst. Suddenly the soldier said, "Wuzang! Aren't you Wuzang from Anshan?"

"Yes, that's right. I am Wuzang from Anshan!" Suddenly, memories came back to Musashi. The soldier had been one of the Chinese laborers at the construction site of his former company, Shinpo-gumi.

The soldier immediately reported his relationship with the prisoner to his superiors, testifying that Musashi had always been kind and fair to his fellow Chinese workers. That testimony worked to clear Musashi's name, and he was released on the tenth day of his confinement.

"Cooperating Personally" with Colonel Liu

Upon leaving the prison, he was taken to the office of a Colonel Liu who was then in charge of affairs related to Japanese in Manchuria. "Wuzang, we are sincerely sorry for the way we treated you. We now know all about you," apologized the colonel in a very polite and respectful manner. "What do you intend to do now?" he asked Musashi.

"I must go around to various places throughout Manchuria where there are Japanese and help in any way that I can with the repatriation of my fellow countrymen," replied Musashi.

"Then we have a proposal for you. As you go about your activities, would you be willing to lend us a hand?" What Colonel Liu wanted was for Musashi to report on the activities in Manchuria, particularly on the movements of the Eighth Route Army. In effect, Musashi was being asked to be a spy for the Nationalist army. The conflict between the Nationalist army and the Communist forces had intensified to such an extent that all of Manchuria was presently in a state of flux.

Hardly able to believe he was being asked to do such a thing, Musashi was about to blurt out, *I did not come back to Manchuria to be your spy!* However, he held his tongue and gave the idea some thought. If he did take on the role as a collaborator for the Nationalists, his movements back and forth between different parts of Manchuria might become much easier. Certainly, there might be danger to himself that he may not have been aware of at this time, but as he weighed the advantages and disadvantages, the advantages won out.

"Colonel Liu, I will do as you ask. However, rather than say that I will collaborate with the Nationalist army, let's say that I am cooperating with you personally." Colonel Liu nodded his head, apparently satisfied with Musashi's answer.

Musashi set out, this time alone, to visit the Japanese association office on Kasuga Avenue in Shenyang. This time, he had more time to discuss matters with the staff members at the office. "The order for the repatriation should start with Japanese living in northern Manchuria or who came from there, and those who are refugees and the sick should be given first priority. I will now depart and go around to visit other Japanese associations and let them know this will be the policy."

The staff members, of course, agreed completely with Musashi's suggested policy and promised full cooperation to insure implementation. The Japanese who were suffering the most were the refugees from the northern regions who had had to flee the Soviet invasion. Most had their personal possessions pillaged, and they had nothing to sell or exchange for food. They were the ones who tried to find shelter wherever they could—in abandoned schools, hospitals, factories, community centers, and anywhere else where there was a roof. Most were suffering from malnutrition and sickness, doing their best to survive in the severe cold of the Manchurian winter, without proper food, clothing, or medicine. They were the ones dying in great numbers.

Based on the document from Chief Secretary to the Prime Minister Narahashi that Musashi had carried and given to Takasaki, Japanese associations began collecting moneys donated by those who still had assets. The funds were used to organize the transporting of refugees to Koroto. Under the leadership of the Japanese associations, repatriation operations commenced in an orderly manner. Observing the work of the associations, Musashi later confessed he felt great pride in their efforts and in the consideration they showed toward the refugees.[1]

Chapter 20

"Save Our Countrymen in Manchuria"

Large-Scale Repatriation Commences

The first U.S. naval vessel to return to Sasebo from Koroto, Manchuria, bearing the first group of Japanese back to their native land was the *LST QIO58*. Carrying 1,219 Japanese citizens, the ship docked at the Port of Sasebo on the southern Japanese island of Kyushu on May 14, 1946. Subsequently, ships of the Q category followed one after another on May 15, 16, 17, 18, and 26 until a total of 13 ships had transported over twenty thousand Japanese citizens back to Japan.

Maruyama and Shinpo were at the dock in Sasebo when the repatriated Japanese began arriving. Because refugees, the sick, and the homeless were given priority, the first groups of returnees were indeed in miserable condition. About the only possession most of the returning Japanese brought back was usually one simple backpack, while many had nothing except the ragged clothes they wore on their back.

Most in the first group of repatriates suffered from severe malnutrition. The first rice they had tasted in almost a year was the food given to them on board the repatriation ships. In

Manchuria, they had survived for months on small amounts of *koryan* (sorghum) and chestnuts. If repatriation had been delayed another month, thought Shinpo and Maruyama as they watched the enfeebled but happy returnees step onto the soil of their cherished native land, many of them would not have survived long enough to be among the returnees.

Repatriated Japanese returned day after day, not only to Sasebo, which was the main port of disembarkation, but to Maizuru (near Kyoto), Hakata, and other ports in Kyushu. After they came off the ship, the returnees were led into a tent where they were doused with DDT, given medical examinations, then were issued blankets and clothing and one thousand yen each to send them to their final destination, wherever that might be.

More than a few, particularly if their homes were in the northern parts of Japan, would stop at the repatriation headquarters at No. 2-609 Kugayama (Maruyama's residence) in the Suginami Ward of Tokyo to say their greetings and express appreciation for their return. As Maruyama remembered it, most expressed their gratitude by saying, "Thanks to your efforts, we were able to return from Manchuria. We heard your broadcast in April and learned for the first time that Maruyama-san, Shinpo-san, and Musashi-san had returned to Japan and had continuously been engaged in earnest effort on our behalf. Since hearing that broadcast, we were able to survive, as that alone gave us hope." Then many would follow with "I am on my way back to my home in northeastern Japan, but I'm afraid I will not be able to find a place to stay with just the money I received upon my landing. I wondered if I could stay here for tonight."

Even in those days, one thousand yen did not go that far. If they ate a little extra, or if they bought medicine, the money would disappear quickly. Lodging in an inn or hotel was out of the question for most. Thus, the Kugayama residence became an overnight stopping point for many repatriates. Because the house was built before the war, it was not a large house, but the newly returned Japanese were grateful for the accommodation. Every day, anywhere from two or three guests to thirty-five or more people crowded into the small house, sleeping in every room and often spilling into the hallways. "When we think about the suffering we endured in Manchuria and reflect back on the living conditions on the repatriation ship, this is almost luxurious! And we feel perfectly safe here." So saying, the guests would happily go to sleep. During the day, they all pitched in to help with preparing meals, cleaning up, and generally taking care of all the household chores. Since there was no budget to feed them, some of the more energetic guests would go to the market and buy yams, potatoes, radishes, and greens with money that the representatives (i.e., Maruyama and Shinpo) gave them and prepare meals for the temporary lodgers upon their return.

On most days, the Kugayama headquarters was left to be run completely on its own by the guests, since Maruyama and Shinpo were not home, busy with their responsibilities insuring that the repatriation operation was proceeding smoothly. In fact, the house was a sort of a society without a government, with no landlord or supervisor, with each guest maintaining public order and self-control. In all the time that repatriates took advantage of the free lodging at Kugayama, there was not even one case of a person speaking out of line or causing a disturbance. They were all complete strangers to each other, but they all shared the common experience of suffering in Manchuria and waiting for the day they would return to their native home. At night, after their meager meal, they would talk to each other, relaxed and feeling safe, finally able to think about the future. After reminiscing about the hardships they had endured for so long, their conversation inevitably turned to sharing their hopes and dreams for the future. Their chats were always friendly and often subdued, and no one ever caused anyone any trouble.

Maruyama often had the opportunity to observe these repatriates as they enjoyed each other's company in such a crowded space. He was amazed and gratified that his house at Kugayama was able to play such an important role in welcoming back so many of the returnees. It was, to him, a reminder of the scenes he remembered reading in Sir Thomas More's *Utopia*, the book that he had so loved as a graduate student in the United States. Man's happiness and peace, he reflected, were not to be measured by the abundance or meagerness of material things. He was also reminded of the Oriental philosophy that said, "There is happiness as long as you have water to drink and have an elbow to use as a pillow."

As he mused melancholically, Maruyama wondered how long it would be before he would be sitting in the very same place, listening to the happy chatter of his wife and four sons. He had no idea how they were faring, but he knew that Dalian was presently under complete Soviet control so that, at least for the time being, no Japanese were expected to be repatriated from that region. Whenever he saw the happy faces of families with children staying overnight at his Kugayama residence, he was reminded of how much he missed his own family. But he knew that, if anyone could take care of his boys and survive the conditions in Manchuria, his wife, Mary, was that person. He prayed that the God his wife had so much faith in would bring her and their children safely back together with him someday soon.

In the morning, the temporary lodgers would express their appreciation for the food and lodging and go their own way to their homes in northern Japan, hoping that their loved ones and homes had survived the devastation and terror of the foolhardy and needless war.

Preparing a Pamphlet to Appeal to the Nation

When Maruyama, Shinpo, and Musashi finally arrived back in Japan on March 13, 1946, at Sasebo, they read their carefully prepared statement describing the present conditions in Manchuria, conditions about which the people of Japan could until then only fearfully speculate. Unfortunately, their statement before a mass of newspaper reporters at the *Asahi* newspaper western division headquarters in Kokura City was completely censored and never saw the light of day. In the following days, the three men did their best to get the word out about Manchuria to the public by speaking at numerous assemblies and meetings throughout Japan. Then, on April 17, Maruyama made a radio broadcast from the central broadcasting station of NHK which, for the first time, described to the entire nation the situation in Manchuria. Even then, two sections of his manuscript had been deleted by the SCAP censors.

Although repatriation from Manchuria had finally commenced, Maruyama and Shinpo were determined to disclose the entire truth about conditions in Manchuria to the public. There were still many Japanese living in regions occupied by the Soviet army, including their own families, who were not included among those awaiting their turn to go to Koroto and find passage on one of the repatriation ships. It seemed that the objective of the Allied Powers' censors was to cover the eyes and ears of the Japanese people about the true situation in Manchuria, even though the same Allied Powers were simultaneously changing Japan from an imperial nation into a democratic nation.

One of the pillars of a democratic nation was the freedom of speech. To fully disclose the entire truth to the public, Maruyama and Shinpo came up with the idea of publishing an appropriate pamphlet. However, there was one problem: Japan, in those days, had a severe shortage of paper. The problem was overcome, fortunately, through the sympathy and understanding of Chief Secretary to the Prime Minister Narahashi, who used his influence so that Oji Paper Manufacturing Company donated a large amount of paper for the cause.

Maruyama and Shinpo went to work putting together the manuscript for a pamphlet. It did not take long to compose a comprehensive manuscript for publication since the two had given so many speeches on the subject in the past several weeks. Then came the hard part. In those days, all material to be published had to be submitted to the censorship division at GHQ for its review and permission. Three days after the manuscript was submitted to GHQ, Maruyama was summoned to GHQ by a censor.

Maruyama Takes on the Censors

The censorship division of GHQ was located inside the Kanto Electric Distribution Center Building in the Uchisaiwaicho section of Tokyo. When he reported to the censorship division, a handsome young civilian in a suit appeared at the reception desk and invited Maruyama to follow him to his office. The young and affable American introduced himself as a "Mr. Pringshuim" and informed Maruyama that he had been assigned to handle the submitted manuscript. (The Tokyo GHQ Telephone Directory of 16 May 1946 does list a Mr. K. Pringsheimer. Because all names in Japanese are written phonetically, there are a few other instances in which the Japanese "katakana syllabary" rendering in Kunio Maruyama's *Why Was Koroto Opened* differs slightly from the English spelling of a name.[1])

When Maruyama seated himself in front of the table in the censor's office, Pringsheimer said, "Mr. Maruyama, as you can see, there were many parts that had to be censored out from the manuscript you wrote. As it is, it may not even be worth publishing." As Maruyama inspected the pages of his manuscript, on every page, and on just about every line, red marks were drawn through those parts that were meant to be deleted. In fact, those parts of the manuscript that escaped the censor's red line amounted to perhaps a mere 2 or 3 percent of the entire document.

"This is certainly a shock. Just about everything has been marked for deletion! With this, there is not much left to be read." Not only was Maruyama shocked, he was extremely angry, but struggled to maintain his composure. In his mind, he immediately thought back to a couple of months ago when the three escapees from Manchuria first landed in Japan and to the joint press conference that was held at the *Asahi* newspaper's western headquarters in Kokura, and how not one meaningful part of their statement appeared in the newspapers the next morning. As at that time, it was obvious that the Soviet representatives among the Allied Powers were involved in suppressing the truth about conditions in Manchuria.

If this is the way things are going to be, thought Maruyama as he stared at the countless red lines on the pages of the manuscript, *we have had all we can take.* Even if Japan was under occupation authority, the suppression of truth was unforgivable. The time had come for Maruyama and his companions to dig in and refuse to give in meekly. With that determination, Maruyama looked up at the young censor and began asking questions bluntly and, without holding back, began stating what he felt he had to say.

His first question to Pringsheimer was "Are we not allowed to make any announcements about Manchuria?"

The censor replied, "There is not any specific rule like that."

Then Maruyama asked, "You mean it is permissible to say thing in words, but it is not permissible to put things in print for people to read?"

"That is not true," replied the censor, "but what do you mean?"

To that, Maruyama replied with sincerity and conviction, "Perhaps you may already know, but I made a nationwide broadcast on April 17 from the Central Broadcasting Station on a theme entitled, 'An Appeal Concerning the Situation in Manchuria.' I submitted the broadcast manuscript beforehand, and it was inspected by the censors; the content of that manuscript was very similar to the content in this pamphlet. Only ten lines were deleted by the inspectors so that I broadcast everything else. Your censoring here is something I have a hard time understanding. May I ask from whom you are trying to keep the true situation in Manchuria a secret? Is it to keep it from the Americans? Or from other foreigners? Or is it to keep from letting the Japanese people know?

"Just one month before I departed from Manchuria, I saw a group of about ten American and European newspaper reporters who were visiting Shenyang under the very strict surveillance of Soviet occupation army guards. I badly wanted to talk to them, but since the Soviet soldiers were guarding them so carefully, I was, of course, not able to do so. I wanted to find out from them for what purpose and by using what route they came to be in Manchuria.

"More than a month later, on our way back to Japan through Tianjin, I purchased and read a copy of *Newsweek* magazine that had been published in the United States, and for the first time I found out. I have that copy of *Newsweek* at my house, so if you desire, I can have it delivered to you. In that issue of *Newsweek*, there was a photo showing several Japanese who had been killed by either Soviet soldiers or Manchurian mobs, with their corpses scattered all about. Several more photos in the magazine captured other horrific scenes. This was just one American magazine, but I suspect that there are other articles and photos in newspapers and magazines in various European countries resulting from their own reporters in that group visiting Manchuria.

"If that is the case, it is most probable that all the peoples of the entire world are aware of the situation in hellish Manchuria where justice and humanity have been trampled on. It is useless to hide the facts. Even for the Japanese, repatriation has already commenced since May, and as the many repatriates return to their native homes, they are surely speaking out about the situation in Manchuria based on their own experiences, which probably include tragedies ten times worse than what I have written in my pamphlet.

"And, yet, after all that, for you to tell me that you are preventing me from publishing the pamphlet that I have written describing the true situation in Manchuria is like trying to push a speeding express train from behind it! Since my two companions and I have been back in Tokyo, we have met many times with key personnel at GHQ; and in the beginning of April, we had a very cordial meeting with General MacArthur himself. To one and all, we have related the truth in detail about the serious tragedies occurring in Manchuria, detailing situations many times worse than what I have written in this pamphlet. Each person who heard our story listened with great attention and empathy. I would be willing to bet that it is *not* at the urging of General MacArthur or any of the senior officers we have talked to that this publication describing the truth in Manchuria is being forbidden.

"I myself lived and studied for several years in the United States and got to know the United States quite well. I also feel that I have a great understanding of the merits and virtues of the American people. Americans value freedom and fairness above all in everything they do, and they will hardly cast a blind eye at things they should know about in other countries. America will never try to enforce despotic or barbaric policies in order to hide and suppress facts that Americans have the right to know about. If, as a matter of course in your occupation policy, you enforce undemocratic methods and steps that are against justice and fairness, such as the handling of our pamphlet, and if you expect the citizens of Japan to follow your leadership, I suspect that the number of people who will go along with you will be a very small number indeed. I, for one, who probably have a relatively better knowledge, understanding, and affection for the American people than the average Japanese, will be the first to firmly oppose such treatment, no matter what the consequences may be."[2]

Thus Maruyama got it off his chest.

"Hmm, I wonder if that is so," chimed in Pringsheimer, rather easily and calmly in view of Maruyama's outburst.

Having anticipated a severe reprimand or at least a counterattack, Maruyama was pleasantly surprised and bowed his head and humbly asked, "In any case, I beg you to read the manuscript one more time and please reconsider the audience you want to prevent from reading all the red-lined sections."

The young civilian censor looked pleasantly at Maruyama and said, "Since your pamphlet was examined by a small number of inspectors, perhaps there were areas where sufficient deliberation was lacking. Therefore, I would like to have it reexamined after consulting with the censorship committee, which is composed of officers. In any case, I will contact you in three or four days, so I hope you won't mind coming back here once more." He then politely placed the manuscript back into its envelope.

"Please do the best you can," Maruyama said, with a bow. Then, after a firm handshake, he left the censor's office. As soon as he got home, he rummaged through his belongings at the Kugayama headquarters and found the *Newsweek* magazine he had bought at Tianjin. He asked an assistant to take it immediately to the GHQ censorship office in Uchisaiwaicho to be handed over to a Mr. Pringsheimer there. (*Author's note*: The magazine that Maruyama bought in Tianjin was the March 18, 1946 edition of *Newsweek*. In a photo accompanying an article headlined, "Rape of Manchuria," a gruesome scene of several dead bodies of Japanese workers left abandoned by the Soviets in Mukden [Shenyang] is shown in the ruins of a factory.)[3]

Only a Couple of Red Lines This Time

The local policeman came to the Kugayama headquarters two days later to relay the message that a call had come from GHQ, asking Maruyama to come to the censorship office at his convenience. When he arrived there, Pringsheimer was waiting for him and again led him to his office.

Placing the envelope in front of Maruyama, Pringsheimer said, "After our meeting a couple of days ago, I resubmitted your manuscript to the officers' censorship committee for reevaluation. As a result, their decision was that if you would alter the wording in a couple of the lines in your manuscript to express them in the way they suggested, the committee is satisfied and approves your manuscript in its entirety." Pushing the manuscript toward Maruyama, Pringsheimer pointed to the minute section that required correction.

Maruyama could hardly believe the good news and replied, "Please allow me to make the corrections right now," and made the necessary changes right in front of the young censor.

It seemed that the only objection that the censorship committee had in the manuscript this time was a sentence that said, "The [Japanese] soldiers in districts outside of Shenyang were also taken in groups to Siberia or to other areas in the Soviet Union." Maruyama changed that sentence on the spot to, "As for what happened to the [Japanese] soldiers in districts outside Shenyang, no one knows how they were treated." That was all it took to have the entire manuscript approved for publication.

Standing up, Maruyama again bowed to the young civilian and then shook his hands tightly as he expressed his gratitude. Pringsheimer wished Maruyama the best of luck in his ongoing efforts to return all Japanese from Manchuria. As he headed home on the train, Maruyama mused about the pleasant attitude of the young American civilian. It was difficult for him to imagine a Japanese official reconsidering a decision already made; in most cases, the Japanese official would be more concerned about losing face than admitting an error. He was grateful that the young American had been such a pleasant and honest individual who was willing to consider Maruyama's arguments and reverse his original decision regarding the contents of the manuscript.

The 35-Page Pamphlet

The pamphlet, which was only thirty-five pages long and about half the size of a magazine, was published on June 15, 1946, by the Koumin Kyouhon Publishing Company. Takegoro Nakanishi, chairman of Japan Koshikai Pharmaceutical Industry and a man who had contributed in many other ways to the effort to bring home the Japanese from Manchuria, took on the entire responsibility for publishing the pamphlet that described the actual situation in Manchuria. It detailed the dangerous conditions for the Japanese still living there and appealed for their earliest possible repatriation.

The pamphlets were priced at two yen each, and the main distribution venue for the pamphlets was the kiosks at National Railway stations. They were also placed in ordinary bookstores throughout Japan. "If someone has difficulty coming up with two yen to pay for them, please hand them out for free," Maruyama and Shinpo had insisted to the various vendors. Thus, there was not much income from the sale of the pamphlets. Besides, people could easily read the contents while standing at the store, so many were read but not bought. Over fifty thousand were donated to associations of families who had loved ones still remaining in Manchuria.

The pamphlet authored by Maruyama was entitled *Save Our Countrymen in Manchuria* and contained the gist of many speeches (including the NHK broadcast in April), presentations, and narratives that Maruyama, Shinpo, and Musashi had repeated countless times.

The Gist of the Pamphlet's Contents

Since much of the thirty-five pages contained description of conditions in Manchuria that have already been presented in this book, only the foreword of the pamphlet as translated by this author is quoted here:

> It was around dusk of March 31, 1946. I was in Shiroyamakan in Nagano Prefecture where I had just concluded a speech at the prefectural meeting on behalf of the Relief Effort for Japanese Countrymen Residing in Manchuria and Korea organization, and just as I was about to depart Shiroyama, an elderly lady who reminded me of my own mother stopped me. She began to ask me many questions regarding the safety of her son who had been ordered deep into Manchuria as a volunteer army recruit to colonize that part of Manchuria. She pointed to the cherry blossom trees lining the streets of Shiroyama and said, "It is spring now, and the cherry blossoms are beginning to bloom. But until I know the whereabouts of my son, those cherry blossoms will not look beautiful to me." So saying, she had tears in her eyes as she bade me farewell, wishing me the best. For some time, I watched as that elderly lady walked away, and I felt a sudden feeling of tightness deep in my chest which was beyond my control.
>
> At the end of the war there were 1.7 million Japanese still left in Manchuria, and if you count the seven hundred thousand soldiers and their dependents, the total is around 2.4 million. On top of that, if you count the Japanese in northern Korea, Karafuto (Sakhalin), and Chishima (the Kuril Islands), the total nears three million. And for each of these three million Japanese who are still left on the other side of the ocean, if we assume that each has five loving persons here in

Japan—wives, husbands, dear ones, and others who care deeply for them—that would mean that there are fifteen million people who, like myself and the elderly lady who I had just parted with, are probably unable to really appreciate the beauty of the cherry blossoms. And it is not just those in Japan with loved ones overseas, but all eighty million Japanese, who cannot be uncaring of our fellow countrymen left behind....

The eyes of the world are upon the defeated nation of Japan, and they are carefully watching every move by the people of Japan. If the people of Japan remain indifferent to the rescue of these Japanese left behind, I would not hesitate to say the following to the rest of the world: "The Japanese people are most zealous when it comes to waging and fighting in a war, but when it comes to humanitarian efforts such as saving these countrymen, they are a decidedly indifferent people, and they have little sympathy for these countrymen in particular who have not been able to come home," and, thus, convey an impression to the world that would be most disappointing since the world may have expected much more of the Japanese people.

Now is the time for all Japanese in Japan to mobilize even greater national efforts than at any time during the war in this humanitarian effort to rescue the Japanese left behind and work until success is achieved....

If, by reading this pamphlet, you are made aware of the actual conditions of the Japanese people still left in Manchuria since the end of the war, and if this can be one more thing to help raise interest in the rescue efforts of those left overseas, we will be most grateful.[4]

The contents of the pamphlet described how, from the time that the army of the Soviet Union invaded Manchuria and declared war on Japan on August 8, 1945, the relatively peaceful and prosperous life of every Japanese in Manchuria abruptly turned into a nightmare. It detailed how the Japanese Kwantung Army, which had guarded and bossed over every aspect of Japanese lives until the Soviet invasion, suddenly disappeared and left the civilians to fend for themselves. The pamphlet detailed the condition of the Japanese settlers, particularly those in the north who were forcibly driven out of homes and villages to become homeless refugees, and how terrorism became rampant as many refugees were killed in their flight, often by bandits, while the Japanese in the cities were terrorized by many Soviet soldiers roaming the streets, robbing civilians, raping women, looting homes, and killing those who resisted. It described how means of earning a living became unavailable to the Japanese; how Japanese bank accounts were frozen; how malnutrition and diseases became rampant; how food and fuel became too costly for the Japanese; and how the entire country was shut off from the rest of the world as all means of communication were severed and no Japanese could enter or leave Manchuria. Finally, the pamphlet urged the people of Japan not to let up on pressuring the Japanese government and SCAP GHQ to negotiate the opening of ports at Yingkou and Dalian in addition to the ongoing repatriation from Koroto, to speed up the repatriation process.[5]

The 35-page pamphlet written by Maruyama entitled *Save Our Countrymen in Manchuria* was the first published document (June 1946) to inform the Japanese people about the dire situation in Manchuria. The illustration on the pamphlet's cover also adorns the cover of this book.
(Author's Collection)

Tearful Responses to the Pamphlet

A few weeks after the pamphlets had been made available to the public, mainly through sales at railroad station kiosks and bookstores, letters started pouring into the Kugayama headquarters, mostly from families with relatives still in Manchuria as well as several from those who had been repatriated and were now safely back home with their relieved families in Japan. As Maruyama and Shinpo and their volunteer helpers read through the letters, many made them choke up with emotion.

Two excerpts are quoted below. The following letter came from a former Japanese army soldier who was demobilized and returned to Japan but whose family still remained in Manchuria:

Dear Sir:

I had the opportunity to read the pamphlet regarding the situation in Manchuria that you published recently, and I want to express my warmest gratitude to you. I was not able to hold back my tears as I read about the innocent children selling goods or seeing visions of them following and clinging to passersby....

Although Japanese are being repatriated every day, they all seem to be coming from only Shenyang, but do you know what the schedule for repatriation from other areas might be? According to the newspapers, there are no plans for repatriation from the Dalian region, but if that is so, that is an extremely sad thing. Why can't ships be dispatched to Dalian? Where does the problem lie that it cannot be resolved? ... If they are not repatriated within this year—rather, if they are not repatriated before winter arrives, their lives are in danger. In my case, I came home first, and I am spending every day constantly fretting that my daughters might be left there to die. Please, please, do whatever you can so that a ship can depart from Dalian before another day passes....

I left behind my wife and three children in Hufangdian, and when I was drafted, I cried as any man would cry, and I returned to Japan from South Korea. There were about four thousand that I know of among my companions. I sincerely apologize for my selfish questions, and I know each individual has his own situation, making it impossible for you to take up every request, but I beg you to do the best you can.

Tomitake Koiwa
July 26, 1946[6]

The next letter came from the wife of another Japanese soldier in Soviet-controlled territory who had not been demobilized yet:

Dear Sir:

Please forgive my rudeness in suddenly sending you this letter. I am a family member of a soldier who is yet to be demobilized.

While I was out yesterday doing some errands, I purchased a copy of your writing entitled *Save Our Countrymen in Manchuria*, and I read it as if my breathing had come to a stop. Although it is a small pamphlet of only about thirty pages, I cannot tell you how many times I reread it while wiping my eyes. The passionate words went straight to my heart, and I was very saddened. My husband was in Karafuto [Sakhalin] at the end of the war, but as you may know, his whereabouts are completely unknown since then.

It goes without saying that if we could but just be allowed to communicate, what hope that would bring to each other. ... One year has passed since the war ended, and how long that feels.... Those who served in the southern islands have all been demobilized. Although we may have lost the war, could we not insist on the articles that are in the Potsdam Treaty? It is said that conjecture leads to more conjecture, but will the Soviet Union return them after three years, or will it be five, or I have even heard that they never intend to return our people, and that is driving my nerves beyond their limit.

At this point, all I want to do is to plead and say, "I don't care about the ration of three cups of rice that is distributed to me. All I want is to have my husband back even one day sooner." Is our government really seriously thinking about what it should do? In recent times, I have begun to believe that their attitude is, "Don't worry, we can bear the pain that someone else is suffering even for at least three more years," but am I wrong? …

Please do whatever you can to bring them home one day sooner. I think about the coming of winter, and I am deeply saddened. If our request for their return before winter comes has no effect, what do you think about getting together a petition by the families and sending it to the Soviet Embassy? All the families are crying. We wouldn't even mind writing it in blood. Please exert all your effort so that we can at least correspond with our loved ones.… I have been rude in asserting only selfish things, and I ask forgiveness. I have brought difficulty upon you on my husband's behalf, and assuming you will hear my requests, I have cried in the dark of the night praying to obtain some hope.

I apologize for the hurried writing, but I pray for your health and also pray that you will continue your work so that your labors will bear fruit and we may see the bright smiling faces of millions, nay, tens of millions of people, soon.

I again beg your pardon for my selfish requests.

Mieko Nakashima
August 17, 1946[7]

Chapter 21

Pressure to Open Ports under Soviet Control

Prime Minister Yoshida Appeals to MacArthur

In the absence of Musashi, who was back in Manchuria helping the various Japanese associations organize the orderly movement of the Japanese to Koroto where American vessels (manned by Japanese crews) were waiting to transport them back to Japan, Maruyama and Shinpo continued their campaign to exert pressure on the Japanese government so that the issue of repatriation of her citizens from Manchuria would remain a top priority. They continued their rounds of speeches and attendance at meetings, always concluding with an appeal to those in the audience to write letters, make phone calls, and even visit government agencies and GHQ to appeal for greater efforts for repatriation throughout Asia. One prominent individual, who apparently had not ignored the pleas of the three men and the citizens of Japan, was the new prime minister of Japan, Shigeru Yoshida.

Yoshida, who had met with Maruyama, Shinpo, and Musashi on March 30 shortly after their return to Japanese soil in his Foreign Ministry office, had bluntly told the three men, "Japan does not have any diplomacy right now...." Two months later, on May 22, 1946, Yoshida became the forty-fifth prime minister. History has largely credited him with bringing Japan out of devastating defeat to eventually join the ranks of the most democratic and wealthiest nations.

Shortly after assuming the highest political office of Japan, Yoshida wrote a personal letter to General MacArthur at GHQ in Tokyo. "My dear General," began the June 14, 1946, letter in Yoshida's characteristic English, "I understand the question of repatriation was taken up at the Allied Council Meeting the day before yesterday.... I know that repatriation has been satisfactory so far and I am entirely grateful to the cooperation and assistance given by you and the Allied Powers. However, there is one regretful exception. That is the repatriation from the Soviet-occupied zones or former Soviet-occupied zones."

Yoshida went on to list the numbers of Japanese his government estimated were still remaining in Sakhalin, the Kuril Islands, North Korea, and Manchuria and to point out that "no repatriation, practically speaking, has taken place from the above zones, with the exception of about 100,000 each of civilians from North Korea and Manchuria. I get letters every day from the anxious families all over Japan demanding the government take some actions on the ground that the repatriation is guaranteed under the Potsdam Declaration, and no doubt you get more letters than I do." Yoshida then stated his understanding that, thanks to the U.S. government, one hundred Liberty ships and eighty-five LSTs would be made available for repatriation in September. However, he continued, unless something was done before then, that might be too late.

He asked MacArthur to "make an issue of the case at your earliest convenience both in Tokyo and in Washington." The prime minister of Japan concluded his letter by saying, "Your assistance in this connection would be deeply appreciated by millions of my countrymen."[1] Yoshida, it seems, had been hearing loudly and clearly the message from the people of

Japan who had, undoubtedly, been encouraged by Maruyama and Shinpo to make their plea for repatriation known to the government.

The Prince's Shabby Socks and the Paltry Meal

On July 6, Maruyama and Shinpo visited the emperor's brother, Prince Takamatsu. (This meeting had been arranged quite some time earlier by Soichi Saito, who headed the Japanese government agency in the Ministry of Welfare responsible for administering the repatriation of Japanese from Pacific regions.) For the first time, a member of the imperial family was personally apprised of the plight of Japanese living in misery under Soviet occupation. Maruyama noted that, just before Shinpo and he set out to visit with the prince, they had each taken out a brand new pair of socks that had been given to them as presents recently, and each was wearing the new socks. Maruyama happened to glance down at the socks the prince was wearing, and they were old and worn and did not even match. A strange feeling of charm and admiration that he could not explain overcame Maruyama at seeing His Imperial Highness Takamatsu, the emperor's brother, unashamedly wearing old and unmatched socks. Maruyama also felt a twinge of guilt that he, on the other hand, was wearing a pair of brand-new socks. Before they parted, Prince Takamatsu made arrangements for Maruyama and Shinpo to visit with the Imperial Household Agency on July 10.

On the appointed day and time as arranged by Prince Takamatsu, Shinpo and Maruyama went to the office of the Imperial Household Agency and were warmly greeted by Chief Imperial Chamberlain Inada, Chief of General Affairs Inumaru, and Minister of Palace Affairs Matsudaira. Once again, the representatives briefed the three officials, who were perhaps the officials closest to the emperor, about the conditions of Japanese in Manchuria awaiting repatriation. Maruyama gave the officials two copies of the just published thirty-five-page pamphlet, *Save Our Countrymen in Manchuria,* which the officials promised would be given to the emperor and the empress. They also promised that their Imperial Majesties would be fully apprised of everything Maruyama and Shinpo had just reported.

At the conclusion of the meeting with the Imperial Household Agency personnel, they were invited to have lunch before their departure. The meals were brought out on a beautifully lacquered wooden tray on which rested two impressive and gorgeous lacquered bowls with the imperial crest on them. When the two men took up the chopsticks and removed the lids of the elegant bowls, they were somewhat taken aback. Instead of the expected rice (which was rationed during those times), the meal consisted of a mix of less elegant noodles and potatoes.

Obviously, even their Imperial Majesties were eating the same foods that all other citizens of Japan were eating. Only two months before, on May 12, a group of demonstrators led by the Communist Party had entered the grounds of the Imperial Palace to appeal directly to the emperor for an increase in rice rations. Calling themselves the Give Us Rice Assembly, they raised a red flag (the symbol of Communism) on the imperial grounds for the first time. Three days later, more than 200,000 people gathered on the open grounds in front of the Imperial Palace demanding more food, and one banner in particular caused quite a controversy. That banner declared: "While I [the emperor] am eating my fill, you, my subjects, are dying of starvation." *Here, in these bowls in front of us,* thought Maruyama, *is proof that the emperor eats no better than his subjects.*

Female Legislators Swarm GHQ

Three days later, Maruyama and Shinpo visited the chambers of both the House of Representatives and the House of Councilors to gather together female representatives to win their support for the cause of repatriation. Over three days, on July 13, 17, and 19, Maruyama and Shinpo met with small groups of female representatives, as their schedule allowed, to discuss the plight of Japanese still remaining overseas, particularly in Soviet-controlled areas. It was not that the two men were ignoring the male representatives, but they thought that strong pressure brought on GHQ, General MacArthur, and Mrs. MacArthur by the lady legislators would have particularly effective results. After hearing firsthand the detailed briefing on conditions in Manchuria from the two men, the women followed with extremely lively and passionate discussions.

After the legislators had expressed their feelings and opinions, the two men always concluded the meetings with the following request: "May we ask you to take the following actions? We urge you to form groups and make appointments to meet with General and Mrs. MacArthur and explain directly to them the sufferings being endured by the Japanese still remaining on foreign soils as well as the sufferings of the families, relatives, fiancées, and friends of those who have not returned yet, and appeal to them to make the necessary arrangements for immediate action. We believe that an appeal by you, ladies, would be much more effective than an appeal by a group of male representatives. We feel you will truly move the hearts of the general and his wife as well as the hearts of his staff. With stark realization that the Japanese in foreign lands are truly hovering between life and death, that each day of delay in repatriating them results in many deaths, we ask that you not be concerned with protocol or loss of face or embarrassment, and we ask that you make your appeal soon, tomorrow if possible."

There were, in those days, thirty-nine female members in the Japanese Parliament. Thirty-three of them met with Maruyama and Shinpo and pledged to lend their support to pressure the government and GHQ to accelerate repatriation, including from Soviet-occupied regions. Several groups of female parliamentarians descended on GHQ to show their support for the cause, some making tearful entreaties to the American officers, who greeted them with much respect. When it became known that the female representatives were paying visits to GHQ, other female groups representing families with loved ones in foreign lands often joined them. One of the notable groups was led by Representative Shizue Kato, who had studied in the United States and was fluent in English. The groups often visited the headquarters of the Soviet delegation in the Azabu District immediately following their GHQ visit.

Several days after some of the female legislators had met with GHQ officers, Maruyama visited GHQ on other matters and was stopped by George Kawamura, an American Nisei officer whom Maruyama had gotten to know. "Mr. Maruyama," he commented, "lately there has certainly been a great increase of female visitors from your side coming to make appeals here. In any case, women are more pleasant to have as visitors than men, so please know that we welcome them here!" Although the comment was offered in a whimsical tone, Maruyama was pleased. Lately, he had been feeling somewhat gloomy, not having seen any progress. The visits, after all, were being noticed by GHQ!

Maruyama replied, "You said, 'from our side,' but I am not sure what you mean. We are certainly not organizing and dispatching any groups to come and appeal to you. However, since the desire to have Japanese from overseas returned home as early as possible is a desire for all Japanese, perhaps you should be ready for groups of young ladies to descend on you and surround you with their appeals! I suspect there will soon be mobs of mothers with babies on their backs as well as grandmothers with canes whose one leg is already in a coffin coming here, and there will be long lines waiting their turn to appeal to you! So I suggest that you widen the road in front of GHQ!" The Nisei officer laughed heartily as the two parted.

Families of the Yet Unrepatriated Press On

Because the fate of many Japanese, both military and civilian, still left in foreign lands was completely unknown, especially those in Soviet-controlled territories including Manchuria, Sakhalin, the Kuril Islands, and Siberia (where many Japanese POWs had been sent), their families in Japan became more and more concerned with each passing day. Many of those family members made calls on GHQ and the headquarters of the Soviet delegation to express their desperate concerns and delivered petitions appealing for action. Several times, Maruyama and Shinpo accompanied those groups and pleaded together with them.

When they visited Prince Takamatsu on July 6, one of the subjects they discussed was forming a nationwide organization whose aim would be to combine forces to strengthen and formalize procedures to welcome home repatriates and rehabilitate them so that they would have every opportunity to become productive Japanese citizens as the nation recovered from the war. With the enthusiastic support of Prince Takamatsu, a national organization calling itself the Alliance for the Rescue of Japanese Living in Asian Countries was formed. Founding members included many prominent businessmen and members of Parliament, including Miki Takeo (who later became prime minister), Kenzaburo Hara (a future labor minister and a life-long friend of Maruyama's whom he first befriended during his graduate study days in the United States), House of Peers Member Fujiemon Takenaka, Yasuo Shimizu (president of the major construction company Shimizu Group), and Minister of State Etsujiro Uehara, among others. Maruyama, Shinpo, and Musashi were appointed as permanent directors.

Chapter 22

The Ordeal in the Tiger's Den

Hurried Evacuation from Anshan

In Manchuria, Musashi was completely engrossed in his mission. He met with key representatives of the many Japanese associations, advising and helping organize the orderly movement of Japanese to Koroto. His Manchurian and Chinese acquaintances who had known him before his escape to Japan were extremely helpful in countless ways. They were people whom Musashi had worked with side by side as sweat poured from their brows in the days before the Soviet invasion. Many were like brothers to him.

He was also eagerly assisted by a group of about ten young Japanese men, all former soldiers of the Kwantung Army who had escaped from Soviet army captivity. Musashi had set up his one-room office in a building in Shenyang. From there he organized the repatriation work, and there the volunteers gathered to lend their assistance. With time, the number of these former Japanese soldiers who wanted to lend a hand with repatriation grew, so that by the latter part of July, they numbered about seventeen or eighteen. Musashi later reflected that, although many of their names and faces had been erased from his memory, his feeling of gratitude to each and every one of them would never be forgotten.

As summer came, the conflict intensified between the Nationalist army and the Communist forces. The Nationalist army had controlled most of the major cities throughout Manchuria early in the conflict following the Soviet invasion and the end of World War II, but the Communist forces steadily began to exert influence in areas surrounding the cities. One city that worried Musashi was Anshan City, his former residence, which had until recently been under firm Nationalist control. Through his connections with former Chinese acquaintances, he began to hear rumors that Anshan was in danger of soon coming under Communist control. Because of Anshan's proximity to Soviet-controlled Dalian in the south and to North Korea, the Eighth Route Army had begun intensifying its activities in the area.

In late June, Musashi paid a visit to the then chairman of the Anshan Japanese Association, Dr. Yoshisuke Ishikawa, a prominent physician who had been active since before the war in activities concerning Japanese in Anshan. Musashi told the doctor, "The situation around Anshan is extremely tense. Anshan is next in line to Changchun to be repatriated, but if things get worse, war between the Nationalists and Communists could erupt before repatriation begins. It is my recommendation that Japanese in Anshan move as soon as possible to Koroto."

"But how can we do that?" replied Dr. Ishikawa. "Trains need to be arranged ..."

"I will talk to the Nationalist army to have them arrange that. However, to get them to agree, there may need to be a 'donation' made for their military financing. Can that be done?"

"I understand. The Anshan Japanese Association will do what is necessary to get the 'donation' ready." Dr. Ishikawa did not hesitate in his response.

Musashi immediately contacted the Nationalist general who was the deputy director of Japanese-Chinese affairs in Shenyang. Upon receipt of the appropriate 'donation,' negotiations were successfully concluded to transport Japanese civilians by train ahead of schedule from Anshan City to Koroto. The first group of Japanese to be repatriated from Anshan boarded trains in early July. Three weeks later, the last group from Anshan headed for Koroto; Musashi was on the train platform at Anshan Station to watch them board trains to forever depart Anshan. It was not long before Anshan City fell to the Communist Eighth Route Army.

Arrested: The Terrible Ordeal Begins

Although Musashi and his helpers made every effort to keep their activities at the small office in Shenyang as discreet as possible, it was inevitable that it would attract attention, particularly with so many young Japanese going in and out throughout the day. Unbeknownst to the Japanese, the Nationalist army had been closely observing the activities at the Shenyang office for quite some time.

One day, as Musashi and one of the former Japanese soldiers named Takahashi were returning to their office in a horse-drawn Chinese carriage, a Nationalist army officer and two men in civilian clothing stopped them just as they were about to enter their office. The officer stepped in front of the Japanese and ordered them to halt. He and his two civilian companions had drawn their pistols. Musashi then saw three other soldiers with rifles at the ready coming out of their hiding places. Any attempt at resistance was foolish, and the two Japanese were placed back in the carriage and meekly led away. As Musashi pondered his bad fortune, he realized that today was August 15, 1946, approximately three and a half months since he returned to Manchuria from Japan. It was also the first anniversary of the end of World War II.

The carriage came to a halt at the back entrance of a large building in the suburbs of Shenyang City. After they were searched in one room of the building, two soldiers ordered them to proceed downstairs to the basement. As Musashi descended, with the two soldiers right behind him, an indescribable fear grew inside him as it became darker with each step. He noticed a bad smell all around, and he began to feel ill. At the bottom of the stairs, two waiting guards took charge, and one led Musashi to an underground cell. With a loud clang of a heavy key, the inner door of the cell was opened, and Musashi was pushed into the cell.

The floor and walls were lined with wood, and Musashi sat down on the floor and closed his eyes against the semidarkness to collect his thoughts. When he opened his eyes, he was again struck with a feeling of utter despair, the likes of which he had never experienced before. As he looked around the dim cell, which smelled of urine, sweat, blood, vomit, and every kind of unpleasantness, he estimated that it was the size of about an eight-*tatami* mat room (or twelve by twelve feet).

In the corner on the floor was a rectangular hole, about one foot square and two feet deep, which was the all-purpose toilet. There was, of course, no hand or face washing facility. Three sides of the cell interior were solid walls, but the wall facing the hallway was constructed of wooden lattice that was about seven inches thick. The spacing of the lattice was about two inches so that no hands or feet could reach through. At the bottom of the wooden lattice was a small opening for food to be passed through. The door to the hallway, also made of wooden lattice, was about two feet by a foot and a half, so that one had to crawl to get in or out. A single five-watt bulb hung from the ceiling, but the amount of light it gave was less than what a candle would have provided. A ventilation opening atop one wall seemed merely cosmetic; no fresh air from the outside circulated through.

As Musashi looked around, he felt as if he was in a warehouse or storage shed that had not been occupied for several years. As his eyes slowly adjusted to the available light in the cell, he realized there was something in the corner of the cell, and it was moving. "It" actually turned out to be six emaciated, pale, and nearly dead human beings. The cell contained seven prisoners in all, counting Musashi. As he looked at his bloodless and listless cellmates who appeared to be no more than skin and bones, Musashi knew he was only one step on this side of hell. He knew now that no one could help him; no one even knew where he was. Unspeakable despair, loneliness, and helplessness penetrated the very depth of his soul.

For the next three days, as he breathed the stifling air, thick with dust, he was left alone with his six companions. He soon found out they were officers of the Communist Eighth Route Army and one Soviet soldier. All had been arrested on suspicion of spying. He also found out that quite a few others had been brought to this same cell in the recent past. Where they were now, one could only fearfully guess.

There were a total of three cells in the underground prison similar to this one. It was said that many died in these cells after being brought back from periodic questioning. The average period of interrogations was estimated to be about one month long, and after that, the questions seemed to cease. Then there was likely to be a summons one evening, and when that came, it was said that the prisoner was taken outside to be executed by gunfire.

The total period of confinement here could last three to four months, and when one of Musashi's fellow inmates told him this, he felt everything go dark in front of his eyes. He held his head in his hands and crumpled face-first to the floor. In utter despair, he lost all physical and psychological will to fight back.

It's the end for me! But how can I be so weak? I've got to fight on! I have been prone to say a lot of brave things every day,

*so how can I be so weak? But my breast is about to tear open!
There is no hope for me! I hurt … it's painful! I can't breathe!
But what about the repatriation of my fellow countrymen?
How can I let them down? But I won't be able to withstand the
tortures that await me! It's better that I not fight so that I can
die as quickly as possible! Why am I so cowardly? Am I not
a third-degree black belt in judo? Didn't some say about me
in the past, "You can try to kill Musashi, but he won't die"?
—Hey, Musashi … you're unsightly, you're a coward, you have
no guts, you're a sissy with no mettle, you are a disgrace …
you really want to keep living that much?* It was as if someone
were whispering into his ears!

Normally not a religious man, Musashi began to call on
Buddha for help. Then he called on God, on Jesus Christ, and
on all the various gods he knew. Then, reflecting that he was
in China, he called on Confucius and on all the great men and
women of the past, including Sun Yat-sen. He shouted loudly
in his heart, and his tears flowed as he cried like a baby. He
hoped beyond hope that he would suddenly wake up from
this bad dream. He prayed the Buddhist sutra, *"Nam myo ho
ren ge kyo."* For what seemed a very long time, he continued
alternately praying, weeping, and crying out within his heart,
feeling utterly sorry for himself, then shaming himself for being
such a miserable coward.

Nonstop Torture

Then, after a few days, the torture began. He was taken
upstairs to a room where two men (the interrogators were
always in civilian clothing) began alternately questioning him
and beating him, initially with their hands, then later with a
belt and a switch. Sometimes they put a burning cigarette to
the most tender parts of his body. They asked why he was
spying and for whom. When he replied he was not a spy,
they beat him again and again until he lost consciousness. He

would later wake up in his cell, pain searing every part of his body. This, with terrible variations, became the daily routine for Masamichi Musashi.

In the beginning, they slapped him with their open hands or their fists or kicked him. However, after a few sessions, it appeared that their hands began to hurt, so they resorted to using a belt. They whipped him with the belt, beginning from just below the chin, then to his chest, then his stomach, then his back. At first the pain was unbearable, then the pain became heat, and everything began feeling hot. After multiple slashes, his chest and back began to swell and become puffy. Then, when the skin broke, a reddish-black blood would seep out and cover his entire body. When that happened, recalled Musashi, he no longer felt as if his body belonged to him, and it seemed that the pain was less unbearable than before. Then, when he fell on the mat that had been placed under him during the torture, his nerves would go into total paralysis, completely unable to move.

While Musashi screamed in pain within his heart, he managed to keep silent and not show his weakness externally. He courageously held back his screams and pleas, and his torturers would say, sneeringly, "Wuzang, you're quite a man. We are impressed." But he knew he could not hang on much longer; his body would not be able to take much more. He felt as if the bones in his body would soon shatter like glass. In fact, he knew he was already only skin and bones. He used to weigh a robust 165 pounds, but he felt as if he now weighed no more than a hundred pounds.

A Variety of Tortures

One form of torture that the interrogators seemed to favor, since it did not require much physical effort on their part, was the cigarette torture. The interrogator would light a cigarette and take several strong puffs to make sure it was well lit, then rub or daub it on Musashi's chest or feet. The heat at contact would be over 1,300 degrees Fahrenheit. The sensation was more painful than hot. The worst part of that torture was that Musashi's body stamina would decline significantly so that a feeling of utter weakness would overcome him. At no time was Musashi allowed to wash his body, much less treat his wounds with medication. The burns and wounds that resulted from the cigarettes and the beatings would develop a whitish-yellowish pus oozing from red, raw skin, and the pus remained even after the skin had peeled off. Then maggots would collect around the wound so that the healing would take forever. Suppurations were most significant on his shins and calves and on the insteps of his feet. Even the interrogators, it seemed, could not stand the sight of the wounds and eventually ceased using the cigarette torture.

A horrific and most unpleasant ordeal was the water torture. A large aluminum teakettle would be used for that particular torture. Musashi was stripped down to only his underwear, and his arms and legs were tied down so he was unable to move. The interrogators would raise the full teakettle and put the spout into Musashi's mouth, and pour the contents into his mouth. In the beginning, since he was never given enough water to quench his thirst, Musashi greedily drank the water until his stomach was full. "*Xie xie*! Thank you very much! *Frou le* (that is plenty)!" The gurgling protest by Musashi did no good, and then the terrible part would begin.

As he clenched his teeth and resisted taking in the water, his three interrogators would pry open his mouth. It was quite a struggle for the interrogators to force open his mouth, but in the end they would succeed in opening it by holding his nose shut tight so that he was unable to breathe. All too soon, Musashi's mouth would open, and the water would pour in. Soon he felt bloated with water, and it felt as if water was seeping out of every orifice and pore of his body. Because of the involved cleanup that followed the water torture, Musashi was made to endure it only about three times, but the terrible memory of those times would stay with him forever. Following the water torture, Musashi could only lie in his underground cell, unable to rest, slipping in and out of consciousness, his body utterly exhausted from the ordeal. He panted like a dog, with his tongue hanging out, and his ceaseless low moaning could be heard all night long by his sympathetic but helpless cellmates.

But the most fearsome torture was conducted with electricity. The interrogators must have had the easiest time with this torture, since they could comfortably sit and administer pain simply by turning a knob. A wooden box with two cables attached, each about nine feet long, was all that was needed to torment the victim. Of all the varieties of torture apparatus, Musashi felt that this had the greatest potential to end his life.

In preparation for the torture, he would be stripped down to his underpants, and the cables were bound to each of his wrists or ankles. His free limbs were also tightly bound by hemp cords to make sure he had no freedom of movement at all. Then the interrogator rotated the handle attached to the battery box, and electricity surged through Musashi's body. Often they doused him with water to intensify the shock and discomfort. As much as Musashi was able to remember, he fainted more than ten times; at least three times he was actually "dead" since his heart stopped. When he was "dead," the interrogators would carry him to his underground cell and would lay him on the floor, covering him with straw mats. Had he not come around in time, they would have carried him off to the place for disposing of dead bodies.

This was the one torture where Musashi could not suppress his screams. Every time the handle was cranked, a cry came out of his mouth, from the depth of his being, as the electric current attacked not only his physical body but his entire nervous system. An indescribable sensation of "da-da-da-da-da" coursed through his body, a frightening feeling that he could neither describe in words nor ever erase from memory.

His entire body felt as if it were crumbling, as if all his bones had turned to cotton. He could almost sense the sparks jumping out of his eyes, and his consciousness was indistinct, as if he were floating through air. When he regained full consciousness, he usually found himself back in his underground cell, unable to remember how he got back there.

Losing Hope

As his blurred eyes cleared, he found his evening meal had been placed next to his thin pillow. Inside a large aluminum bowl was a small portion of *koryan* (sorghum), cooked without the husk removed, a meal that even a horse would be reluctant to eat. There were also two pieces of pickled Chinese radish. The meal was completed with water in an aluminum can slightly bigger than a coffee cup, barely half filled. The same meal was always repeated, never with any alteration.

With each torture session, with the passage of each day, Musashi feared for his life. He felt that his mind was becoming dull. He was losing all his senses. His tongue seemed to merely be dangling, rendering him unable to speak intelligibly. Because of the lack of water, he urinated very little. His stool was like that of a horse and barely had any smell due to his diet of *koryan* and pickled radishes. His body dwindled away to mere skin and bones. He began to lose hope. He stopped caring whether he survived.

But then, he would sometimes remember a delicious meal he had had in the past, or a wonderful musical he had seen at the Nichigeki Theater in Sukiyabashi in Tokyo. These occasional memories would jolt him back to reality and rekindle in him the need and desire to live. He was not even married yet; how utterly regrettable that he had never had the joy of living with someone he loved. And how about his work in repatriating the Japanese from Manchuria? Were not millions in Japan counting on him to succeed so that they could once again reunite with cherished relatives and friends abandoned in Manchuria? Were not Maruyama and Shinpo counting on him to succeed? Did he have the right to give up when so many depended on him?

Heeding His Cellmates' Advice

It may have been his cellmates who, in the end, saved his life. Seeing him so often dragged back to his cell either completely unconscious or utterly beaten and obviously unaware of his situation, they said to him, "Wuzang, you are too straightforward. You need to become craftier. When tortured, you need to shout at the top of your lungs that it hurts, that it's painful, then make as much noise as possible and make a scene."

"Of course, I am a human being, and like everyone else, I'd like to scream out that it hurts. I am in pain, but I have been holding it inside of me," he replied. But he thought his cellmates might be right. Perhaps by screaming and diverting attention, he could make the ordeal more bearable, even more comfortable. Perhaps his torturers would ease up on the amount of pain they inflicted.

When he was dragged up the next time for his interrogation session, he decided to resist no more. As his wrists and ankles were bound up with electric cables, and at the instant the interrogator grasped the manual handle, Musashi yelled as loud as he could and exhibited a completely uncharacteristic scene of pain and agony. In fact, the torture had not even begun, but seeing that their victim was acting so completely different this time, the interrogators must have thought that the man before them did not have much longer to live. From then on, the interrogations and torture came to an almost complete stop. Musashi was convinced that, had he acted in such an exaggerated manner from the beginning, the interrogators would have ignored his screams and tortured him until he was dead. In later years, he often thought of his cellmates with gratitude, fondness, and sympathy. They had probably all ascended to heaven shortly after his encounter with them, and he prayed for their happiness in the next world.

Years later, Musashi also often thought about all the torture he had endured—by beatings, cigarette burns, water, and electricity—and a chill always ran through him at those thoughts. He had difficulty talking about his ordeal to others, but he finally gave a detailed account in his autobiographical book *The Dawning of Asia: Crossing the Lines of Death*, published in 2000, more than fifty years after he had endured the horrendous experience.

Has the End Finally Arrived?

In the early evening of October 5, 1946, more than seven weeks after his arrest as a spy by the Nationalist army, he heard the footsteps of several people in the hallway coming toward his cell. When the footsteps stopped, one of them called out, "*Wuzang Zhengdao* (Masamichi Musashi)!"

Musashi thought the time had finally arrived for his execution. The soldier who yelled out his name asked if he had any personal belongings, so Musashi replied, "*Mei you* (no, I don't have any)."

"*Wai bian zou* (step outside)!" said the same soldier, and Musashi resolved to face the end calmly. As the door was opened with two loud clangs, he looked toward his cellmates (there were then three), and they silently exchanged glances of understanding with their eyes. Without a word, the three and Musashi nodded and exchanged a last wordless farewell. Then he stepped through the latticed door and joined the five guards who were awaiting him.

Musashi failed in his attempt to appear brave. As he reflected that he would never return to this cell and that this was the end, his entire body suddenly became as soft as an octopus, and he had difficulty standing up. Two of the guards supported him and kept him from falling down. As they began walking down the hallway, Musashi was once again able to feel the ground, and he indicated that he could walk unassisted. The walk seemed much longer than when he first arrived at the underground prison.

In a room that Musashi vaguely recalled, he was given some fresh underwear and the top and bottom of a civilian uniform by one of the guards. He was also given a pair of shoes in exchange for the slippers he had worn in prison. *When one is executed*, mused Musashi sadly, *the sentence must be carried out wearing clean clothing.*

Musashi was later unable to recollect step by step all that happened that day. His mind and body were not under his control. He simply did whatever the guards told him to do; his head, his body, and his spirit were all a complete white. He was led up the stairs, and he could see from the windows that it was dusk. Had it been the middle of the day, he would probably have been barely able to open his eyes to the glare. While he was in his underground cell, he had sometimes heard five or six simultaneous gunshots, followed by a single gunshot about a second later and then complete silence.

I suppose I will be executed on the rooftop, thought Musashi as he was led up the stairs by the guards. *It will probably be troublesome for them to carry my corpse down the stairs*, he thought as the guards indicated they only had a few more steps to climb. He expected at any time to be met by a clergyman, after which the execution would be carried out. He saw the skies darken as the bright red sun began setting, and his worry turned to the aiming accuracy of his executioners. If they could not see well, and if they missed their mark and only wounded him, he might not be able to die immediately but might lie wounded in agony, awaiting death. With each step, Musashi worried about various things with trepidation and panic. Suddenly they stopped outside an office door, and one of the guards directed Musashi to enter.

Reprieve!

As soon as he entered the room, he experienced the surprise of his life and wondered whether he was dreaming. Standing to greet him was Colonel Liu, the Nationalist officer who was in charge of affairs related to Japanese in Manchuria, to whom Musashi had entrusted his safety. Standing next to Colonel Liu was a Colonel Mou, whom Musashi later learned was the commander of the Northeast Operations Intelligence Command. Both were wearing their dignified Nationalist army uniforms.

Speaking in Chinese, Colonel Liu said, "*Ayaa, Wuzang, xian sheng* (Dr. Musashi)! *Dui buqi, dui buqi* (forgive us, forgive us)!" Then, both took Musashi's hands warmly and with humility, bowed their heads, and again repeated, "*Dui buqi, dui buqi!*" as they expressed sincere apology.

From the time of his arrest, Musashi had been harboring anger, malice, and hatred against those who, mistaking him for a spy, had tortured and tormented him, robbing him of all dignity. But at this moment, he felt utter happiness and relief. It was as if he had gone to hell and met Buddha himself. He felt as if he had actually committed a great crime and had been sentenced to death, and yet he had suddenly been found innocent, and the death penalty had been lifted. It was if all his sufferings until now were blown away, as if everything was forgotten and only a feeling of gratitude remained in Musashi's heart. "*Xie xie! Xie xie!*" cried Musashi to the two officers over and over again. He could not hold back the tears of joy that streamed from his eyes. For reassurance, he held on to the two colonels' hands tightly and could not let go for quite some time. Truly, Masamichi Musashi had come back to life after he had been dead. The word "miracle," thought Musashi, had been invented just for an occasion such as this!

After some time, Colonel Mou opened the door and gently led him outside, where an official car was waiting. The air outside was, Musashi still remembers, the most delicious he had ever breathed. They headed to the residence of Colonel Liu, where Musashi was allowed to bathe for the first time in months, have a delicious feast, and rest in a bed of soft mattresses, pillows, and blankets.

Many years later, every time Musashi reflected on his captivity, torture, and reprieve, he could not hold back the tears of gratitude for his salvation. Even today, he thinks he is a most fortunate human being, someone who was given a second chance to return to the paradise of this world. He continues to humbly give thanks to Buddha and to all the divinities who allowed him to live.

Going Home for Good at Last

As soon as he regained enough strength, he went back to the building on Kasuga Avenue that had been his repatriation headquarters. Hoping to find some of the young Japanese men who had been assisting him before his arrest, he was disappointed to find no one there. He asked Colonel Liu if he knew the whereabouts of the young man, Takahashi, who was arrested at the same time with Musashi, but Colonel Liu was unable to tell him anything. Heartbroken but determined to learn Takahashi's whereabouts, as well as to continue his work in the repatriation effort, Musashi informed Colonel Liu that he intended to work alone.

The colonel was straightforward and blunt in his advice to Musashi. "Wuzang, what are you talking about? Almost all the Japanese in the various regions of Manchuria have already returned to Japan. Ships will soon cease to come to Huludao, and repatriation there will soon come to an end. You too had better return to Japan as soon as you can." By then, it was a fact that over a million Japanese had returned to Japan from Koroto. Japanese who still remained in Manchuria were those who had been interned for various reasons, including suspected war crimes, as well as those Japanese who lived in regions still under Soviet control.

Colonel Liu continued, this time using an admonishing tone, obviously not expecting any rebuttal from Musashi. "I am going to assign an escort officer to you, Major Tian Bao Min. You must depart as early as tomorrow for Huludao."

When Musashi reflected back to that conversation much later after he had safely returned to Japan, he realized that Colonel Liu had acted in a stern but kindhearted manner and had extended an extraordinary consideration to Musashi. Colonel Liu was probably fully aware that by this time, the standoff between the Nationalist army and the Communist Eighth Route Army was at its height, and the situation in Manchuria could explode at any time. The Nationalist army was in control of the major cities of Manchuria; on the other hand, the Eighth Route Army was in control of the areas surrounding the major cities as well as most of the agricultural regions of Manchuria.

(Two years later, the Communist Eighth Route Army, under the command of Lin Biao, surrounded Shenyang, and the Nationalist army under Chiang Kai-shek fled from Shenyang Airport without putting up a fight. The common wisdom on both sides of the conflict was that "If you lose Shenyang, you lose Manchuria; if you lose Manchuria, you lose China." That saying proved true as the Nationalists fled to Taiwan in 1949, and Mao Zedong's Communists eventually took complete control of mainland China.)

Musashi wisely took the advice of Colonel Liu. Escorted by Major Tian Bao Min, he traveled by train from Shenyang to the Port of Koroto. On October 26, 1946, he secured passage on the last repatriation ship from Koroto returning to Japan. As Musashi watched the receding land of Manchuria from the deck of his ship, he was filled with many emotions. Closing his eyes and clasping his hands together, he silently gave thanks for his safe deliverance from almost certain death in that dark dungeon in Shenyang. "Good-bye, Manchuria. Good-bye, Anshan, my second home." The great continent slowly receded as Musashi felt the warm tears of sorrow slowly flowing down his cheeks.

More than six months since departing Japan on the first repatriation ship bound for Koroto, Musashi returned to the Port of Sasebo (in Nagasaki Prefecture) on November 1, 1946, on the last ship carrying Japanese repatriates from Koroto.[1]

(*Author's note: All quotes in this chapter were excerpted and translated by the author from Masamichi Musashi's book* The Dawning of Asia: Crossing the Lines of Death, *pages 141–181.*)

Chapter 23

A Speech to Rouse the Nation

Celebrating Musashi's Return

"Musashi-san, thank you for all you have done." Both Shinpo and Maruyama were elated to see their comrade again on November 3 when Musashi got off the train at Tokyo Station on the last leg of his return journey from Manchuria, and the two bowed deeply in gratitude to their young companion. That evening, the three celebrated at the Kugayama headquarters with a feast in honor of Musashi's return and heard all the details of the horrendous ordeal he had endured. Maruyama and Shinpo could do nothing but repeatedly thank their young companion as they shed tears of joy for his safe return and tears of sympathy for all that he endured.

"By the way, what is the latest news on your families?" asked Musashi as the evening was winding down. "They have not been repatriated yet," said Shinpo. It was nine long months ago when the three bade them farewell in Dalian after entrusting them to the care of Bishop Lane and the Catholic Church there. Dalian was presently under the firm control of the Soviet army. The family Shinpo left behind consisted of a total of four: his wife, Takeko; his two young sons (Takaaki and Nariaki); and his wife's brother, Kunihisa Musashi (no relation to Masamichi

Musashi). Maruyama's family consisted of six: his wife, Mary, his four sons (Robert, Joseph, Paul, and Xavier) along with Toki, Mary's young relative from Yamaguchi Prefecture who had accompanied the family to Manchuria. Not one word had been heard from them since they parted in Dalian.

When Maruyama made the nationwide radio broadcast from the Central Broadcasting Station in Tokyo on April 17 reporting to the Japanese nation and to the world for the first time the grave situation in Manchuria under Soviet occupation, there were many in Manchuria who secretly possessed radios (most had been kept hidden in cellars or under floorboards), and in defiance of grave consequences if they were found out, they constantly listened to broadcasts coming from Japan. Thus, almost all Japanese in Manchuria were soon aware that three men had escaped Soviet clutches and were now working desperately to bring them all home. Shortly after the broadcast, word had reached the ears of the three men (from those who had already returned via Koroto) of a widespread rumor that the families of the three men had been left behind in Manchuria. Fortunately, the families had all changed their names so that no one in Dalian was aware of any Maruyama or Shinpo in their midst.

To no one in particular, Maruyama said, "Although we left our families in Dalian for their safety, we have surely caused them a great amount of worry, since even now we cannot predict when their repatriation will commence. However, when we consider the mission we set out to accomplish, and when we consider the gravity of the responsibility we had to shoulder, I think we did the right thing. If they had stayed in Anshan, they might have returned to Japan a long time ago via Koroto. However, considering our own situation, if our families had returned home safely already while many others remained in Manchuria, we would be feeling guilty. God must have decided that our families would be among the last to return home. I wager that, by the time our families are repatriated, the last of our countrymen, including the refugees, will have come home. God has made arrangements so that our families and the last of the refugees will share the same fate. We must accept the ordeal and fate that God has granted to us. Our families are bearing the same cross that we are carrying. Let us just keep doing all we can and accept the will of God." Shinpo and Musashi silently nodded in agreement to the comments of Maruyama, a non-Christian, who spoke then like a devout Christian.

"We must now bring about the repatriation of Japanese from those areas under Soviet control without delay," said Shinpo with a grave countenance after a few moments of silence. "We still have a lot of work to do."

"We'll begin anew tomorrow," said Musashi.

"No, you need to rest for some time and heal both physically and spiritually," said Maruyama.

"I cannot do that. Until both of your families return safely to Japan, we cannot declare that the goals of the plan we set out to fulfill have been completely accomplished," replied Musashi with a firm conviction.

Another Visit to the Prime Minister

On November 7, the three men paid a visit to the residence in Nagatacho of Prime Minister Shigeru Yoshida (who had been the foreign minister when Musashi left for Manchuria). Musashi gave him a full report on the current situation in Manchuria. He related how he had delivered Japanese government documents to the appropriate officials in Manchuria and assisted in organizing repatriation through the various Japanese associations. Then he related his horrific ordeal of confinement and torture upon being arrested as a suspected spy. The prime minister listened with sincerity and intensity to the vivid narration and said at the conclusion in a most serious tone, "I thank you for all that you did and had to endure."

The three then brought the prime minister up to date regarding all the work they had been doing as the Representatives to Petition for Saving Our Countrymen Living in Manchuria, including their countless visits to GHQ and the personal visit with General MacArthur in April. They informed him of the many assemblies they had participated in to appeal for repatriation and the countless meetings they had had with families who were still awaiting the return of their loved ones. They told Prime Minister Yoshida about the latest assembly held on October 11 at Hibiya Public Auditorium; a huge crowd had attended and seemed to have been deeply stirred. Finally, they appealed to the prime minister for his cooperation in a national effort to bring about the return of Japanese still in Dalian, Sakhalin, the Kuril Islands, and other Soviet-controlled regions; many of those Japanese, they reminded him, would probably not be able to endure another harsh winter under the cruel conditions of Soviet occupation.

Prime Minister Yoshida listened intently from beginning to end. Then he bluntly and honestly shared his opinions and hopes in his present role as the top Japanese government official under the complete supervision of GHQ. As he spoke about the things he hoped he would be able to do, sympathy welled up in Maruyama for this sincere man who the Japanese public often referred to as the "One Man," an autocrat. At that moment, he was certainly not acting like an autocrat; he was honestly informing the three men that his authority was completely checked and limited by the American occupation machinery. Yet Maruyama felt that Japan was fortunate that the man at the helm of the nation in these critical times was this blunt and honest man in front of them.

Maruyama related in his book *Why Was Koroto Opened*, that in the midst of their meeting with Yoshida, Minister of National Affairs Takao Saito quietly came in to see the prime minister. Saito took a chair just a little distance from them and sat down patiently, evidently waiting for the conversation to end so he could speak to the prime minister on some urgent matter. Realizing that it was rude to keep Minister Saito waiting too long, Maruyama quietly whispered aside to the prime minister, "Mr. Saito is waiting to see you, so I think we had better excuse ourselves."

The prime minister replied, "I can see Minister Saito at any time, so you need not be concerned. This conversation with you is also very important, and I want to hear more, so please continue without hesitation." So the conversation continued. Shortly thereafter, probably because Saito thought the conversation would continue much longer or because he had other things to do, he quietly stood up and left the room.

Maruyama thought back to his first meeting in London with the then Japanese ambassador to Great Britain, involving the incident of the ticket for the gallery of the British Parliament (see chapter 14). Maruyama concluded that this was a man who did not make distinctions based on rank or status. Prime Minister Yoshida was a man of clear conviction who treated everyone equally. Maruyama had great admiration for such a man.

A Rousing Assembly at Hibiya Park

As Maruyama and Shinpo reported to Prime Minister Yoshida during their meeting on November 7, a historically successful assembly had been held in Hibiya Public Auditorium on October 11 that drew the largest crowd to date of family members who still awaited the return from overseas of missing relatives as well as a large contingent of the press. While many similar assemblies had been held since the escape of the three men, this time the hall was filled beyond capacity.

At the conclusion of the assembly, those present signed a petition urging the earliest repatriation of Japanese still left behind in foreign countries, and it was submitted to GHQ. Additionally, petitions containing the same request were delivered to the various delegates of the major Allied Powers, including U.S. Delegate George Acheson, British Delegate Shaw, Soviet Delegate Terebianko, and Chinese Delegate Shang Zheng. A special note to each Allied Powers delegate was included in the petition, requesting the earliest return to Japan of those Japanese military and civilian personnel who had been forcibly transported to the Soviet Union.

The assembly was sponsored by the *Asahi* newspaper, and the Hibiya Public Auditorium began filling beyond capacity well before the start time of 1:00 PM. Maruyama delivered the speech to the crowd. Because the speech was probably as significant as the NHK radio broadcast that Maruyama had made in April, especially in light of the petitions to be submitted to the Allied Powers delegates following the speech, key passages are excerpted as follows:

> Today, as we welcome so many earnest people who have come to pack this Hibiya Public Auditorium, we reflect on the miserable conditions of our countrymen who are still stranded in foreign lands. The purpose of this assembly is to establish some quick method for their rescue, and I feel that this meeting has a historic significance and an enormously meaningful purpose. Today, as the second winter since the war ended is about to descend, if only those Japanese who have been stranded in faraway lands across the seas knew how so many of you have come together this day to this assembly with overflowing sincerity, I know not how gladdened they would be....
>
> At the end of the war, the Japanese government once made an announcement regarding the prospects of repatriating all the Japanese, but according to that announcement, it was to take four years to return all the Japanese. That is to say, they declared that it would take until 1949 to complete the project. Yet, in a period of just one year and two months, 65 percent or four

million five hundred thousand Japanese (who had been stranded overseas, including in Manchuria) have been able to return and set foot again on their beloved land. We are indebted to the magnanimous consideration of the Allied Powers Headquarters for this progress, and we can hardly find the words to express our sincere gratitude. However, at the same time, there are still 2.5 million countrymen on the other side of the ocean who are stranded as I speak … hoping beyond hope to return home before one more day goes by.…

Based on our experience engaged in our activities for the past eight months, we feel there will be no resolution in solving the problem of rescuing the Japanese who are still living overseas and returning them to Japan unless we and you and all the citizens of Japan stand up and combine forces. Today, most people are saying, "The present government of Japan has no power, and it is useless." We too, as the Representatives to Petition for Saving Our Countrymen Living in Manchuria, have appealed since March to relevant agencies in the government and have met with many key personnel in government and have discussed matters with them. Unfortunately, however, on the issue of repatriating our countrymen stranded overseas, the government has absolutely no power.

Prime Minister Yoshida has declared in our National Parliament that, "In regards to the repatriation problem, the government has no power. All we can do is request the help of GHQ." I believe that Mr. Yoshida is simply making an honest declaration. As you probably know, on October 25 of last year, GHQ ordered the overall cessation of Japan's foreign relations functions and ordered the handover of all foreign relations agencies so that Japan has no ability to conduct any foreign diplomacy. To say that the government has no power is proof that the nation of Japan has changed that much. The right of independence of the Japanese government is now in the hands of the Supreme Commander for Allied Powers, so that it is not an exaggeration to say that today's Japanese government is, to put it bluntly, no more than one of the administrative agencies subordinate to GHQ. But I would like to say to all of you that, although we say that our government has no power, we are forbidden to use that as an excuse to abandon the problem of repatriating our countrymen from overseas. Can we simply say things such as "Since our government is powerless, no matter what we, the people of the nation, do, it is a waste of time. So let's just let happen whatever happens" and simply watch our wretched countrymen die? I, for one, do not want to be in the presence of even one person who whines with such a perverted way of thinking....

Just the other day, on September 26, there was a news report from the Supreme Headquarters that negotiation will soon open between the Soviet delegate in Tokyo, Lieutenant General Terebianko, and GHQ, on the matter of repatriating Japanese presently interned in Soviet territories. Our interest has been immensely aroused by this good news, and we are praying for the negotiation's success. From that point of view, I believe that there is a need to aggressively petition both GHQ and the Soviet representatives to make repatriation a reality as soon as possible.

Recently, newspapers are reporting on the situation regarding the Far East War Crimes Tribunal taking place in Ichigayamitsuke. I had an opportunity to go to observe the tribunal ... I am sure that some of you have also gone to observe the trial. They have remodeled the building of the former Department of the Army and have set up a beautiful courtroom where judges from eleven nations sit in a row at the front. Behind them are the flags of eleven nations, and right under the flags are the prosecutors and the various attorneys facing them, and the stenographer and interpreters sit at desks between them. The twenty-eight war crime defendants, accompanied by military policemen, sit facing the judges. Surrounding all of this is the gallery for observers.

I managed to get a seat in the gallery at the very front so that I was able to get a very close look at the countenance and attitude of all twenty-eight defendants, starting with former Prime Minister Tojo. As I looked into the faces of the defendants, I had the following thought: Were these, after all, the highest-ranking leaders of Japan during the war? When you take away each one's rank and scrape away his authority and see him as simply just another naked individual, each seems to me a mere powerless, incompetent being. As I continued to reflect on this and stared into the faces of the defendants, my heart unconsciously turned in the direction of our countrymen still left behind in Manchuria.

Notwithstanding the fact that the crimes of those defendants are fairly obvious, they are still judged by the judicial method of civilized nations; not only were they assigned Japanese attorneys to defend them, they were also assigned American defense attorneys. They were granted plenty of opportunities to present their assertions to their advantage so that they are being given an extremely fair trial. When they go to sleep at night in the prison at Sugamo, they can wrap themselves in warm blankets so as to not catch a cold, and they are even eating foods that are considerably more tasty and nutritious than what we are able to eat.

Contrasted to this, those many good Japanese who are still left in Manchuria, particularly those babies and innocent children who do not even know the meaning of war—what about them? In spite of the fact that war has come to an end and peace has reigned for over a year now, they are still frightened by the sound of gunfire and are victimized by robbery and pillaging so that they are suffering torment that is many times worse than that which the war crime defendants are undergoing. And they are not given any opportunity whatsoever to say a word in defense of their lives or freedom. They simply become refugees and quietly die away due to hunger, cold, and sickness. When one compares the plight of those war crime defendants in Tokyo with that of the unfortunate countrymen who saw the end of the war arrive while they were living in Manchuria, there is a gap of a thousand miles! Can there be a greater contradiction in this world than that? The old saying of a rock floating while the leaves of a tree sink—truly, that proverb must have been meant for a contradiction such as this....

As I looked upon the faces of the twenty-eight defendants at the Far East Trials, one more thing flashed significantly in my mind. That is, all throughout the war, these war crimes defendants commanded the people of Japan to "Make possible the things that are impossible." And the people of Japan, regardless of whether they agreed or not, blindly obeyed that command and cooperated in the war efforts. Yet, while war has come to an end, and while the world is now supposed to be at peace, 2.5 million Japanese whose safety is unknown are still stranded on the other side of the ocean, with the vast majority of them on the verge of death. This, then, is a most grave tragedy for the nation of Japan herself and is many times worse than the problems we face here, such as the shortage of food. To quickly solve this tragic situation and return all our countrymen to their native land, to give each and every one of our citizens the chance to help in the construction of a new Japan whose objective is a peaceful and democratic nation—this, after all, is the responsibility of all in the Japanese government and is likewise the responsibility of each Japanese citizen. This is the time for our nation to come together as one and to exert efforts that exceed by many times the efforts we exerted during the war, for the sake of rescuing our countrymen overseas, for truly, this is our opportunity to "make possible the things that are impossible."...

I personally believe that the twenty-eight war crimes defendants ... should stand before the great courtroom of the international tribunal and speak with sincerity and repent their transgressions of the past, confess everything, and apologize. They should then make an appeal, while they are still standing on the floor of the court, to the heads of state of the United States, England, the Soviet Union, and China, who are party to the Allied Powers, and beg for the earliest return of those Japanese still left behind in foreign countries, since those Japanese are truly the ones who are suffering a great tragedy that goes against justice and humanity. That appeal by the defendants should be made with tears of blood flowing.

However, like a bird in a cage, they are merely cowering. They have not said one word about rescuing the multitude of Japanese still suffering such tragedy, which merely demonstrates that they are insincere toward the people of Japan and to those countrymen overseas. All we can conclude is that they have completely abandoned their responsibilities. As I watched the faces of the war crime defendants ... it was all I could do to hold back the angry frustration that welled up from the bottom of my soul....

I want to tell all of you that, while Japanese from Manchuria are being repatriated at this moment from one place—that is Koroto on the Bay of Liaodong— that one place will freeze over once December arrives, and this is something that worries us greatly. According to the latest information we have, however, GHQ has increased the number of repatriation ships and is accelerating the rate of repatriation. They have revised their planning to complete the repatriation before the middle of December when the waters of Koroto are expected to freeze. Additionally, GHQ announced that one ice-breaking ship will be sent over to help.

I am grateful to GHQ's kindness from the very bottom of my heart, but at the same time, we need to ask even more from GHQ. We must ask GHQ to open up ports for picking up repatriates even beyond Koroto, and expand to Dalian, Yingkou, Andong, as well as Qingjin in Korea, and without fail have all repatriation completed before the ports freeze up.... As of now, not one person of the 300,000 of our countrymen from Dalian, Port Arthur, and surrounding areas has been repatriated, so if the opening of the port at Dalian cannot be agreed to for some reason, we must call upon GHQ to make arrangements to conduct repatriation from other appropriate places such as from nearby Shahekou, Jinzhou, or even Chufangshen.

If repatriation is postponed so that the Japanese stranded in Dalian, northern Korea, Chishima (the Kurils), and Karafuto (Sakhalin) are made to live through a second winter, the expectation that the number of victims who will die as a result is clearer than seeing light with the break of day. If that happens, it is my belief that historians in later times will record this miserable plight of the Japanese left behind in

foreign lands as the greatest tragedy to befall a people
in the history of mankind....

Here, to illustrate the importance of even a single person
taking action, Maruyama told the story about the young mother
who, during the American Civil War, directly petitioned
President Abraham Lincoln to allow her court-martialed husband
to see his infant son before his execution. (See chapter 4.)

Parliament has just established a new constitution which
is the fundamental basis for all laws for the nation of
Japan. The underlying reason for adopting the new
Constitution is to establish a democratic nation that
protects the dignity of each and every individual, with
justice and humanity as the undergirding of a peaceful
culture. When we think about the ideology in establishing
this new nation of ours, in this present time when war
has ended and peace has reigned for one year and two
months, I must ask the following questions: Where is the
peace, where is the culture, where is the justice, where
is the humanity, and where is the democratic nation
that assures the dignity of each individual in the nation
if we are not even able to rescue the 2.5 million of our
fellow countrymen still left behind in faraway lands on
the other side of the ocean? In just the space of time I
have been speaking to you, which is only a little over
an hour, several tens of Japanese have died. The time
has come when we must express sincerity in our fervent
desire to bring home immediately all the Japanese who
have been left behind in foreign lands, and I urge that
we appeal together to GHQ to resolve this issue at the
earliest time.... And [I ask] that each of you help us in
our efforts. I bid you farewell.[1]

The rousing applause at the conclusion of the speech seemed
as though it would never end.

Chapter 24

Reunited at Last!

Negotiations to Open Dalian for Repatriation

Documents dated as early as May 1946 indicate that negotiations had been conducted by the United States with the Soviet Union to allow repatriation of Japanese from Soviet-occupied territories in Manchuria. A May 11 secret message from the United States Army Forces Commanding General in China addressed to SCAP states, "For planning purposes only, negotiations are now underway to establish Repat[riation] Team at Dairen approximately 1 June with planned one thousand per day lift.… This is for information only and not for action until further notified. If negotiations succeed, can SCAJAP [the Shipping Control Authority for the Japanese Merchant Marines as established by the Allied Powers] shipping be made available?"[1] Another secret message from the CG (Commanding General) China a couple of weeks later, on May 28, discusses the estimated number of Japanese in Manchuria (1.3 million) and concludes that "Negotiations for use of Darien [Dalian] as a port for repatriation are being taken up on a higher level" and "No definite information available at this time."[2] At this juncture, no resolution had been reached in the negotiations; in fact, resolution was not officially reached until December.

A secret message from SCAP dated December 19, 1946, regarding "repatriation from Soviet and Soviet-controlled areas" reported that "on 19 December, agreement was reached between SCAP and General Derevyanko [Terebianko], member of the Allied Council of Japan from the USSR, under which Japanese now in Soviet and Soviet-controlled areas will be returned to Japan," along with an agreement that about ten thousand "Koreans in Japan who were born in Korea north of 38 degrees north latitude" would be repatriated to Korea. The message stated that the agreement was reached as a result of resumption of negotiations on September 26, 1946. Under the agreement, Japanese POWs as well as Japanese civilians "will be returned at the rate of fifty thousand per month, the maximum rate desired by the Soviet side. SCAP had offered to increase the rate to as much as 360,000 per month." The message went on to name the ports to which the Soviets would deliver the Japanese for repatriation, including Dalian. Finally, the message reported that, under an interim agreement of November 26, a total of 16,865 Japanese had already been repatriated from Dalian and other ports in Soviet-controlled areas, including Siberia. That number included 6,239 Japanese military personnel.[3]

The Soviets Finally Agree to Open Dalian

Maruyama, Shinpo, and Musashi were informed by GHQ about the progress that had been made between the Soviet Union and GHQ as early as the beginning of December. At long last, repatriation of Japanese, both military and civilians, from Karafuto (Sakhalin), the Kuril Islands, Dalian, northern Korea, and Siberia was to become a reality. While the decision was long overdue, the three men, along with the entire population of Japan, were overjoyed at the news. Repatriation from Koroto had commenced in May; seven months later, repatriation from Dalian and other Soviet-controlled ports was now about to commence. Their work since escaping from Manchuria almost a year ago had been directed ultimately toward this final goal.

The three wasted no time in calling on the various Japanese government agencies, including the Foreign Ministry, Ministry of Health and Welfare, Repatriation Relief Agency, and other bureaucratic organizations to request that all necessary measures be taken to welcome the returning Japanese who had had to wait so long to come home.

Although the United States and the Soviet Union officially reached the agreement to open up the Soviet-controlled port of Dalian in Manchuria effective as of December 19, 1946, repatriation for some commenced from December 3.[4] Maruyama, Shinpo, and Musashi took turns to await each ship that returned from Manchuria to the Port of Sasebo in Nagasaki Prefecture in the southernmost island of Kyushu. The first ships to bring home Japanese from Dalian were the *Eicho Maru* and the *Tatsuharu Maru,* which arrived at Sasebo on December 8, 1946, carrying over six thousand passengers. This first group of repatriates from Soviet-controlled areas of Manchuria included mostly Japanese who had fled to Dalian from deep within northern and eastern Manchuria; most were not longtime residents of Dalian.

Most had fled to the Dalian area as the Soviet army invaded Manchuria at war's end, only to become refugees and to be interned in various refugee camps. Many in the group had been subjected to violence and pillaging by soldiers of the Soviet army or personnel of the Communist Eighth Route Army at the outset of the Soviet invasion and had fled to Dalian without any concrete plans, other than to flee oppression, thinking that, because Dalian had such a major concentration of Japanese, they would readily find ships to take them back to Japan. Others had been ordered by the Japanese Imperial Army in the closing days of the war to make their way south to Dalian; after issuing the orders, the Imperial Army was nowhere to be found. After living as refugees for a year and a half, and after suffering almost every kind of hardship and cruelty that man and nature could inflict on them, somehow they managed to survive. Just about every person who disembarked at Sasebo on the first repatriation ships from Dalian was mere skin and bones, wearing only rags as clothing and possessing only what they carried on their backs.

A Pitiful Sight

Upon the arrival of the first ship carrying repatriates from Dalian, Maruyama and Musashi were joined at the Port of Sasebo by Colonel Howell, the director of G-3's repatriation affairs section at GHQ. As the ship approached the wharf, they could see the refugees on the deck staring wide-eyed toward the pier, many looking to see if someone they knew might be on the dock waiting for them. Musashi and Maruyama stood at each side of the American colonel as they prepared to welcome the pitiful-looking refugees. It was often hard to distinguish between males and females in their tattered clothing, with their hair uncut and unkempt. As they began descending the gangplank, several were staggering, barely able to walk, and some were supported by others as they descended.

As Colonel Howell looked on at the unfolding scene, he muttered, "How pitiful!" and the two Japanese at his sides saw him wiping away tears. Maruyama too could not hold back the choking sensation he felt in his throat, and tears flowed from his eyes. He noticed Musashi too had the same reaction. All that the three could do for some time was to stare in a trancelike state of dismay and disbelief at the flow of returnees coming down the gangplank, trying to hold back their tears of pity and sympathy. Each wondered if these people, mostly the sick and refugees, had not actually crawled out of hell itself.

When Maruyama finally found his voice, he turned to Musashi and said, "I'll bet that Colonel Howell has never seen a sight like this, even on the battlefield." Musashi could only nod in agreement.

The bedraggled returnees slowly walked away from the ship and were directed toward a large tent where they would be welcomed and where the necessary processing would be conducted. Some of the returnees recognized a loved one among the waiting crowd on the deck and began to cry and wave frantically. The waiting relatives too had tears in their eyes as they waved and called out the names of loved ones they had not seen in years. As Maruyama eavesdropped on the conversations between the waiting relatives who desperately searched for a familiar face as each returnee came down the gangplank, he heard them saying, "I don't care how shabby they look!" and "It's okay if they come back with nothing but their lives! As long as they come back, how happy I will be!" With each reunion, there was joy in the air.

Maruyama returned to Tokyo after welcoming home the first group of returnees, leaving Musashi to take care of all the chores that needed to be done at Sasebo. Back in Tokyo, he and Shinpo reviewed all the processing and welcoming arrangements that would be necessary when the refugees began streaming into Tokyo on trains from Sasebo before reaching their final destination, wherever that might be. After about two weeks, when he was satisfied that not much remained to be done in Tokyo, he again left everything in the capable hands of Shinpo and returned to Sasebo for a longer stay. He spent the first few days back in Sasebo visiting with the senior American military officers of the repatriation affairs section of GHQ, who had been stationed in Sasebo since the end of November, to discuss the administration of landing procedures to insure smooth and quick processing so that the repatriates could return to their homes as quickly as possible.

Postpone Return to Tokyo—Your Family May Be on Board

Each time Maruyama saw a family disembarking from a repatriation ship, a deep emotion coursed through him as he observed them reuniting with relatives. Family members waited anxiously in a designated area on the pier, and upon recognizing a relative descending the gangplank, they ran as close as they were allowed, to wave and cry out their names. He knew it would not be long before he would be the one rushing to greet his wife and sons.

Not a day had gone by since his return to Japan almost a year ago when he did not think longingly about Mary and his four boys and their helper Toki. Were they safe? Had they been able to obtain food? Were they well? Were they surviving the brutal cold of a Manchurian winter? Although he never once regretted leaving them behind under the care of Bishop Lane and the Maryknoll sisters and fathers in Dalian as that was the only right thing to do, that did not erase the pain and feeling of longing he constantly felt. He tried to comfort himself with the thought that there was no one to whom he could have entrusted everyone's safety and welfare more confidently than to his loving and capable wife. Yet he still worried constantly, since he had had absolutely no news about his family in almost a year. He often inquired of some of the recent repatriates from Dalian whether they knew anything about his and Shinpo's families, but since both families had changed their names, no one could shed any light. Maruyama had heard rumors that his family had changed their name to Mary's maiden name, Takeda. No one could guess which ship might bring them home or when.

As soon as ships from Dalian began to arrive with their precious cargoes, Maruyama discussed the possibility of the return of his family with the Sasebo Security Bureau supervisor he had come to know. The supervisor promised he would let Maruyama know at once when his or Shinpo's family were among the returnees. Each time a repatriation ship arrived at Sasebo from Dalian, the supervisor meticulously studied the passenger manifest to identify a likely family or group as that of Maruyama's or Shinpo's family.

On the morning of January 10, Maruyama had made plans to return by train to Tokyo to take care of some pressing business as well as to relieve Shinpo, who had stayed in Tokyo during most of the past several weeks. He notified the Repatriation Aid Bureau, with whom he had worked closely, that he intended to return to Tokyo. After packing his bags to depart, he had just sat down to breakfast in the room he had been assigned during his stay at Sasebo when the phone rang.

The call was from the supervisor of the Repatriation Aid Bureau's Sasebo Security Office. The caller said, "Maruyama-san, there is a group that fits the description of your family among the passengers on board the ship that arrived early this morning. At this time, of course, this is pure speculation based on going through the passenger manifest, and since I have not seen anyone, I cannot confirm it at all. But we have one of our staff members accompanying the quarantine officer on board the ship right now, and he will try to see the group as soon as he can and will inform us as soon as he has confirmation. Therefore, may I suggest that you postpone your departure to Tokyo until tomorrow?"

Shinpo's Family Not on Board

Trying to keep his dancing heart under control and sound calm, Maruyama thanked the supervisor and said he would postpone his travel and await further news by phone. He had not seen or heard from his family since February 22, 1946, when he, along with Hachiro Shinpo and Masamichi Musashi, left the Maryknoll Church in Dalian as the priests and nuns sent them off with their prayers. In less than a half hour, the same caller rang him and said, "As I previously relayed to you, we are sure that they are your family. They will be disembarking in a very short time, so please go right away to the designated waiting area along the dock for those welcoming returnees."

Hastily, before the supervisor could hang up, Maruyama asked, "Do you know anything about the family of Shinpo? Are they with my family also?"

"We searched with care for Mr. Shinpo's family as well, but it does not seem they are on this ship. Perhaps they will arrive on the next ship or perhaps a later one," he replied with obvious disappointment in his voice.

Maruyama thanked him profusely and rushed down toward the pier where the ship had docked earlier in the morning. As he ran, he thought, *At least with my family back, I will be able to ask them the status of Shinpo-san's family*, and with that thought he began to feel very cheerful. When he reached the waiting area near the ship's side, where a crowd of others also waited eagerly, he was relieved that disembarkation had not started yet. As he looked up at the deck of the ship, he saw many returnees peering down at them in wonderment, some waving frantically when they saw a loved one in the crowd waiting below. As Maruyama looked on at the many rejoicing relatives, some unashamedly crying with joy, he was unable to control his tears as he too was caught up in the emotion. As more and more repatriates disembarked from the ship and made their way toward the tent, it became difficult to look for his family because of the large crowd.

Maruyama noticed that the returnees on this ship were considerably healthier, better dressed, and less shabby than those who came on the first ships from Dalian. They were considerably better groomed and carried more personal belongings, and most were able to walk unassisted, unlike the earlier groups. As it had been planned, those in charge of repatriation on the Manchurian side had set up an order of departure so that those who were destitute, the refugees and the ill, were the first to be given passage home.

The repatriates lined up and entered the tent for processing, and each was checked and recorded by the disembarkation officials. One necessary step was a healthy dose of DDT sprayed on the returnees to disinfect them from typhoid, cholera, dysentery, and any other germs they might have been exposed to and could spread in Japan. When that was done, they were released to walk over to the crowd of loved ones who had been eagerly awaiting them. For the first time, returnees and waiting loved ones were able to reunite, embrace, and cry in each other's arms. It was a joyous scene that could not be witnessed without shedding tears of happiness and joy.

At Long Last—Reunited!

Maruyama continued to anxiously search for his family as the crowd grew larger. Afraid that he would miss his family if he stood among the crowd, he walked a little distance to a higher ground from the milling crowd and intently watched as returnees emerged from the processing tent. After a while the crowd began to thin somewhat, and Maruyama worried that there had been a mistake and that his family was not on board this ship, or that he might have somehow missed them.

Then, as it seemed the last of the repatriates were coming out of the tent, he spotted a group that looked like his family. They walked separately, one by one, separated by a few steps from each other. He first recognized his oldest son Kunitake (Robert), and the moment he saw him, Maruyama muttered to himself, "My goodness, he has gotten as thin as a stick!" Right behind Robert walked his third son, Kuniaki (Paul), followed by his youngest, Kuniteru (Xavier), and Kunihiko (Joseph), his second oldest. Bringing up the rear together were his wife Mariko (Mary) and the helper, Toki. Maruyama was shocked at how thin each had gotten. It was hard for him to believe that malnutrition could make everyone so skinny.

He immediately ran toward them and was about to shout their names and let them know how glad he was to see them, but for an instant, he became choked up and no sound would come out of his mouth. As soon as the children saw their father, they ran to him and embraced him simultaneously crying and yelling with joy. Then, Maruyama looked at his wife, who stood watching the joyous reunion with tears streaming down her face, and wordlessly he took her hands and held them tightly for a long time. Then he hugged her tightly, an act in public culturally uncharacteristic for a Japanese, but not a single soul seemed to mind.

Finally finding his voice, Maruyama said to Mary, "For all that time that I was not with you, you endured so much suffering so ably, and how well you brought the four children through the ordeal. Thank you for all you did. I am so grateful to you!" Maruyama renewed his grip on Mary's hand as they looked lovingly into each other's eyes, and both cried quietly but with sheer joy. Then, turning his attention to their helper, Toki, he expressed his sincere gratitude for all she had done to help his wife and children come through the long ordeal.

Feeling that he had regained his composure and could talk normally again, Maruyama began chatting happily with his children as they walked together toward the building of the Repatriation Assistance Bureau. At this moment, he felt like the luckiest man alive, without a care in the world.

On the way, Mary filled her husband in on the situation concerning the Shinpo family. "Mr. Shinpo's family is doing fine," she began. "I think they may be a little delayed in coming back. Someone secretly reported to the occupying authorities that Mrs. Shinpo's husband had escaped to Japan as a representative to rescue us and that he was involved in Japan in repatriation efforts. Their lives were in imminent danger, so I immediately went to see Bishop Raymond Lane and asked him to take Mrs. Shinpo and her entire family under the wing of the Maryknoll Catholic Church. Ever since then, they have been living in the church. And because the church is an American church, the Soviet army could not touch it, so the Shinpo family was able to feel completely secure and safe. Since we lived at Momogendai, and since the church that the Shinpo family stayed in was at Fushimicho, which was some distance away from us, it did not work out that we could all get on the same ship back to Japan. I am sure their turn to be repatriated will be very soon. They are now all very safe. There is nothing to worry about. Please explain everything to Shinpo-san as soon as you can."

Maruyama felt great relief after hearing his wife's narrative. As soon as he could, he found Musashi, who was also at the Port of Sasebo working to make the processing of the returnees as smooth as possible, and related all that Mary had told him concerning the Shinpo family. Musashi returned to Tokyo on the next train and passed on Mary's assurances to Shinpo. Hearing concrete and uplifting news about his family for the first time in almost a year, Shinpo was extremely relieved and happy and was able to concentrate on his chores on behalf of the retuning Japanese with renewed vigor.

Maruyama spent that night at Sasebo with his family in the dormitories set aside by the Repatriation Aid Bureau for returning Japanese. The next morning, after a hearty Japanese breakfast, specified supplies (including a blanket) were distributed to each repatriate along with one thousand yen in cash. Before boarding the train for Tokyo, Maruyama stopped by the Repatriation Aid Bureau office to coordinate various activities for the future and thank the supervisor of the security office who had been so kind in helping him reunite with his family. Then, Maruyama, Mary, their four sons, and Toki boarded the train for a joyous ride to Tokyo, with Kugayama as their final destination.

More than three years after their reunion, the Maruyama family poses
for a family portrait, the troubles and turmoil of Manchuria now only
a disturbing memory. The four boys (l-r: Xavier, Joseph, Robert, and
Paul) have regained their weight, and Mary is now working as a U.S.
Department of Defense civilian employee at Tachikawa Air Base near
Tokyo. Kunio is about to begin his career as a professor of economics at
his alma mater, Meiji University. (Kunio Maruyama Collection)

Chapter 25

The Voice of Authority Prevents a Strike

A Labor Union Calls for Nationwide Strike

Although the Maruyama family was happily back together, there was anxiety about the Shinpo family. While no one doubted that they would soon return safely, until they actually set foot on Japan and Shinpo could embrace them in his arms, the joy of the Maruyamas' return was somewhat subdued. The Repatriation Aid Bureau continued to stay alert for a returning family that fit the description of the Shinpo family, and the three men made sure one of them was at Sasebo each time a ship arrived from Dalian.

One postwar organization that became quite active and even vigorous in its activities even before barely a year had passed since the defeat of Japan was a workers' rights advocacy group called the Joint Struggle Committee of the Public Employees' Union (*Kyoutou*). This committee represented mainly those who worked for the National Railway as well as workers involved in communications, and they began making demands on the Japanese government to seek improved benefits for all its members. They became increasingly aggressive in their demands so that on January 18, 1947, they held a large assembly in the park in front of the Imperial Palace to call for a general strike. They declared that all railway and communications workers throughout Japan would cease work and participate in a general strike on February 1. After their assembly in front of the Imperial Palace, union members marched through the main streets of Tokyo carrying their union flags and banners to drum up enthusiasm among the general public.

The repatriation of Japanese from Soviet-controlled Dalian, which had recently commenced, was estimated to take at least another three or four months to complete. Ships coming in to the Port of Sasebo always returned from Dalian with a full load of returnees, including many who had been refugees and those afflicted with serious illness. Upon stepping on Japanese soil, every returnee was most anxious to reach their home as soon as possible and to reunite with relatives and friends from whom they had been separated for so long. Maruyama, Shinpo, and Musashi had spent most of their efforts in the past few months negotiating and preparing with both Japanese and GHQ agencies to minimize the delay before returnees would be welcomed home by their loved ones who had undoubtedly been waiting almost beyond hope. There were some among the repatriates who were so gravely ill, elderly, or weak from more than a year of abuse and neglect that a mere few hours delay would be enough to kill them before they had the chance to see their loved ones.

A general strike of the National Railway could be devastating to the newly arrived repatriates since all means of land transportation would be shut down. There would be no way for the pitiful returnees to make their way home. Of course, it was not only the repatriates from Manchuria who would suffer from a general strike, but incalculable damage and suffering would be inflicted on all eighty million people of Japan, since the entire nation would be paralyzed and all communication would come to a halt. The Japanese people were already struggling mightily as they went from day to day trying to recover from the war. Was it right for a tiny group of Japanese, the labor leaders of the railway and communications workers, to take such a selfish action and, on their own terms, inflict such large-scale disturbance on the people of Japan? Was this not a challenge directed at the entire nation? Was the government going to allow this grave injustice and do nothing about it? Was the government so ineffectual that it was incapable of eliminating the threat? These were the questions Maruyama, Shinpo, Musashi, and countless citizens had on their minds as each day passed and the promised date of the general strike drew closer. The criticism and reproach by the general public against the impending inconvenience increased daily in volume.

Urging a Halt to Strike Falls on Deaf Ears

Maruyama and his two companions wasted no time in visiting the headquarters of the National Railway Labor Union, which was located in front of Tokyo Station. They met with the executive officers to make them aware of the hardship a transportation strike would cause to the returnees from Manchuria. The three men politely and calmly explained the harm the strike would cause, not only for the repatriates who had waited so long to return to their loved ones, but to everyone in Japan who would have no means to travel. In view of Japan's present situation, still struggling to recover from the war, the three demanded that the general strike be cancelled.

When it appeared from the demeanor of the executives that their words were having absolutely no effect on their decision to press on with the strike, Maruyama said to them, "If you are going through with the strike no matter what, you must make exceptions for the repatriates who are returning from overseas and make special arrangements so that they will not be

stranded at the Port of Sasebo." The three men were determined
to continue negotiating with the union leaders. They refused
to lose hope and visited the union headquarters several more
times in their desperate effort to convince the union leaders to
cancel their selfish plan.

January 31 came, and unless a miracle happened, the strike
would begin at midnight, and all trains of the National Railway
would cease to operate. Shortly after noon, Maruyama and
Shinpo made one more visit to the union headquarters office
in a last-ditch effort to move the union executives to cancel
the strike for the sake of the next group of repatriates who
would be arriving at Sasebo the next day. Maruyama explained
to the executives who sat facing them with blank or irritated
countenances as follows:

Since the group of repatriates arriving tomorrow is
coming home so much later than expected, there will
be many ill refugees, many much worse off than those
who have returned before them. We know that there
are many seriously ill and elderly persons among
the group who are close to drawing their last breath.
They have courageously persevered until now, telling
themselves, 'If I am going to die, I will do so only
after I return to my native land. Before I die, I want
to see the faces of my parents, or of my wife or of my
husband, or of my children one last time.' For many,
that earnest desire is the only thing that has carried
them on until today.

We Japanese must do all we can to return those
people to their homes as soon as we can after their
landing. We fear greatly that the slightest delay in
transporting them to their homes will be the cause
of the worst possible situation. I will give you one
concrete example: Shichiro Shinpo, the brother of
Hachiro Shinpo who now stands in front of you, was

repatriated from Koroto last August. Unfortunately, on his voyage back to Japan, he became acutely ill just before boarding the repatriation ship due to all the hardships he had endured in Manchuria. Tragically, he never recovered, and he took his last breath on board the very ship that was taking him home, away from all the sufferings he had endured, and he became only yet another precious victim to be buried at sea, just before reaching Japan.

If all means of transportation become completely paralyzed because of the general strike of the National Railway workers, we are convinced that such incidents (of untimely deaths) will be repeated over and over again.... Truly, this is a major humanitarian issue. Who will bear the responsibility for the unnecessary hardship on our fellow countrymen who have already suffered so much? Will it be the labor union of the public workers? Will it be the government? In either case, this is a challenge being directed at the citizens of the entire nation. In particular, we cannot condone any action that demonstrates hostility to the pitiful repatriates coming home from a foreign land just as they are returning to their beloved homeland. At the least, we ask that you exempt all transportation from your list of categories that will go on strike tonight. If you still insist that the strike be carried out in spite of our appeals to you, then we demand you institute special treatment for the repatriates who will disembark at Sasebo and insure they are transported back to their native homes as soon as possible.[1]

For the next several minutes, both Shinpo and Maruyama pleaded and cajoled and appealed to the executives with all their might. As Maruyama looked around at the faces of the union leaders who sat silently around the table, he thought he detected some look of sympathy and feeling in a couple of them. However, when they broke their silence to express their reaction, Maruyama and Shinpo were thoroughly disappointed and disgusted with their arrogance. They stated in effect that, at this late juncture, they would not change the set course of action and that the strike would proceed as scheduled. By now, Maruyama and Shinpo were quite aware that it was pointless and simply a waste of time to continue to argue. Nevertheless, the two frustrated men no longer held back and vented their anger at the heartlessness and cruelty of the union executives who had no concern about the inconvenience they were about to impose on the entire Japanese nation, not to mention the heartbreak and disappointment they would cause to the thousands of repatriates from Manchuria and their awaiting families whose long ordeal was finally about to end.

A Miraculous Order from SCAP

Then something happened that can only be described as miraculous! Just as Shinpo and Maruyama were helplessly venting their anger, a union official burst into the room to announce that an order had just been issued by General MacArthur to halt the strike. With the single voice of authority from the Supreme Commander for Allied Powers, this enormous issue that had made the blood of Maruyama and Shinpo to boil and their stomachs to convulse had been resolved! It was now the union executives who were disappointed, angered, frustrated, and bitter as they digested the news. They knew there was nothing they could do; there was no appeal possible.

Maruyama and Shinpo instinctively grasped each other's hand and rejoiced at the news. Their joy at that instant knew no bounds. As the two walked out of the union office and toward their train at Tokyo Station, they simply repeated to each other over and over again, "Thank goodness!! Thank goodness!!"

It was at 2:30 PM on January 31, 1947, when Maruyama and Shinpo were in the midst of passionately, yet fruitlessly, appealing to the leaders of the National Railway Labor Union at their headquarters office in Tokyo Station, that GHQ's public relations section issued a press release to the Japanese media announcing that General Douglas MacArthur had issued a cease-and-desist order to the Joint Struggle Committee of the Public Employees' Union to cancel their general strike. The two-page order from General MacArthur read in part as follows:

Under the authority vested in me as Supreme Commander for the Allied Powers, I have informed the labor leaders ... that I will not permit the use of so deadly a social weapon in the impoverished and emaciated condition of Japan, and have accordingly directed them to desist from the furtherance of such action.

[W]ith great reluctance, I have deemed it necessary to intervene ... to forestall the fatal impact upon an already gravely threatened public welfare. Japanese society today operates under the limitations of war defeat and allied occupation. Its cities are laid to waste, its industries are almost at a standstill, and the great masses of its people are on little more than a starvation diet.

A general strike, crippling transportation and communications, would prevent the movement of food to feed the people and of coal to sustain essential utilities, and paralysis which inevitably would result might reduce the large masses of the Japanese people to the point of actual starvation and would produce dreadful consequences upon every Japanese home.... Even now, to prevent actual starvation in Japan, the people of the United States are releasing to them quantities of their own scarce food resources.

[Plunging the great masses of the Japanese people into disaster] would impose upon the Allied Powers the unhappy decision of whether to leave the Japanese to the fate thus recklessly imposed by a minority, or to cover the consequences by pouring into Japan, at the expense of their own meager resources, infinitely greater quantities of food and other supplies to sustain life than otherwise would be required.... I could hardly request the Allied peoples to assume this additional burden....

I do not intend otherwise to restrict the freedom of action heretofore given to labor in the achievement of legitimate objectives. Nor do I intend in any way to compromise or influence the basic social issues involved....[2]

The National Railway Labor Union issued a directive at 7:45 PM that day to all its members to desist from going forward with the strike, but almost everyone had been made aware of General MacArthur's order by that time, so all preparations for a transportation strike had already been abandoned. On the same day (January 31), the Joint Struggle Committee of the Public Employees' Union, to whom MacArthur's order had been targeted, disbanded. As a result, there was no disruption to any transportation facilities so that the returnees, who had been stranded for so long in Dalian and other Soviet-occupied areas of Manchuria, were able to return home, with no obstruction, into the arms of anxiously waiting loved ones.

Repatriation from Soviet Territories Winds Down

Thanks to the agreement reached by the United States with the Soviet Union, effective December 19, 1946, repatriation of Japanese from Dalian continued uninterrupted through January (sixteen ships returned over 52,000), February (fourteen ships brought back over 40,000), and March of 1947 (when nearly 60,000 were brought back in twenty-three ships in a large-scale operation).

On March 10, Shinpo's long and patient wait finally came to an end as his family of four—his wife, Takeko, and his two sons (Takaaki and Nariaki), together with her younger brother, Kunihisa Musashi—arrived safely at the Port of Sasebo, all in relatively good health in spite of the obvious malnutrition they had endured for so long. It had been one full year plus one month since the Shinpo family was separated. Both Shinpo and Musashi were waiting at the port when the Shinpo family disembarked. For Shinpo, this was the happiest day of his life as he embraced his wife and sons, tears of joy and relief trickling down his cheek.

The happy reunion was marred by one sad piece of news which Takeko Shinpo's group was hearing for the first time. Shinpo's older brother, Shichiro Shinpo, was not there to celebrate the reunion. (Maruyama had related the story of his death to the high-ranking officials of the National Railway Labor Union on January 31 while imploring that the impending strike be cancelled.) Hardship, neglect, and malnutrition from living in Manchuria had taken quite a toll on the elderly Shinpo as he awaited his turn to return home, and it was only through the kindness and support of others around him that he survived to make his way to Koroto to finally board a ship bound for Japan in August 1946. It was surmised that once on board the ship, he apparently felt such relief that he ceased his struggle for life just as the Japanese mainland came into view. As others clambered on deck to rejoice and marvel at the sight of the green mountains of Kyushu, Shichiro quietly died before reaching his beloved homeland. As Shinpo and Musashi escorted the Shinpo family to the processing tent, their thoughts and silent prayers turned to Shichiro and the many other souls who never returned home.

In reality, recalled Maruyama, there were many who met the same fate as Shichiro Shinpo, never quite making it home, only to be buried at sea as the Japanese land mass came into view. Mothers, fathers, daughters, sons—death was not selective. Particularly sad were the deaths of the many infants, who only recently had first seen the light of day, and of the elderly, who were quietly buried at sea. Had the opportunity for repatriation come to them only a few days sooner, thought Maruyama, they might have had a better chance to make it home.

Repatriation ships with names like *Daizui Maru* and *Dai-ichi Yamato Maru* continued to bring home Japanese citizens from Dalian during the latter part of March and into April. Then on April 3, 1947, the ship *Takasago Maru* docked at Sasebo carrying six thousand Japanese returnees. This, for all intents and purposes, concluded the repatriation from Dalian. (Small groups of Japanese continued to be repatriated from Dalian sporadically until the summer of 1947.[3])

Chapter 26

The Story of a Young Girl Trapped in Dalian

"Why, Yes! I Knew Your Mother"

While conducting research in the summer of 2008, this author and his younger brother Xavier visited the Maryknoll Mission in Ossining, New York, where the Maryknoll Archives are located. A Japanese visitor who happened to be there doing her own independent research mentioned that she had just met and interviewed a retired nun who said that she had been in Manchuria as a youth. Intrigued, the author immediately made a phone call to the nun in her dormitory, which was only a few minutes away from the archives, and introduced himself by saying, "Sister, my name is Paul Maruyama, and I understand you were in Manchuria during the Soviet occupation. We (my brother and I) too were there in Dalian, and we'd like to come and talk with you."

The nun said, without one moment of hesitation, "Why, yes! I knew your mother well!" Momentarily stunned, the author and his brother immediately went to see Sister Grace Mary Kuji, MM, in the lobby of the sisters' residence.

Awaiting the two brothers at the door was a petite, elderly, and gentle-looking lady in civilian attire who smiled warmly at them through her tinted glasses. After bowing to the nun in the Japanese fashion and then grasping her hands tightly as long-lost friends would, the brothers were led into a comfortable receiving room where they all sat down to chat. The conversation was conducted mostly in Japanese, the language Sister Grace Mary was more comfortable with, but was interspersed on occasions with English.

The brothers told the nun that they were in the midst of doing background research for an eventual book that would relate the story of three Japanese men, including their father, who escaped from Manchuria and ultimately succeeded in persuading GHQ to dispatch ships that resulted in the repatriation of 1.7 million Japanese stranded there as a result of Soviet invasion and occupation just as World War II came to an end. The author related to Sister Grace Mary that, just before the three men made their secret exodus from Anshan, the Maruyama family and the Shinpo family were entrusted to the care of the Maryknoll Church in Dalian, which was then headed by Bishop Raymond Lane.

As memories flooded back to the elderly nun, she remembered that she had known the brothers' mother, Mary Mariko Maruyama, in Dalian and later in Tokyo in the early 1950s. "There was always something different about your mother," said Sister Grace Mary, who until now had not known that Mary was a Seattle-born U.S. citizen. "She was not like other Japanese women. She was always confident, always optimistic, and always friendly. Unlike other Japanese women, who were taught in those days to be quiet and unassertive and to always stay in the background, your mother was always cheery, helpful, and outgoing. She was always warm and was like a bright sunshine during those trying days!"

Trapped in Dalian

Yasuko Kuji, who later became Maryknoll Sister Grace Mary Kuji, was born in Tsingtao, China (also known as Qingdao, where the best-known Chinese beer is still made), across the bay and to the south of Dalian where her parents had crossed over from Japan before her birth. Life was exciting, cheerful, and comfortable in those days for Japanese living in China, and Yasuko enjoyed her childhood and teenage years in Tsingtao.

However, Japanese children living in China generally returned to Japan for their higher education, and at eighteen years old, she returned to Japan to enroll at Nihon Joshi Daigaku (Japan Women's University) in Mejiro. As she tried to concentrate on her studies, rumors were abuzz that, in spite of the glowing propaganda claiming victory after victory by the Japanese military in little-known locations of the Pacific, things were really not going well. Soon, there were rumors that the Japanese homeland was about to be invaded by American forces, and if that happened, there would be no mercy for military and civilians alike. The cruelty to be inflicted on the Japanese populace, especially on women, by the barbaric American soldiers was to be so terrible that all should prepare to take their own lives, went the rumors. If the rumors were true, Yasuko wanted to return to Tsingtao and be with her family when the end came.

With eight other schoolmates, Yasuko boarded a ship and left Japan to return to her parents. She got as far as Japanese-controlled Dalian by way of Pusan, Korea, without any problem, but a visa was required for her to go on to Tsingtao in China. She settled in Dalian as she awaited documents from her parents in Tsingtao to prove that she had a legitimate reason to apply for a visa to China. The documents never arrived, and she was stranded in Dalian as the war came to an end with the Japanese surrender, and all of Manchuria fell into chaos as it fell under the control of the Soviet army and Communist Chinese.

Fortunately for Yasuko, she was taken under the protective wing of the Hama family, wealthy Japanese relatives of a college classmate. The Hamas were very kind to Yasuko, treating her like a family member. But without a job and feeling guilty about "freeloading" on the Hamas, she looked for something to do. Hearing about a school run by the Maryknoll Mission that was doing many good things for the refugees and the displaced Japanese who were pouring into Dalian, she sought out the Maryknoll Kaisei Gakuin (Maryknoll Star of the Sea Institute) to volunteer to help. She soon befriended two Japanese nuns, Sisters Sabina and Roseanne, as well as other Korean and German sisters. Yasuko immersed herself in the good works the sisters were doing and, at the same time, took English classes.

Sisters Sabina and Roseanne soon introduced Yasuko to a White Russian family engaged in the business of making chocolate and encouraged her to work for the family. Although the Hama family was reluctant to see Yasuko working for a living (since they felt it was below her dignity), the sisters convinced the Hamas to allow the young girl to earn her own keep. Initially, the arrangement went smoothly, but Yasuko found that her cultural distance from the kindly White Russian family was too wide and uncomfortable to bridge. She, therefore, requested and received permission to live in the Maryknoll residence, to work full-time in helping the nuns with their enterprises. Her encounter with the numerous poor, destitute Japanese who came begging to the church was a shock to her. She had never seen Japanese in such conditions. More than anything else had, it brought home to her that Japan had lost the war.

Maryknoll Compound Becomes Home

Living with five nuns, Yasuko observed the daily life of the sisters who, in spite of having almost nothing themselves, spent their days helping the refugees and the poor, giving away money, food, and clothing without complaint. When it seemed that there was nothing more to give away, when the kitchen was empty of food, the nuns never despaired, always saying with a smile, "God will provide."

In spite of observing, and being a part of, the kindness, charity, and blessings the sisters demonstrated on a daily basis, there were many things the non-Christian Yasuko found difficult to accept. When she was asked by Sister Margaret, a Korean nun, to help teach the Old Testament Bible to a group of young students, she had difficulty comprehending stories about Abraham and Moses and Jacob and about sheep and shepherds and beasts of burden, all of which were strange tales to her, stories she felt she could never have much interest in. Christianity, to the young Japanese girl from Tsingtao, was indeed alien, and she did not like many aspects of the foreign religion.

But one day, on her birthday, the sisters surprised her with a wonderful feast to celebrate the occasion. She did not know how they learned of her birthday, but the unexpected generous (and delicious) gesture in midst of all the poverty and sufferings moved her to tears. Reminiscing about the birthday feast even more than sixty years later, she wondered how the sisters were able to find all the wonderful foods in Dalian for the memorable meal. Two months later, when she was asked to again teach a Bible class, her attitude had changed, and things began to make sense. Shortly thereafter, she asked to be baptized and became a Catholic.

By then, the situation in Dalian had worsened for all people, especially the Japanese. Rumors were rampant about Russian soldiers attacking Japanese women. Doors were always kept closed, and windows were shuttered. No strangers, particularly men, were let into homes. Women, including Yasuko, cut their hair short and wore men's clothing to disguise themselves as much as they could. While Yasuko herself was never attacked by any Soviet soldier, she heard many stories of Russian soldiers chasing and violating Japanese girls; women lived in constant fear. She remembered that the Chinese were not, in most cases, unkind to the Japanese. While some did seek revenge on those Japanese who had mistreated and discriminated against the "inferior" non-Japanese during the glory years of Japanese dominance, many Chinese showed pity and even sympathy toward the Japanese who were suddenly impoverished, unemployed, and unprotected by any government. The greatest concern that Yasuko recalled, besides the menace of the Soviet soldiers, was the chaos and rampant banditry against the unprotected Japanese. She recalled that a very large gate at the main entrance to the Maryknoll compound completely disappeared one night without anyone hearing a sound or witnessing the theft.

Sister Grace Mary Kuji, shown during a visit to Japan in 2008, at age eighty-one. Now retired and living at the Maryknoll Headquarters in New York, Yasuko Kuji (then a Japanese college student) became trapped in Dalian when she tried to return to her parents in Tsingtao, China, in the last days of the war. Kuji later became a Maryknoll nun. (Grace Mary Kuji Collection)

Keeping the Caucasian Intruder Out

One day, a large Caucasian came and knocked on the door of the church residence where Yasuko stayed. Gripped by immediate fear, she cracked open the door just enough to ask what the man wanted. As he tried to push his way in, Yasuko pushed back with all her might to close the door. Then the man said in Japanese, *"Watashi wa ookii desu ... motto akete kudasai* (I am a big man ... please open the door a little more)!"* It was Bishop Raymond Lane who had come to deliver some cookies and cakes to the sisters as he sometimes did! Bishop Lane, whose Japanese was good enough to carry on casual conversation, lived with some Salesian Order fathers and brothers in the same compound as the nuns. The embarrassed Yasuko opened the door wide as the other sisters gathered around happily to see what goodies the bishop had brought for them.

Although everyone, including the occupying Soviet army, knew that the Maryknoll Catholic Church property was a United States entity and was thus left alone by the officials, both Chinese and Soviet, it was still not wise for Americans to become too visible in Dalian. Thus, Bishop Lane, his fellow American priests, and the American sisters maintained a relatively low profile and avoided leaving the church property as much as possible. What help and aid they gave to the poor, the refugees, and the sick were done mostly out of sight of the authorities. Another group that stayed even more careful were the German nuns whose country, until very recently, had been a bitter enemy of the Soviet Union. (Bishop Lane was elected at the Maryknoll Headquarters in New York to be the next superior general of Maryknoll Mission, and on June 28, 1946, he left Manchuria on board a U.S. naval vessel to return to the United States in time to attend the ceremony that installed him to that position.[1,2])

Yasuko often saw both Mary Maruyama and Takeko Shinpo while residing at the Maryknoll residence. Mary, who lived with her family a few miles away from the Maryknoll compound, taught English at Maryknoll Kaisei Gakuin. Sister Grace Mary remembered that she knew Mary then only as Mrs. Mariko Takeda. (Shortly before the Maruyama family departed Dalian for Japan in early 1947, they once again changed their name, since rumors were heard that someone had reported them to the authorities as the family of Kunio Maruyama who had made the NHK radio broadcast in April 1946.)

Yasuko also saw Mrs. Takeko Shinpo at the Maryknoll compound often. She remembered that Mrs. Shinpo had requested that her two boys, Takaaki and Nariaki, be baptized. They were given the baptismal names of Peter and Paul. The Shinpo family also lived a few miles from the Maryknoll compound; however, when a rumor was heard that someone had denounced them to the local occupying authorities as families of one of the three men who had escaped to Japan, they moved inside the Maryknoll compound and stayed there until their departure for Japan in March 1947.

Returning to Japan on a Clunker

When the Soviet Union finally agreed to open up the Port of Dalian for repatriation of Japanese in late December 1946, relief, elation, and bittersweet emotions spread through the Japanese communities as they began preparing for departure and anxiously awaited their turn to seek passage on the repatriation ships. Yasuko Kuji's turn did not come until March 1947. She later learned that her family in Tsingtao had returned to Japan more than a year before (in December 1945) on board a ship of the U.S. Navy. Yasuko, along with nuns whose nationalities were Korean, German, and Japanese, was among the last of the residents at the Maryknoll compound to be allowed to return to Japan. The five or six American nuns who had also lived at the compound had been repatriated to the United States several months earlier.

The ship that carried Yasuko and her fellow repatriates was a Japanese vessel named the *Seattle Maru*, a broken-down clunker that experienced many mechanical problems as it set out from Dalian to Sasebo. On board the same ship were Yasuko's friends, the Shinpo family. As the ship pressed onward across the Yellow Sea toward the East China Sea and finally through the Korea Strait to its destination of Sasebo, its boiler failed completely so that the ship literally drifted into the Port of Sasebo. Needless to say, the anxious passengers celebrated not only their return to Japan after nearly two years of captivity under Soviet occupation, but they also celebrated that their clunker of a ship had been able to miraculously make it back to Japan at all.

After proceeding through the required administrative and medical procedures, Yasuko boarded a train bound for Tokyo and coincidentally sat near the Shinpo family of four. She then noticed that there was a gentleman in a suit and tie sitting with the Shinpo family, chatting happily with the Shinpo children. She assumed the man was some kind of an official since he was wearing an armband. The coach that Yasuko and the Shinpos boarded was filled mostly with ordinary Japanese residents on their way to Tokyo for business or pleasure. As the train was about to depart, the man with the Shinpo family stood up and, in a loud voice, announced to the other passengers that the group with him were repatriates from Manchuria and had just returned from Dalian after years of hardship, isolation, and neglect. The passengers all applauded to express their welcome to the repatriates. Yasuko was surprised, because she had assumed the man accompanying the Shinpo family must be some important Japanese government official, which meant that the Shinpos were a very important family. Later, she was informed that the man with the armband was none other than Hachiro Shinpo, husband and father of the Shinpo family.

The Sister Finally Learns the Truth

When Sister Grace Mary related this incident to the two brothers, Paul and Xavier Maruyama, at Maryknoll in the summer of 2008, she had not been aware of the story of the three men who had escaped from Manchuria to Japan in early 1946, and who had carried on a successful campaign to implore General MacArthur to dispatch repatriation ships to Koroto. She had not been aware that the reason Mary Maruyama and her four boys, as well as Mrs. Shinpo and her two sons were frequently seen at the Maryknoll Church in Dalian was because the three men had entrusted the families to the care of Bishop Lane and the Maryknoll Church upon their escape. She had never realized that not one word about the escape of the three men could be divulged to anyone by either the Shinpo or the Maruyama family or by the Maryknoll sisters and priests, including Bishop Lane, who knew the true identities of the Shinpos and Maruyamas, lest the secret became known to Soviet or Communist Chinese authorities.

Until she met the two Maruyama brothers, she had continued to assume that Mr. Shinpo, who appeared out of nowhere on the Tokyo-bound train from Sasebo on that March day in 1947, was some kind of an important Japanese government official. (Even many years later, in the mid-1950s when she became closely reacquainted with Mary Maruyama in Tokyo, the story of the three men was never brought up, not because it had to remain a secret, but simply because no one thought to bring it up!) After the two brothers explained that Hachiro Shinpo had been anxiously awaiting his family's return to Japan ever since repatriation from Manchuria began, Sister Grace Mary's face brightened as if a great mystery had been solved, and she said, "I had always wondered why I never met a Mr. Maruyama or a

Mr. Shinpo while at the Maryknoll compound in Dalian! And I always wondered why Mr. Shinpo appeared out of nowhere on that train to Tokyo from Sasebo. Now it all makes sense!"

After reuniting with her family, who had returned to Japan from Tsingtao more than a year before she did, Yasuko Kuji, now a baptized Catholic, could not forget the goodness, charity, and kindness that the Maryknoll sisters had demonstrated toward the sick, the hungry, the impoverished, and the suffering, both Japanese and Chinese, who had come knocking on the doors of the Maryknoll Catholic Church in Dalian. Inspired by all the sisters she lived and worked with in Dalian, she crossed the Pacific Ocean in 1951 to the United States and arrived at Ossining, New York, where she entered the novitiate and became a Maryknoll sister. She was assigned to Tokyo where she renewed her friendship with many people she had known in Manchuria, including the many foreign and Japanese nuns who had been so kind to her when she was stranded in Dalian at the time of Japanese defeat and the invasion by the Soviet army. She also again befriended Mary Maruyama and her family and even remembered visiting their house at Kugayama. Until she was informed by the Maruyama brothers in 2008, she had not known that that very house had been the headquarters for the committee known as the Representatives to Petition for Saving Our Countrymen Living in Manchuria headed by Kunio Maruyama, Hachiro Shinpo, and Masamichi Musashi.

Sister Grace Mary Yasuko Kuji, who turned eighty-two in 2009, retired as an active nun after having served her God for more than fifty-seven years and lives quietly today in good health at the retirement facilities at the Maryknoll Headquarters in Ossining, New York, occasionally traveling to her native Japan.

Chapter 27

Letters of Appeal to Truman, Marshall, and Stalin

Appeals Sent to World Leaders

The number of Japanese repatriates returning from Dalian, Manchuria, decreased dramatically in the months following the peak in early 1947. The last ship returned to Japan in August of that year carrying a handful of the last of the remaining Japanese who desired to return to their homeland.[1] Thus, the main mission of the three men who escaped and returned to Japan from Manchuria in early 1946 was, in essence, finally completed. There were, of course, some Japanese who chose to remain in Manchuria. Some were detained by Chinese authorities for various reasons, and some married Chinese and could not return to Japan for other reasons.

There were, however, some loose ends to be tied. While the three men's main objective was to bring back to Japan their fellow countrymen left behind in Manchuria, they were often approached by anxious family members of Japanese still left behind overseas, particularly former military personnel who had been transported to Siberia and other parts of the Soviet Union as prisoners of war or whose whereabouts became completely unknown. Because the enfeebled Japanese government was not much help in those days, these families and loved ones had practically nowhere to turn for help. They, therefore, turned to the Representatives to Petition for Saving Our Countrymen Living in Manchuria and pleaded that attention be focused on the yet unrepatriated Japanese throughout Asia. While passion for the issue of repatriating Japanese began to cool among the public, especially as repatriation from Dalian wound down, the desperation and feelings of isolation of those who still had family members and cherished ones overseas increased.

To realign their focus to Japanese still left behind, not only in Manchuria, but in other parts of Asia as well, a new committee called the All-Japan Association for Realizing the Quick Return of Japanese Left Behind was formed on June 28, 1947, with its headquarters office located at the Maruyama residence in Kugayama. With Kunio Maruyama as its chairman and Hachiro Shinpo as vice chairman, several prominent citizens served on its board. Several, including former Manchurian Mining Machinery Company president Yoshiei Tamai and Hideo Konishi (later elected to the House of Representatives and the House of Councilors), had returned from Manchuria themselves via Koroto. Masamichi Musashi was one of three managing directors of the committee. A recently demobilized Japanese soldier, Kenji Kameyama, worked passionately as a director on behalf of soldiers who were still held in Soviet captivity. As time passed, the committee gained national renown and support so that branch offices were established throughout Japan, thus expanding its communications network and strengthening efforts to keep the issue of unreturned Japanese soldiers and civilians fresh on the public's radar.

On August 15, 1947, a national assembly of the All-Japan Association for Realizing the Quick Return of Japanese Left Behind was convened at the Kugayama headquarters to mark the second anniversary of the end of the war. The assembly adopted a resolution to send a petition letter appealing for the return of Japanese still in foreign captivity and control to U.S. President Harry S. Truman and to Secretary of State George Marshall as well as to Soviet Premier Josef Stalin. The letters for President Truman and Secretary of State Marshall were taken that day by Maruyama and several members of the committee to the foreign affairs bureau of the Supreme Commander for Allied Powers (SCAP) located on the fifth floor of the Mitsui Main Office Building in Nihonbashi (in Tokyo) and were handed over to U.S. Consul Bruner in the absence of then U.S. Ambassador to Japan, George Acheson.

The letter to President Truman said, in summary:

We, who represent the members of families of those Japanese left behind in foreign lands, humbly petition with one voice to Your Excellency, Harry Truman, president of the United States....

Of the seven million Japanese countrymen who were residing overseas at the time of the end of the war, six million have already returned.... This is solely due to the great effort ... of the Allied Forces ... and is the direct result of sympathetic arrangements granted to us ... beginning especially with General MacArthur.

However, even now, when we reflect on the plight of one million Japanese who still remain in foreign lands, mainly in Soviet territories ... we are unable to bear the grief in our hearts. At the same time, when we think about the more than ten million family members and friends who have someone they love dearly still overseas ... we cannot put into words the sympathy we feel for them. As Your Excellency must be fully aware, Article 9 of the Potsdam Declaration states, "After members of the armed forces of Japan have been completely relieved of all their arms, each member will return to his home and will be given the opportunity to live peacefully and productively." We have had both gratitude and faith in this most generous article by the Allied nations and have come to this present day awaiting the earliest realization of this public pledge.

However ... one million of our innocent countrymen are still held in internment in faraway lands under foreign skies, separated yet from their beloved wives, fathers, mothers, children, brothers, sisters, and fiancées....

We ask you to personally review this situation, and our earnest desire is that Your Excellency will make the arrangement, based on your overflowing sympathy, to return our fellow countrymen still left overseas to their families ... our only wish is that all those who have waited beyond hope will be able to feel the joy of reunion and to have the happiness of pleasant conversation with each other once again....[2]

The letter of appeal to President Truman was signed by Kunio Maruyama and the key directors of the All-Japan Association for Realizing the Quick Return of Japanese Left Behind. A postscript expressing deep sympathy and regret for the recent passing of Truman's mother, Martha Truman, was added.

The letter to Secretary of State George Marshall was similar to the one sent to Truman. But the letter to Stalin was more direct and cool. Stalin was reminded of the sufferings of the over ten million grieving friends, relatives, and family members of Japanese military personnel still under internment in the Soviet Union and territories under his nation's control, and how they were shedding tears every day, praying and waiting for those loved ones detained abroad. The letter asked that Stalin have complete understanding of the spirit of Article 9 in the Potsdam Declaration, and concluded with a plea that the Soviet premier take the necessary action to return the Japanese to their homeland before another day passed.

The dispatch of petition letters to the heads of state of the United States and of the Soviet Union, appealing for the return of unrepatriated Japanese, was reported by the Japan Broadcasting Station (NHK) during its news broadcast that evening and on the following morning.

The Tragic Death of a Great Friend

A tragic event took place on August 17, two days after the petition addressed to President Truman was submitted to the SCAP foreign affairs bureau for dispatch to the White House. Maruyama and his fellow committee members had hoped to hand the letter to Ambassador George Acheson who had been the right-hand man to General MacArthur in carrying out occupation policies. Unfortunately, Ambassador Acheson was not in at the time of their visit, and the letter was entrusted to one of the U.S. consuls. As the highest-ranking American civilian among occupation personnel, Acheson had been assigned in September of 1945 to act as MacArthur's political advisor and chief diplomat. In 1946, he became the chairman of the influential eleven-nation Allied Council for Japan, which administered postwar Japan. Maruyama had come to know, respect, and admire Acheson in his numerous meetings with him. Many were the times when he and others involved with various repatriation issues would conclude a discussion that needed resolution by saying, "We must go and present the problem to Ambassador Acheson." Delegates who came to Tokyo from all over Japan, representing families of cherished members overseas bearing petitions and pleas addressed to the U.S. government, inevitably presented them to Ambassador Acheson, and their numbers were countless. The number of Japanese who shook the ambassador's hand was, Maruyama reflected, extremely large indeed.

Acheson had written a secret letter to Secretary of State James F. Byrnes, on August 26, 1946, to inform him about the mood of the Japanese people regarding repatriation, particularly among those who were anxiously awaiting return of their loved ones. The letter was written when ships were returning Japanese from Koroto and during the height of Maruyama and Shinpo's nationwide campaign to rouse the public to appeal to GHQ for the opening of Soviet-controlled ports in Manchuria, particularly Dalian. "The Japanese are showing ever-increasing apprehension and unrest concerning fate of nationals in Soviet-controlled and Communist Manchuria areas," wrote Acheson. "An increasing number of petitions signed by many thousands interested relatives as well as heavy daily mail of personal letters are being received by General Headquarters and Chairman Allied Council. On August 20, Special Committee from Japanese Diet ... stated pressure upon Diet members has reached points where situation is almost beyond control. Japanese press continues to ... reflect the growing Japanese public concern regarding effects upon Japanese nationals during the approaching cold season....

"Japanese Government has recently submitted to SCAP petition on repatriation of nationals from Manchuria and Siberia.... Japanese Government now estimates that some 570,000 nationals in Manchuria alone have no prospect of being repatriated before next spring unless ports other than Hulutao (Huludao or Koroto) are made available. Japanese Government estimates the number of deaths of nationals last winter in 11 districts of Manchuria from lack of fuel and food and from epidemics was 111,250 and points out conditions will be infinitely worse this coming winter...."

Acheson concluded his letter to the secretary of state by suggesting that the State Department "may wish, as interim measure and because of humanitarian considerations, to (1) request Chinese and Soviet Government to render all practicable relief and assistance to Japanese nationals in their respective areas and (2) request governments concerned to allow (subject to censorship, if necessary) mail communication between Japanese nationals in their areas and Japan proper...." The letter was obvious evidence that Ambassador Acheson was well aware of and wholly sympathetic to the plea from Maruyama, Shinpo, and thousands of Japanese citizens to put pressure on the Soviet Union to cooperate in the repatriation of Japanese in Soviet-controlled territories in the summer of 1946.[3]

One of Maruyama's fondest memories of Acheson was when he and a large delegation of Japanese, still awaiting their detained kin and friends to return from foreign lands, visited the ambassador in his office in the diplomatic section of GHQ in October 1946. Ambassador Acheson was kind, gracious, and empathetic to the families and offered them valuable advice. At the end of the meeting, a little Japanese kindergarten girl presented the ambassador with a bouquet of flowers which he graciously accepted. In spite of his busy schedule, Acheson took time to pose for several photographs with the visitors.

On August 17, 1947, Acheson was returning to the United States on a U.S. B-17 to coordinate some urgent diplomatic business with the State Department when the plane suddenly crashed into the ocean about seventy miles west of Honolulu, killing all on board. Only fifty-one years old at the time of his death, Acheson was in the prime of his career with expectations of an even greater future. While his death was lamented in the United States by all who knew him, large numbers of Japanese also mourned his death. In particular, those Japanese families, relatives, and friends who still had loved ones overseas were touched and saddened at the untimely death of the American diplomat who always showed understanding, sympathy, and compassion to his Japanese visitors.

Maruyama wrote a heartfelt letter of condolence on behalf of all the Japanese who had come to know the warmhearted and sympathetic American and who now grieved the tragic passing of a great friend, United States Ambassador to Japan George

Acheson. The letter was addressed to Acting Ambassador William Siebold, who responded several days later on August 28 to Maruyama by writing, "On behalf of the Diplomatic Office of the Supreme Commander for Allied Powers, I wish to express my sincere appreciation for your expression of profound sympathy regarding the unfortunate demise of Ambassador George Acheson and for your tribute to the soul of the late ambassador."[4] Siebold was soon appointed to succeed Acheson as ambassador to Japan.

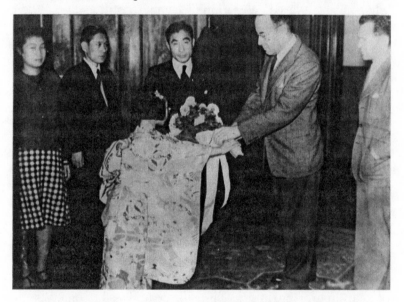

A little Japanese girl presents a bouquet of flowers to Ambassador to Japan George Acheson Jr., as Hachiro Shinpo (second from left) and Kunio Maruyama (third from left) look on. Tragically, Acheson was killed near Hawaii in a plane crash on August 17, 1947. (Kunio Maruyama Collection)

A Member of Parliament Questions the PM's Sincerity

On October 23, 1947, Ambassador William Siebold sent an emissary to Maruyama's home in Kugayama to hand-deliver a letter to Maruyama acknowledging that the letter from the All-

Japan Association for Realizing the Quick Return of Japanese Left Behind had indeed been received and acknowledged by the president of the United States. Maruyama immediately dispatched a reply letter thanking the ambassador for the wonderful news and promised he would insure that all members of the association were informed immediately. Two weeks later, this matter was brought up on the floor of Parliament to chide Prime Minister Tetsu Katayama for his lack of passion regarding the issue of the Japanese not yet returned from foreign lands.

At a time when the issue of still unrepatriated Japanese in foreign lands seemed to fade from the national headlines and particularly from government attention, Nobuo Asaoka, a House of Councilors member and an advisor to the All-Japan Association for Realizing the Quick Return of Japanese Left Behind, made a motion on the floor of Parliament on November 8 calling for greater government effort to repatriate Japanese still overseas. The motion passed unanimously, and during the debate, Asaoka delivered an exceptionally energetic and convincing speech that had the undivided attention of all in attendance. The following paragraphs from Representative Asaoka's speech were extracted from parliamentary records for that day by Maruyama and quoted in *Why Was Koroto Opened*:

In conclusion, I would like to request that Prime Minister Katayama make comments on his enthusiasm and his resolve [regarding the repatriation issue]. A simple comment would be satisfactory. Following the formation of the Katayama Cabinet, I listened to the prime minister's speech to the House of Councilors on his administration's policies, which was less than an hour long. Upon conclusion of his speech, I was sincerely disappointed. The issue that is of such great concern to the people of the entire nation was taken up at the very last and was dealt with in a matter of a few seconds. The fact is, I want to tell you about a repatriation group that I am involved with as its advisor. As a result of their prudent enthusiasm regarding their efforts to promote repatriation, disregarding the fact that the Japanese nation was defeated in war and disregarding that her people belong to a defeated nation, they decisively made the decision to dispatch a letter of petition to President Truman, to Premier Stalin, and to Secretary of State Marshall on August 15, urging their assistance in the repatriation effort.

And what do you think resulted? They received a response from President Truman and Secretary of State Marshall informing them that the letters were indeed received! This was reported in the *Asahi* newspaper in their October 23 issue. I have that article here in my hand. According to the *Asahi* newspaper article that I will read to you, they reported as follows: "A Petition to U.S. President Truman: On August 15, which marked the second anniversary of the end of the war, the All-Japan Association for Realizing the Quick Return of Japanese Left Behind held a national assembly during which they sent off a petition letter urging repatriation to President Truman and Secretary of State Marshall. A letter from Acting Ambassador Siebold of the Supreme Commander's Diplomatic Branch was delivered to Association Chairman Kunio Maruyama that stated that the president of the United States and the secretary of state acknowledged receipt of the petition letter."

The Katayama Cabinet came into existence during the first National Parliament, and it began administration with a clean slate under the new constitution, and each step and every advance that is made within our hall will be picked up by electronic wire to be reported in Washington, in Moscow, in London, in Nanking, and in every corner of the world. Thus, concerning the issue of Prime Minister Katayama having spent only a few seconds to take up this problem [of repatriation], it indicates to me that, in the entire world, the person who has the greatest concern and whose heart is most grieved by this problem, and who is working the hardest on behalf of humanity in the world, is none other than President Truman. Furthermore, I believe that the person who is laboring tirelessly in his busy post on this problem is none other than Secretary of State Marshall.

Both their excellencies, the President of the United States Truman and the Secretary of State Marshall, went to the trouble of informing one citizen of a nation which was defeated in war that they had received his letter of petition regarding repatriation. Reflecting on all the facts regarding this issue, I would like to leave it to each of you to come up with your own conclusion. On this occasion, I have presented to you this one issue, and I would like to have a response from the prime minister and from various agencies in the government regarding their future resolve and their sincere will.[5]

House of Councilors member Asaoka's speech was interrupted numerous times by thunderous applause. Prime Minister Katayama took to the podium shortly after Asaoka's speech had ended, and when the applause had died down, he made the following brief comment in response:

"While I understood the speaker to say that my having taken up this issue in simple words demonstrated my indifference and lack of enthusiasm, I assure you that I spoke on many issues at that time and I have no thought whatsoever to take up the issue in only a simple manner."[6]

Chapter 28

Death Does Not Wait

An Unexpected Telegram

Even though the issue of repatriating Japanese from overseas began to slowly fade from the national radar, primarily since the majority of Japanese civilians had been returned, even from Soviet-occupied regions, Kunio Maruyama, Hachiro Shinpo, and Masamichi Musashi continued their efforts on behalf of those still stranded overseas, whose relatives and acquaintances continued to look to the three men for leadership on the issue. They continued to be invited to speak at rallies and assemblies calling on the Japanese government not to ignore those still overseas.

On February 11, 1948, a major rally on behalf of unreturned Japanese was held at Hibiya Public Auditorium in Tokyo, which was attended by many notable dignitaries, including Minister of Health and Welfare Yoshiichi Takeda. Because that day was Empire Day (now called Founding of the Nation Day), a national holiday, turnout was exceptionally large as thousands came to participate. Snow had been falling since the previous night, but it had stopped by the time of the assembly, and a bright and shiny day greeted the attendees. Musashi spoke first, followed by Shinpo, and then it was Maruyama's turn. As he was speaking, a piece of scrap paper was placed on the podium next to his notes, and the message on the scrap paper said, "Please conclude your speech quickly." Maruyama quickly wrapped up his speech and hurried off the stage amid thunderous applause and sought out the reason for the message. The moderator handed him a telegram which Maruyama immediately realized was from his older brother, Tadao. The message on the telegram was brief and to the point: "Mother in critical condition. Come home now."

With a sinking feeling, Maruyama quickly informed Shinpo and Musashi about the telegram from his brother and headed directly to Ueno Station to catch the train to Nagano. Although it had been almost two years since his return to Japan from Manchuria, he had not had the time to visit his ancestral home deep in the mountains at a place called Tomikura (now Iiyama City) in Nagano Prefecture. Suddenly, he felt very guilty for having neglected his family for so long, particularly his loving mother.

His father had died at age sixty-nine on June 2, 1945, while Maruyama was working at the steel manufacturing company in Anshan, Manchuria. When he received a telegram two months before the war's end informing him that his father was gravely ill, ships were no longer able to cross the ocean so that there were no ordinary means of returning to Japan. However, since Maruyama had contacts in high places because of his position as the public relations officer for his company, he was able to make arrangements to be flown on a Kwantung Army plane back to Japan. The plane could not be made available for another three days, however, and Maruyama prayed that his father's life would be extended until he was able to return home. On the day before his departure, however, another telegram came from his bother Tadao, which said, "Father passed away. Postpone any difficult return home." Sadly, unable to hold back his tears, he called his army contact to cancel his plans to return to Japan.

"This time," Maruyama thought to himself, "this time, I will be home in time!" He had not had any particular news informing him that his mother had been ill, so he wondered if she had had some kind of an accident. The train followed its schedule as it chugged along northwestward, but Maruyama could not suppress his impatience and anxiety. When he arrived at his destination of Iiyama, a blizzard was raging; two of his cousins met him at the station with boots and snow gear. The only way to get home was on foot, since no car could make it in the heavy snowstorm and there were no other means of transportation. During the nearly seven-mile trek through wind and snow, Maruyama stopped at a grocery store that still had its lights on to buy apples for his mother in spite of protests from his cousins who advised him that it was more important to hurry than to buy presents. Hours later, when they finally arrived at his native home, several people came out the door to greet him, including his brother Tadao.

Mourning His Mother's Death

"How is Mother?" Maruyama blurted at once. No one responded, but they all began crying. "Oh, no! I didn't make it?" A desperate choking feeling coursed through him.

Finally Tadao replied, pain obvious in his features, "It's good of you to come such a long way. Mother has already taken her last breath." Maruyama suddenly regretted having stopped to purchase the apples, but Tadao said, "No, that little bit of time was not a problem. It was probably about the time you were climbing up to Usui Pass that mother took her last breath. In any case, this is fate." It was fate that Maruyama was not able to be at the side of either of his parents at the moment of their passing.

Maruyama immediately took off his snow gear and boots, entered the house, and went to the room where his mother lay. Yoshi Maruyama lay silent, cold, and serene on the futon bedding on the *tatami* floor, no longer breathing, no longer alive, surrounded by several relatives including Maruyama's younger brother Katsuei. Her features now looked waxen, but her kind face was relaxed and clear; she had attained Buddhahood (died) at seventy-two years of age. Maruyama knelt next to his mother, hugged her cold body, and silently murmured his apologies for not having returned in time, heedless of the tears that streamed down his cheeks. After some time, those sitting nearby said, "We are so glad you came. It must have been quite hard getting here. We tried so hard to encourage Mother to keep her spirits up at least until you arrived, Kunio-san. But no matter how much we encouraged her, it seems she was in a great hurry to go to meet Buddha." Those comments suggested the deep faith Maruyama's mother had had; they were also meant to console Maruyama.

Maruyama sat beside his mother's body, reflecting on the love his mother had always shown him, feeling guilty that his long absence had made it difficult for him to reciprocate equally and adequately. *Her love for me*, thought Maruyama tearfully, *was deeper than the ocean, and her kindness was higher than the mountains. Forgive me, Mother, that I was not able to do anything to pay you back while you were alive.*

Yoshi Maruyama was raised in a farming village in an even more remote village, and her education had been extremely rudimentary so that one could almost say she was uneducated. But she was a woman who possessed great natural intelligence, aesthetic appreciation, and a broad and open mind, and she had great common sense. The Maruyama family belonged to the Jodo Shinshu sect of Buddhism, which followed the teachings of Shinran Jonin, a senior disciple of Honen, the founder of the Jodoshu sect, and Yoshi had been a particularly devout believer. She often composed songs that praised Buddha; she then would ask a young person in the village to make mimeograph copies so that she could share them with others in the village. Whenever a high priest came to the neighborhood to give a sermon, Maruyama's mother would always be in attendance, no matter how far away the assembly was. As he reminisced about all that was good about his mother, Maruyama felt an acute loneliness that he could not describe in words.

Then, like an ever-changing panorama running through his mind, his thoughts turned to his fellow countrymen in Manchuria. His mother had passed away in this old but magnificent house in a country village in Nagano, Japan, lovingly nursed to her last breath, surrounded by her relatives and friends, in all probability secure in her mind of the love everyone had for her as she passed on to Buddhahood. In contrast, how many refugees in Manchuria went to their deaths feeling abandoned, far from the country of their birth, unable to fight against hunger, bitter cold, and disease, alone and separated from their loved ones? Although Maruyama could not be at her side at the moment of her death, his mother had at least died peacefully and in warmth in spite of the raging snowstorm outside, surrounded by love. For that, Maruyama was grateful and thanked Buddha for his divine kindness.

Maruyama spent the rest of the night lying next to his dead mother in bedding that had been spread out for him. The next day, a funeral service was held, attended by almost everyone in the village. Then, for the first time in a long time, Maruyama paid a visit to the graves of his father and his ancestors and silently reported his activities on behalf of the repatriation effort of all the Japanese who had been left behind in Manchuria. The next day, after bidding a sad farewell to his two brothers and other relatives, he returned to Tokyo to rejoin Shinpo and Musashi to continue their activities on behalf of their fellow countrymen still overseas.

Bogus Accounting Issued by TASS on Japanese POWs

An unclassified GHQ document dated 7 May 1948 indicates that by May 6, 1948, 218,179 Japanese had been evacuated from Dalian (with approximately three thousand more left). The same document estimates 1,040,555 Japanese had been evacuated from other parts of Manchuria (through Koroto) with 65,282 yet to be repatriated.[1] In Koroto (Huludao), a large stone memorial has been erected in recent years, which has the number 1,050,000 prominently etched to commemorate the number of Japanese repatriated from that remote port across the Liaotung Bay from Liaoning Province in what was then southwestern Manchuria. Although probably no full and accurate accounting will ever be known regarding all the Japanese who were stranded in Manchuria as a result of the Soviet invasion and subsequent occupation of Manchuria in the week before the Japanese surrender, the vast majority of Japanese, particularly civilians who wanted to return to their homeland, were brought back by the end of 1948. There were certainly some Japanese who chose to stay in Manchuria, such as Japanese women who married Chinese with the intention of remaining in Manchuria. (Many, of course, married because that was the only way they or their families could survive.) Some demobilized Japanese soldiers chose to join the Nationalist forces of Chiang Kai-shek or the Communist army of Mao Zedong and chose never to return to Japan. Many Japanese children were sold or given away for adoption to Chinese families since their parents could no longer feed, clothe, or care for them.

A stone memorial commemorating the repatriation of Japanese during 1946–1947 stands in a lonely spot near the Port of Huludao (Koroto). The number 1050000, etched above the Chinese characters declaring that this was the place from where "temporary Japanese captives" returned home, indicates the number of repatriates who returned from this port.
(Asian Complex Collection)

An estimated 179,000 Japanese civilians died of starvation, neglect, illness, and other causes throughout Manchuria, many of them infants and children, in the harsh winter that followed the Soviet occupation. The number of Japanese soldiers who perished in Manchuria following capitulation to the Soviet forces has been estimated at 66,000.[2] The most egregious and untruthful accounting of Japanese deaths was provided by the Soviet Union on the matter of Japanese soldiers who surrendered and became POWs in the days following the Soviet invasion of Manchuria. Most were transported to various Soviet territories, mainly to Siberia. According to Maruyama's research contained in *Why Was Koroto Opened*, the Soviet Union issued a declaration on May 20, 1949, in *TASS*, the Soviet News Agency, which stated, "the total number of Japanese ... that became prisoners of war was 594,000; of this number, 70,880 were released on the spot.... Moreover, from December of 1946 to May 1 of 1949, a total of 418,166 were returned to Japan. This year [1949] ... 95,000 were returned to Japan."[3] *TASS* declared a few days later that 95,000 Japanese POWs still remained under Soviet custody and that, except for those still under investigation for war crimes, all would be returned within the year.

Both the Japanese government and GHQ refuted the numbers provided by *TASS*. While the Soviet News Agency declared there were approximately 95,000 Japanese soldiers still held in Soviet captivity in 1949, American and Japanese calculation estimated that the actual number should have been around 400,000. More than 300,000 Japanese POWs remained unaccounted for.[4] Maruyama pointed out in his book that the claim by the Soviet Union that 70,880 Japanese soldiers were released "on the spot" in various battlefields was more than suspicious. All reliable sources indicated that all Japanese prisoners who surrendered on the battlefield were forcibly transported to the Soviet mainland, and not one source or witness could be found who attested to being released by the Soviets on the battlefield anywhere.[5]

John Dower relates in his book *Embracing Defeat*, that in April 1950, an appeal from 120,000 citizens of Shiga Prefecture was sent to General MacArthur, accompanied by an embroidered portrait of the general. More than 120,000 people, who were relatives of Japanese soldiers still missing and unaccounted for by the Soviet Union, had each contributed a stitch to the portrait. During the war, it had been customary to send a Japanese soldier off to war with a cloth stomach warmer sewn with a thousand stitches, each by a different individual. A *sennin-bari haramaki* (belly scarf stitched by one thousand people) symbolized the closeness between the soldier fighting in a foreign country and his community, especially the womenfolk in the soldier's native village or town.

The appeal to MacArthur thanked him for his concern up to the present but asked him to continue his efforts on behalf of bringing back to Japan those soldiers still unreturned. More than four decades after the end of World War II, the Soviet Union finally provided the names of 46,000 Japanese that were known to have been buried in Siberia, but those numbers never matched information held by Japan and the U.S.[6] In the end, most grieving Japanese never learned what happened to their loved ones in the military who disappeared into Soviet hands— and they never had proper closure to their grief.

Chapter 29

Repatriated Eight Years after the End of the War

Forced to Stay

There was at least one group of Japanese (of course, there were others) who were forcibly retained until 1953, eight long years after the fall of Japan, because they were unlucky enough to have the technical and scientific skills needed in Manchuria to repair steel manufacturing facilities, furnaces, heavy (and even light) equipment, and factories destroyed during the war and subsequently dismantled by the Soviet army. About ninety engineers and technicians of the Showa Steel Manufacturing Company (Showa Seiko) in Anshan, the same company that Maruyama was working for when he made his escape to Japan, and their families (a total of 280 Japanese) were made to lend their engineering skills, knowledge, and labor, in turn first to the Soviet army, next to the Communist Chinese, then to the Nationalist army of Chiang Kai-shek, and finally again to the Communist Chinese after they drove out the Nationalist forces. They were made to serve different masters for eight years following the war, all because their high level of education, technical expertise, engineering skills, and vast experience in the steelmaking industry were needed by each of the masters.

Kazusada Hara, whose involvement in dismantling his own company's facilities so they could be shipped to Russia was narrated earlier (see chapter 4), was born in Oita Prefecture in 1910. He entered the employment of Showa Steel Manufacturing Company immediately after his graduation from Ryoujun University of Engineering near Port Arthur in Dalian and was the section chief of the machine tool engineering department when the war ended. He experienced the same bombings Maruyama experienced when a fleet of American B-29s descended without warning on the company compound on July 29, 1944. The war that he and his fellow workers thought was in far-off places like Midway, Saipan, and Guadalcanal, was suddenly upon them. Major damage was inflicted on key facilities, and the following days were spent repairing and salvaging what they could to get the factory running again. Like hawks that had been watching the repair process, B-29s again descended on the factory on August 4, again dropping bombs to destroy what had been repaired from the previous bombings and inflicting even greater damage. Subsequent bombing raids occurred on August 27, September 8, and September 26 to almost completely cripple Showa Steel Manufacturing's ability produce steel; an ability that was so critical for Japan to continue her war efforts. Production capacity after the bombings fell to a third of the previous capacity.

When the Soviet army invaded and occupied Anshan, all former Japanese and Chinese employees of Showa Steel Manufacturing were forcibly recruited to dismantle and transport factory facilities and equipment under the watchful eyes and guns of Soviet soldiers. In just two months, Showa Steel Manufacturing Company, consisting of twenty-five factories and more than sixty thousand tons of facilities, was dismantled and hauled off by train to the Soviet Union by an average of ten thousand furiously toiling workers each day. During the period that Hara was engaged in the dismantling project, public order was relatively safe and calm since former members of the Japanese Kwantung Army were used to supplement Soviet troops in maintaining public order. However, on October 30, all Japanese military personnel were ordered to disarm, were arrested, and began to be transported by train to Siberia; public order deteriorated dramatically thereafter. When the massive dismantling project was completed on November 12, 1945, the Soviet army officers and men supervising the dismantling disappeared, never to be seen again. Other Soviet soldiers remained, but they, along with the Communist Eighth Route Army soldiers, were involved in occupation tasks, which included pillaging civilians and making life miserable for Chinese and Japanese alike.

Ignoring a Japanese Soldier's Plea for Help

Hara vividly recalled an incident that happened during the Soviet occupation, which haunted him until his dying days. One day in late November (1945), all Japanese were ordered by the Communist Chinese Army Headquarters to assemble in an open field hastily set up as an assembly area for a major announcement. It seemed that a large group of former Japanese soldiers were holed up and resisting surrender in a nearby mountain called Chiyama. Because they had been under siege for some time without food or water, it was likely that they would make an attempt to escape and seek help from Japanese residents in the community below. The Chinese commander explained the situation to the assembled Japanese and made it clear that if anyone helped the soldiers, every Japanese in Anshan, regardless of age or gender, would be marched thirty miles out of town to an open field without food, shelter, or water in the bitter cold of winter that was settling in on Anshan. The Japanese were already precariously near starvation and were suffering from the bitter cold even in their own homes, so the threat was taken most seriously. The Japanese returned home after the assembly and tightly locked their doors, spoke only in whispers, darkened their homes, and prayed that no one would come begging for help.

Not many days after the warning, there was a very light tapping sound on Hara's wooden shutter that covered the windows of his house at night. Fearful that someone might be observing his house, Hara whispered without opening the door, "Who is it?"

"I am a Japanese draftee, and I am on my way to Chiyama, but in the darkness I have lost my way. Could I have lodging for just this night?"

Unable to find his voice for a while, Hara finally replied, "I am very sorry, but by order of the Eighth Route Army, we are prohibited from helping former Japanese soldiers. Please forgive me." Shortly thereafter, Hara heard the sound of shuffling footsteps fading away. As that night wore on, Hara could only feel pain in his chest. The terrible guilt and shame would not subside. He wondered if he should have done something for that soldier whom he never saw. Many years later, he asked his now grown daughter if she remembered that incident, and she said, "I can never forget it. Grandmother kept crying, 'What a pity, what a pity,' all night long."

Several days later, when rumors spread that the Nationalist army was nearing Anshan, the holed-up Japanese soldiers tried to take advantage of the situation to engage the Eighth Route Army and were defeated in a fierce battle that took the lives of several of the Japanese soldiers. Survivors were captured and taken away to Liaoyang. Hara's guilt and misery only deepened upon the bloody conclusion of the siege.

Watching Others Depart for Koroto

Although ships began arriving around May 1946, at Koroto across the Liaodong Bay to repatriate Japanese stranded in Manchuria, it was not until July 10 that Japanese residents in Anshan were allowed to travel by train to Koroto. Approximately three thousand Japanese per day boarded the trains from Anshan Station to journey to the waiting repatriation ships. By July 28, more than sixty thousand Japanese had departed Anshan for Koroto. But seven thousand, including Hara and his family, were not among the group. Those left behind, all engineers, technicians, and their families, were declared essential by the Nationalists (who now occupied Anshan) to rebuild and reconstruct the factories that had been dismantled and destroyed by order of the Soviet army. Each day, those left behind quietly and sadly bade farewell to those returning to Japan, wondering if they would ever meet again and if their turn to return would ever come. As for those departing, while the long-awaited journey home was finally here and soon they would be reunited with their loved ones back in Japan, their concerns for those left behind dampened their joy as they quietly waved good-bye from the trains that slowly chugged out of the station.

By the fall of 1947, Anshan's relative calm and peace that Hara and his family and other families left behind had been enjoying under Nationalist army control came to an abrupt halt. As the Chinese Communist forces intent on retaking Anshan grew closer, cannons and guns could be heard in the distance. A decision was made by the Showa Steel Manufacturing senior staff to send all but a handful of Japanese to Koroto for their repatriation to Japan. Only ninety engineers and their families, totaling 280, were held back, including Hara.

Hara, whose family of seven consisted of himself, his wife, his mother, a son, and three daughters, was at least able to make arrangements to send his quite elderly mother and three daughters back to Japan. Saying farewell to his mother and three daughters was the hardest thing he had ever done, and he wondered if they would all still be alive when they next met. Hara's wife was too stricken with grief to even come to the station to bid farewell to her daughters and mother-in-law. Never in his life had Hara felt so lonely as when the cargo train carrying half his family chugged away to Koroto. The train took seventeen days (normally a two- to three-day trip) to arrive at its destination since so much of the railroads and so many bridges had been destroyed by the approaching Chinese Communist army.

Life in Anshan in early 1948 worsened as the Communist forces expelled the Nationalist army from Anshan. Food became scarce. Soon the only thing left to eat was *koryan*, the tasteless sorghum normally used as animal feed. Skirmishes became frequent throughout the city, but fortunately the 280 Japanese were not harmed. Fear mounted among the Japanese that, once the Chinese Communist forces controlled the city, there would be a heavy price to pay by the Japanese, as had happened with each change in regime in the past: attacks on women, pillaging, demand for "donations," arrests, people's trials, spying, arbitrary punishment, and other fearful retributions. After all, the 280 Japanese had been directly involved, even if they had no choice, in repairing and rebuilding vital industrial infrastructure on behalf of the enemy Nationalist forces. The Japanese could only wait in trepidation to see what would befall them.

To their complete surprise and relief, the Communist forces did not act maliciously toward them. In fact, the Japanese were given special treatment; the day after the Nationalists capitulated, an extra supply of *koryan* was distributed to the Japanese by the Chinese Communists. Hara learned much later (in fact, almost forty years later, from a Chinese who had been an interpreter on behalf of the Japanese in Anshan in those days) that the most influential Chinese "boss" in Anshan had been persuaded to insure the safety of those few Japanese who remained. The "boss" (much like a Mafia boss) had such great influence in Anshan that no one dared oppose his policies. Fortunately, no Japanese was harmed in the rampage and pillaging that followed the hasty departure of Nationalist forces from Anshan.

Always at the Mercy of Whoever Rules

Hara, his wife, and his son, along with the other Japanese, lived relatively comfortably in Anshan under Communist control. The sound of gunfire was no longer heard, and food was distributed periodically, so that the only anxiety was the question of when they might be allowed to return to Japan. Not a day went by for each of the Japanese without thinking about and longing for their homeland. But at least, they no longer walked in fear or shuttered their homes at night or talked in whispers; they could even enjoy celebrating birthdays and anniversaries and other special occasions. But that did not last long.

On March 5, 1948, an order was issued to all the Japanese that, in two days' time, they were to be taken to Andong (presently Dandong City) near the Korean border. No amount of appeal did any good. Loading all their personal belongings on trucks and horse-drawn carts, they traveled over narrow and sometimes frozen, sometimes muddy mountain passes and valleys and spent their nights in various crude lodging facilities, most without toilet or heat, and after seven days and nights, they arrived in Andong. Before and even during the war, it was normally a ten-hour journey by train.

The Japanese spent the next eight months in Andong, where the men were assigned to oversee engineering tasks at various factories. For a while, Hara worked in a munitions factory where he was involved in the manufacture of hand grenades. The Chinese workers there, Hara remembered after his return to Japan, had great respect for the Japanese engineers and technicians and were most cooperative and obedient. In spite of that, all the Japanese remained depressed and unhappy during their entire stay in Andong. While in Anshan, there was always the hope that they would someday be able to return to Japan. That hope appeared to have faded completely in Andong. Some of the Japanese in the group came up with a plan to escape to Japan by first dashing across the border to North Korea and then making their way to what is now South Korea. That plan, however, never materialized since the Japanese were again ordered to return to Anshan to assist in the city's repair and recovery of steel manufacturing capacities. This time, in December 1948, the Japanese returned by train to Anshan.

Life back in Anshan was not particularly difficult or busy for the Japanese group. By about 1950, correspondence with Japan became possible so that they were able to contact their families and friends in Japan and learned how difficult postwar life in Japan had been. One of the main concerns among the Japanese in Anshan was the education of the children who had stayed behind with their parents. The adults took on the role of teachers and insured that all the children received instruction in math, science, Japanese, history, geography, and all basic curricula so that when they returned to Japan, they would be able to smoothly fit in to regular schools at the proper level for their age. And they continued to wait their turn to return home.

A Young Japanese Mother Who Chose to Stay

Hara had an encounter in 1950 that made him realize they were not the only Japanese still living in Manchuria. Early one morning, there was a knock on the door of his house. When he opened the door, a young woman stood there, and Hara immediately recognized that she was not a Chinese but a Japanese woman. "May I help you?" asked Hara in Japanese. The young woman immediately sat down on the dirt floor of the entryway, as if collapsing, and Hara helped her come inside his house.

The woman explained, "I am a Japanese whose life was saved immediately after the war by a Chinese man whom I married, and I gave birth to a child. That child is now gravely ill and suffering. I have come to you to beg for medicine for my child. I am not of your group that has been forced to stay and work. I am merely too poor to seek help from a doctor."

Hara called for his wife, and together they consulted a doctor in their group and gave the young woman as much medicine and food as they could gather together. The woman went away after profusely thanking Hara and his wife for their kindness. Hara never saw her again and never knew if her child recovered. Most regrettably, Hara had forgotten to ask her name or where she was from in Japan. Later, he heard rumors that at least forty Japanese girls just in Anshan had married Chinese men following the turmoil that accompanied the Soviet invasion and the defeat of Japan. And these Japanese girls, as well as the unknown but high number of Japanese children (later termed *zanryukoji* or "left-behind orphans") who had been adopted by Chinese families, were never included among the Japanese who were offered the opportunity to be repatriated to Japan. When Hara finally returned to Japan, he learned from official Japanese government reports that 3,500 to four thousand Japanese women who married Chinese citizens were left behind in Manchuria following the tumultuous period of Japan's surrender.

Hara and the 280 Japanese in Anshan were finally given permission to return to Japan in August 1953. The entire group was transported to the Port of Tanggu near Tianjin (the same port where Maruyama, Shinpo, and Musashi boarded a U.S. naval vessel on their final leg during their escape from Manchuria in March 1946), where they boarded the *Koan Maru* and arrived back in Japan on August 13, 1953, almost exactly eight years after the end of World War II.

Until he died in 1999 at age eighty-nine, Hara spent much of his free time as a volunteer working on behalf of the cause of Japanese orphans (*zanryukoji*) and women who had been left behind in China and Manchuria at the end of the war and were now seeking reunion with their long-lost families in Japan.[1]

(Author's note: The above was excerpted, translated, and paraphrased by this author from Yoko Tanoue's Manchuria's "August 15" as Related by Parents and Their Children.*)*

Chapter 30

The Matter of the Loans

The Last Repatriation Ship

The *Takasago Maru* became the last ship to carry home Japanese repatriates from Dalian, Manchuria, when it docked at Sasebo on April 3, 1948. By then, Musashi had, for all intents and purposes, left the repatriation work in the capable hands of Maruyama and Shinpo and launched a new life and career in the construction business in his burning desire to play a role in rebuilding a new Japan. With the arrival of the *Takasago Maru*, Maruyama and Shinpo gradually concluded their involvement in repatriation efforts. They too felt it was now time to take part in reconstructing their devastated homeland. Maruyama went on to finally fulfill his original lifelong goal of teaching, and in 1952, he became a lecturer, later professor, at his alma mater, Meiji University in Tokyo. Shinpo, who had been the founder and president of Shinpo-gumi, a most successful and respected architecture and construction company in Manchuria, resumed his career in the construction industry.

To be sure, nearly five hundred thousand Japanese were still thought to be awaiting repatriation to Japan in Siberia, in various parts of Korea, in the Soviet-controlled Kuril Islands, as well as in other scattered areas. However, it was by no means an exaggeration to say that the mission of the Representatives to Petition for Saving Our Countrymen Living in Manchuria, headed by Kunio Maruyama, Hachiro Shinpo, and Masamichi Musashi, had been successfully accomplished, since the vast majority of the Japanese stranded in Manchuria had now been repatriated back to Japan. The Japanese government had assumed immediately after the war that it would take over four years to return home the estimated six million Japanese who resided outside Japan. In fact, thanks to the vigorous, benevolent, and humanitarian efforts of the U.S. military commanded by the Supreme Commander for Allied Powers (SCAP), General Douglas MacArthur, the majority of Japanese, except for those living in territories under Soviet control, were returned within two years following the end of the war.

The Japanese Government Refused to Honor Loans

The efforts of the three brave men who escaped from Manchuria, and who went on to mount a campaign in Japan to spur the Japanese government, the Japanese people, and, in the end, GHQ and General MacArthur, to bring about the early dispatching of ships to Koroto (Huludao) in Manchuria, have not been fully recognized even to this day. In fact, not only have the Japanese government and the citizens of Japan failed to properly recognize the heroic deeds of the three men, but the Japanese government never reimbursed the money that was raised in Manchuria by Musashi, who borrowed from those Japanese able to access their funds. Instead, the loans were repaid for the most part out of the pockets of the three men.

When the decision was made by GHQ to send ships to Koroto in May 1946, to begin the long-awaited repatriation of Japanese from Manchuria, Musashi boarded the first ship back to Manchuria. He was entrusted to accomplish several vital tasks: (1) to take medical and other supplies that were greatly needed by Japanese residents, especially the ill and the refugees; (2) to distribute vital government documents required for repatriation to the various Japanese associations; (3) to deliver letters and documents to key Japanese leaders in Manchuria from the Japanese government; and (4) to assist Japanese associations throughout Manchuria to bring about a smooth and orderly repatriation. Much money was needed to assist the various Japanese associations to bring about the mass transport by train to Koroto of thousands of Japanese, most of them homeless and penniless refugees, many with no food or clothing to tide them over until they reached the waiting ships. Musashi had carried with him "marching orders" issued by the Representatives to Petition for Saving Our Countrymen Living in Manchuria that stated the following:

> If, in the process of repatriation or during the rescue of refugees, funds become necessary, [Musashi] will take appropriate measures to borrow money from influential Japanese in Manchuria. If by so doing he accumulates expenditures, those debts become completely the responsibility of this Headquarters of the Representatives to Petition for Saving Our Countrymen Living in Manchuria and on a later date, all moneys will be returned to the lender by the Japanese government or other related agencies. To make sure this will take place, he [Musashi] will insure that the name, address, birth date, place of loan, and other vital information regarding the lender is clearly recorded and kept, and a receipt will be issued to the lender.[1]

The authority for the provision contained in Musashi's "marching orders" came from the then Chief Secretary to Prime Minister Shidehara, Minister of State Wataru Narahashi. One of the documents the three men brought back with them upon their escape from Manchuria was a letter from the chairman of the All-Manchuria Japanese Association, Tatsunosuke Takasaki. In effect, Takasaki was the individual who spoke for all Japanese in Manchuria during those days of Soviet occupation when all communication between Japan and her citizens in Manchuria was completely severed. Takasaki had written to Minister Narahashi to request a letter from the Japanese government guaranteeing that "money borrowed on behalf of repatriation efforts from wealthy Japanese residing in Manchuria would be fully refunded by the Japanese government upon their return to Japan." Realizing that the lives of 1.7 million Japanese were at stake, Minister Narahashi issued the letter upon consultation with the then Finance Minister Shibusawa; that letter was entrusted to Musashi when he returned to Manchuria, and Musashi handed the letter over to Chairman Takasaki in Shenyang.

On June 1, 1949, the Japanese government enacted legislation entitled "Law No. 13: The Law for the Auditing Committee to Prepare Arrangements for Money Borrowed by Government Agencies in Foreign Countries." According to this law, "borrowed money" was defined as "those funds which were borrowed from Japanese living in foreign countries by governmental agencies located in said foreign countries or by autonomous Japanese organizations or by organizations that conform to such groups, with the stipulation that such funds would be repaid at a later date by the Japanese government."

The law was interpreted narrowly so that the three men (Maruyama, Shinpo, and Musashi) and their self-governing and self-proclaimed committee were considered to be outside the law's application. The problem lay in the fact that, when they escaped from Manchuria in early 1946, the three men had acted completely on their own, in secret, using their own funds and resources, informing almost no one, coordinating their efforts with no one connected with the Japanese government or the All-Manchuria Japanese Association. They had not been directed or requested or sanctioned to take on their mission of rescue by any Japanese government entity or by an organization recognized by the Japanese government. The only discussion they had had was with Takasaki, chairman of the All-Manchuria Japanese Association, who was incredulous that the three were about to carry out their secret mission and probably did not take them completely seriously when told of their plan.

It was precisely because the three men acted completely in secret and on their own that their escape succeeded. Had their plan been discovered by the Soviet occupation army or by any Chinese, or even by a Japanese who might have reported their plan to the authorities to gain favors or a reward, the retaliation against the three would have been quick and final. Not only that, the retribution against their families, friends, and anyone who may have known them would have been brutal, swift, and merciless. But now, the Japanese government was refusing to recognize the self-proclaimed entity called the Representatives to Petition for Saving Our Countrymen Living in Manchuria as an organization eligible to be reimbursed for any money it borrowed in Manchuria for the repatriation effort. The money Musashi raised upon his return to Manchuria, before his arrest and torture by the Nationalist army, was not recognized by the Japanese government to have been borrowed by a Japanese government-recognized entity in spite of the letter from Minister of State Narahashi.

Maruyama and Shinpo were stunned and felt betrayed by the narrow interpretation of the law. They immediately protested to applicable government agencies, including the Foreign Ministry. The response they received from the various bureaucrats was as follows: "We fully understand your feelings and outrage. There is no one who does not recognize the heroic actions you have accomplished. We fully agree that any expenses used for your activities on behalf of repatriation should be fully refunded by the nation. Unfortunately, however, a separate legislative action would be necessary, so we suggest you go to all the different political parties and request that parliamentary representatives use their legislative power on your behalf."

When Musashi, who was by now well on his way to a successful new career, was informed of the bureaucratic runaround, he said to his former employer and mentor Hachiro Shinpo, "Let's not waste any more time and effort on this issue. I am personally ready to make repayment on all the loans." In the end, the three proud men concluded that they could never demean themselves to go around bowing their heads to political leaders in order to ask such a favor.

All the money that was borrowed in the name of their organization was eventually repaid out of their own personal assets or was resolved by other means. The bulk of the money was provided by Musashi whose construction company was in great demand in postwar Japan.

On June 13, 2009, the author met with Masamichi Musashi and his wife, Mitsuko, at their residence in the Shibuya District of Tokyo. It was an emotional meeting that the author had looked forward to for several years. The last time they had seen each other was when the author was barely five years old and had been entrusted, along with his mother and siblings, to the care of the Maryknoll Catholic Church in Dalian as Musashi, Shinpo, and Maruyama set out into the unknown, to escape out of Soviet clutches. Musashi was a youthful-looking, vigorous man of eighty-eight, and one would never have known that this energetic and still ambitious man with a full head of handsome hair was the same man who, nearly sixty-five years before, was tortured so severely in a Nationalist Chinese prison that, on at least three occasions, his tormentors prepared to carry him to the morgue because he showed no signs of life. Shortly after returning to Japan for the second and final time following his horrendous ordeal in Manchuria in 1946, while assisting in the orderly repatriation of Japanese, Musashi felt that the bulk of the work in the repatriation effort was completed, and whatever more needed to be done could now be handled by Maruyama and Shinpo. Thus, he turned his attention to playing a part in rebuilding his defeated and ruined country.

As a contractor in the construction business, Musashi was enormously successful. At one time, he employed several hundred workers; he credits his success to lessons learned while under captivity: no hardship could stop him, no obstacle could overwhelm him, and no goal was beyond his reach. During the "bubble years" when Japan's economy took a sharp dive downward in the 1990s, he suffered staggering losses that reached into the billions of yen; even that did not deter him from recovering. Today, he owns a vast piece of land on the northern-most island of Hokkaido with beautiful landscapes and plentiful hot spring water that he, with his eldest son Hironobu, hopes to some day turn into one of the most beautiful resorts in the world. "I think," said a friend of Musashi's at a dinner party that the author attended, "when Musashi-san was tortured by the Chinese back in 1946, they somehow altered his DNA so that he is forever immune from aging and slowing down!"

Asked if he had ever returned to the former Manchuria (now northern China) to look at the changes that have taken place in Dalian, in Anshan, and in Koroto, Musashi replied in the negative, a shadow crossing his face as he said that memories are still very painful to him. He has lost contact with the Chinese he knew in those days, some who now live under Communism and others who were driven out with Chiang Kai-shek to Taiwan. Most have probably passed away by now, he mused.

Even now, he is occasionally invited to give speeches to reminisce about his role in the repatriation of Japanese from postwar Manchuria. Recently, he was invited to give a speech in Iiyama City in Nagano Prefecture, Maruyama's hometown. There, he gently reprimanded those in attendance for not being aware of the heroic role played by one of their native sons, Kunio

Maruyama, in the repatriation of Japanese from Manchuria. Recalling the first time he met Maruyama, Musashi commented with a chuckle, "He had hairy arms and his eyebrows were thick! It was because of Professor Maruyama that Japanese were able to return. I beseech all of you in Iiyama to always preciously remember his contributions."

"Your father," said Musashi to this author during the June 13, 2009, meeting, "was a most honest and honorable man. One of the things I admired about him was the way he could give a speech. In normal conversation, he was not the best conversationalist, with a lot of 'ums' and 'ahs' in his sentences. But when he stood in front of an audience, you could not help but be swayed by his oratorical skill!"

In a letter that Musashi wrote to this author several months before their long-awaited meeting, he stated the following when told that a book in English about the courageous actions of the three men was in preparation, targeted mainly for American and English-speaking audiences: "The lives of 1.7 million Japanese who lived in the former nation of Manchuria at the end of World War II were saved, not by the Japanese government, nor by the Soviet Union, nor by Great Britain, nor by China; they were saved by the United States of America, and we owe everything to the people of America. The Japanese people must never forget that great kindness."[2]

Masamichi Musashi was a remarkable man in his early twenties when he worked heroically to rescue his fellow countrymen from Manchuria; now in his late eighties, he continues to amaze all who know him with his vitality, his alertness, his ambition, and his optimism.

The author stands with Masamichi Musashi, the only surviving member of the three brave men who escaped from Manchuria in 1946. This photo was taken in June 2009, in the art gallery inside Musashi's office in the Shibuya Ward of Tokyo. His sharp mind, astuteness, and youthful vigor at the age of eighty-eight amazed the author. (Author's Collection)

Chapter 31

Why the Three Succeeded

Reflecting on the Three Men's Selfless Actions

In the concluding remarks in his book *Why Was Koroto Opened*, Kunio Maruyama wrote:

> While this may sound like a lofty statement, the mission that we, the Representatives to Petition for Saving Our Countrymen Living in Manchuria, set out to accomplish, in which we shouldered the burden that decided the fate of 1.7 million Japanese countrymen, had its origin in our sincere love for our fellow man. We simply persevered ceaselessly and consistently in pursuing our goals; eventually, perhaps, our efforts were recognized in heaven so that peace, happiness, and prosperity finally arrived, not only for the many million countrymen who had been stranded overseas, but also for their loved ones at home awaiting them. I do not believe it would be an exaggeration to say that, in the end, we all welcomed the beginning of a new and glorious dawning of Asia.[1]

Indeed, over six million men, women, and children from Japan had left their homeland in the years before August 1945, leaving their relatives and loved ones, to toil in foreign lands throughout Asia to help with the war effort. Most believed that the emperor was a living god; few questioned the veracity of the propaganda spewed out by the military-controlled media. The invincibility of the Imperial Army and Navy was an unquestioned fact; the military was the law of the land. Each Japanese was expected to unquestioningly obey the orders of the military oligarchy; each Japanese was expected to "make possible that which was impossible" on behalf of the war effort. One million seven hundred thousand of the six million Japanese living overseas were in a vast northern territory of China and Inner Mongolia called Manchuria which had been declared by Japan to be the Great Manchurian Empire in 1932 with its own emperor. Rich in natural resources, Manchuria was the lifeline for the imperial military machine which used her coal, iron, and other vital mineral resources as well as her soy, barley and other agricultural products that grew so readily in her rich soil.

Life in Manchuria was relatively comfortable for the Japanese living there until August 8, 1945, when the vast army of the Soviet Union invaded without warning from the north and northeast to quickly control and occupy the Japanese puppet state. Overnight, the good life turned into an endless nightmare, and virtually all freedom was taken away from the Japanese, who were no longer welcome in Manchuria but had no means of returning to their homeland. Homes, jobs, savings, personal belongings, and even lives were indiscriminately taken. Farmers and pioneers from the many Japanese settlements, mainly in the north, were driven southward with only the clothing on their backs, too frequently assaulted by Soviet troops and gangs of bandits as they sought refuge in cities where there were other Japanese residents. Japanese in large cities such as Anshan, Dalian, Changchun, and Shenyang were not much better off since they no longer had any means of earning an income. All

353

their bank accounts had been frozen, and they lived in constant fear of robbery, assault, and incursion by Soviet soldiers and unruly gangs intent on exacting revenge on the now former occupiers of Manchuria. With no money for food, clothing, heat, medicine, and other essentials, the Japanese paid a heavy toll during the harsh winters of Manchuria. This toll fell most heavily on the very young, who did not even know the meaning of war. It was only a matter of time before the life of every Japanese in Manchuria was in jeopardy.

It was remarkable that three ordinary men, men of no particular rank or distinction with no history of extreme bravery, came together to successfully concoct and execute a plan to evade and escape through the extraordinary curtain of iron that had been drawn by the Soviet Union and her ally, the Chinese Communist army, to prevent anyone from entering or exiting the Manchurian Empire. Remarkably, the three men carried out their audacious plan without the help of the Japanese government or organizations in Manchuria associated with the Japanese government. The help for their escape came from the Nationalist army of Chiang Kai-shek, the Maryknoll Catholic Church in Dalian, and the U.S. military, which put them on a ship that transported them back to Senzaki, Japan, from the Port of Tanggu in China.

What was perhaps most remarkable about the three brave men was their persistent activity after returning to Japan. From their first (wholly censored) news conference in Kokura City in southern Japan to their meetings with Japanese government representatives (including future Prime Minister Shigeru Yoshida) to their frequent, often adversarial meetings with SCAP GHQ personnel until the first ship to Koroto was dispatched after they met with General Douglas MacArthur, Maruyama, Shinpo, and Musashi never faltered in their resolve to initiate the rescue of their fellow countrymen stranded under cruel Soviet occupation in Manchuria.

Musashi undertook a nearly impossible mission as he returned to Manchuria, back into the tiger's den, to carry supplies, vital documents, and pharmaceutical goods and to assist in bringing about a successful repatriation. For his trouble, he paid an extraordinary price as he was mistakenly arrested, confined, and tortured for more than seven long weeks, in the end miraculously escaping with his life. Even after the stream of repatriates began returning home, the three men continued their mission, speaking at rallies and assemblies, meeting with government, imperial, and civilian representatives and organizations, and doing all that was within their power to keep the repatriation issue fresh in the consciousness of the people of Japan.

Undoubtedly, the fact that the families of Maruyama and Shinpo still remained in Soviet-occupied Dalian, even after nearly a million Japanese from Manchuria had been repatriated through the Port of Koroto, gave the three men powerful incentive to continue their campaign to open Dalian as a port for Japanese exodus. Even after the families of Maruyama and Shinpo had safely returned home, the self-proclaimed Representatives to Petition for Saving Our Countrymen Living in Manchuria (which was essentially the three men) continued their campaign. They expanded their focus from Manchuria to those still unreturned Japanese throughout Asia, including Japanese POWs who were forcibly transported to Siberia. The Soviet Union never demonstrated much interest in the POWs, to judge by how they were tracked and accounted for.

When the Public Employees' Union, including the railway workers, called for a general strike on February 1, 1947, Shinpo and Maruyama wasted no time in storming the headquarters of the labor union at Tokyo Station to demand that the leadership abandon the strike. The two were in the middle of a tense and emotional shouting and haranguing of the union leaders when it was announced that the Supreme Commander for Allied Powers, General Douglas MacArthur himself, was ordering the union to desist from carrying out the strike. Nothing could stop the men's dedication and commitment in their efforts to bring the stranded Japanese home. Most fortunately, the three men were able to count on General MacArthur and his GHQ personnel throughout their campaign. The same could not always be said of the Japanese government, whose passion on behalf of the unreturned appeared to subside from time to time, as pointed out on the floor of the Japanese Parliament on November 8, 1947, by House of Councilors member Nobuo Asaoka.

Truman Always Wanted All Japanese Out of China and Manchuria

There is ample evidence to indicate that the U.S. government had always intended to bring home the millions of Japanese who had been trapped overseas after the unconditional surrender of Japan. That intention included those trapped in Manchuria. In an NHK (Japan Broadcasting Corporation) documentary aired in Japan on December 8, 2008, it was stated that President Harry Truman met with Secretary of State George Marshall and other key personnel in Washington on December 11, 1945, to discuss the evacuation of Japanese from Manchuria.[2] A few days later, on December 15, President Truman stated in a speech that it was the United States's intention to remove any possibility of Japanese power remaining in China.[3]

The first time Koroto (Huludao) was mentioned as a candidate port for Japanese evacuation seems to have been during a U.S.–China conference on the Issue of Evacuating Japanese POWs and Civilians that was held in Shanghai on January 5, 1946. A key participant at the conference was a Colonel Richard C. Wittman who stated that at least two ports would be required for evacuation from Manchuria. One was Koroto, and the other, if allowed, would be Dalian, and preparation for executing the plan would begin around April 1,

1946. By that time, a commander would be designated to enter Manchuria. Colonel Wittman also stated that, by then, sufficient intelligence about Manchuria would be required.[4]

Since no U.S. presence then was allowed in Soviet-occupied Manchuria, it is this author's assumption that much of the intelligence needed by Colonel Wittman, about the present conditions in Manchuria and the status of the port of Koroto, was provided by the three men (Maruyama, Shinpo, and Musashi), who engaged in numerous discussions with GHQ personnel during the weeks before the first repatriation ships were dispatched in May 1946. Thus, the sudden appearance at GHQ on March 20, 1946, of three men who had just escaped from Manchuria was probably an unexpected stroke of fortune that allowed GHQ to fill in crucial intelligence gaps, namely the present situation in Manchuria and that of the Port of Koroto. Perhaps the confusion in not being able to locate Koroto (chapter 13) was caused by the three men who used the Japanese name for the port, Koroto, rather than the Chinese name familiar to Americans, Huludao.

No Public Tribute Conferred Yet on the Three Men

It has been stated previously in this book that the heroic exploits of the three men have not been widely recognized. Although Maruyama was awarded a certificate of commendation from the Foreign Ministry (in 1974), and a posthumous medal of honor (*kunsho*) was presented to his wife Mary on his behalf by then Prime Minister Zenko Suzuki in 1981, these presentations were done in private and without fanfare. No official or public tribute to date has been conferred upon Musashi and Shinpo (now deceased) for their roles, whose heroism equaled that of Maruyama.

The most likely reason for the neglect is that these men acted completely on their own and in complete secrecy, so that very little record is available to verify their exploits. No government order or letter was ever issued. The few people in places of influence who would have been able to testify to the details of the heroic actions of the three have all passed away. Finally, because of the pain and suffering Japan had to endure for many years following her defeat, recognitions and awards were the last thing on anyone's mind during those days when memories were still fresh.

The relieved and thankful repatriates who made their long-sought journey to Koroto to board the ships that would take them back to Japan in those tumultuous days only had energy to bask in the happiness that they were finally returning to their homeland. It is likely that hardly a soul stopped to ask how it came about that ships suddenly sailed from Japan to pick them up and repatriate them. Among the returnees who spent a night or two at the Kugayama headquarters of the three men before completing their journey home, there were some who had secretly heard Maruyama's April 17, 1946, NHK broadcast even in Manchuria; these repatriates, upon recognizing Maruyama as the man who spoke on the radio, made it a point to profusely thank the three men for all they had done on behalf of the stranded Japanese in Manchuria. But other than that, most of the repatriates had too many other things on their mind to even wonder who, if anyone, outside of GHQ and the Japanese government, had played a significant role in the repatriation of Japanese from Manchuria.

Three Reasons Why the Three Succeeded: Takako Tominaga

One person who did become aware of the three men's extraordinary deeds was Takako Tominaga, author of several books including *Dairen: 600 Days of Vacuum*, first published by Shinhyouron Company, Limited, on July 30, 1986.[5] Due to its immense popularity, more than ten reprintings of the book followed the initial publication. Born in Yamaguchi City in

1931, Tominaga lived as a young schoolgirl in Dairen (Dalian), Manchuria, from 1943 until she was repatriated in 1947.

An entire chapter in her book was devoted to relating the story of the three men. At the time of the Japanese surrender, she was a thirteen-year-old junior high school student residing in Dalian with her family. Trapped with her family and all other Japanese under Soviet occupation for six hundred days following the end of the war, her book is a superbly researched chronological accounting of postwar life of the Japanese people in Dalian until their eventual repatriation. While engaged in researching archival materials at the Kagoshima City public library in March 1982, prior to writing *Dairen: 600 Days of Vacuum*, she came across an article that had appeared in the *Asahi* newspaper's western edition that began with, "The true situation in Manchuria as related by escapees...."

The article, dated March 17, 1946, reported on the present and terrible conditions in Manchuria as related by three men who recently escaped from there. According to Kunio Maruyama, Hachiro Shinpo, and Masamichi Musashi, the article reported, Japanese in Manchuria were suffering immensely from hunger, severe cold, and rampant diseases under the harsh occupation of the Soviet army and the Communist Chinese Eighth Route Army, with additional threats from violent Manchurian gangs. With no means to earn a living and with all bank accounts frozen, all Japanese residents were in extremely dire straits, reported the three men, who planned to relate these facts to the people of Japan and to General MacArthur to rouse up support to rescue their countrymen trapped in Manchuria.

Ms. Tominaga immediately made every effort to locate "the three unknown heroes" and discovered that one of them, Kunio Maruyama, had written a book entitled, *Why Was Koroto Opened*. When she finally contacted the Maruyama residence in Kokubunji just west of Tokyo (where the Maruyamas had moved from Kugayama in the early 1950s), she found that Maruyama was bedridden and unable to give an interview. But she later had an interview with his wife, Mary, who provided all the information Tominaga needed. (*Author's note: Kunio Maruyama died on October 17, 1981, so that when Tominaga contacted Mary Maruyama, presumably in 1982, Maruyama had already passed away.*) Subsequently, Tominaga had an extensive interview with Masamichi Musashi. As for Shinpo (who died of cancer in his late fifties), although Tominaga was never able to interview him, she found out that the main character in a novel of that time, *The Ruffian of Manchuria* by Tetsuro Morikawa, was modeled on Hachiro Shinpo.

Until she discovered the March 1946 *Asahi* newspaper article, she had never heard about the three men and their escape out of Manchuria. She had been aware that Tatsunosuke Takasaki, then the chairman of the All-Manchuria Japanese Association, had dispatched two sets of secret emissaries carrying letters addressed to Foreign Minister Shigeru Yoshida on September 22, 1945. The plan itself was executed by Toshio Hirashima who, at that time, was the vice president of the South Manchurian Railroad Company. A Japanese resident in Changchun, with special talent for writing tiny characters, each about half the size of a grain of rice, wrote the letters that described the dire situation of Japanese in Manchuria under Soviet occupation, and the letters were sewn into the clothing of the secret emissaries. Both groups of secret messengers did succeed in reaching Japan (on October 10), but probably because the Japanese government was in no position then to be able to do anything about the appeal from Takasaki, no action was taken.

In contrast, Tominaga suggests that there were three reasons why the three men (Maruyama, Shinpo, and Musashi) succeeded so brilliantly in their mission. One was the significant help they received from the Catholic Church which never severed its ties with Imperial Japan, in peacetime or during war. The letters from Bishop Lane of Dalian that the three men carried sewn into their clothing addressed to Papal Nuncio Paul Marella, as well as to Father Patrick Byrne, not only opened many doors for the three men, including to General MacArthur, but the plight of the trapped Japanese in Manchuria was undoubtedly reported to the Vatican and to the pope himself.

A second reason for the three men's success, theorized Tominaga, was Maruyama's background and character. Having spent several years studying in the United States, the pro-American Maruyama was able to communicate as an equal with the officers at GHQ. Although a citizen of a defeated nation, he did not let that hold him back as he bluntly and straightforwardly stated his case with honest conviction on behalf of the suffering Japanese in Manchuria, even to General MacArthur himself. "That he spoke from the heart without self-interest undoubtedly moved the high-ranking personnel at both GHQ and in the Japanese government," wrote Takako Tominaga in *Dairen: 600 Days of Vacuum.*[6]

The final reason the three succeeded, Tominaga proposed, lay in the fact that the time was ripe for repatriating Japanese from Manchuria. She cites a report published in a document entitled "Chronological Table of Repatriation Assistance" which stated that on February 20, 1946 (a few weeks before the return of the three men to Japan), "The Headquarters of the Supreme Commander for Allied Powers General MacArthur formally sent in a request to the U.S. government for the repatriation of Japanese countrymen in Soviet-controlled territories." The situation was such that GHQ and the Japanese government were seriously assessing what concrete step would be taken to repatriate the Japanese, and the arrival of the three escapees from Manchuria lit the fuse that energized their actions, theorized Tominaga.[7]

Chapter 32

One Last Battle

Reform at Meiji University

From the time Maruyama graduated from Meiji University and went abroad to study in the United States, first at the University of Puget Sound in Washington, then at George Washington University in Washington DC, and finally at Columbia University in New York, his goal was always to return to Japan and pursue a career as an educator. Those plans were set aside, however, since when he returned to his homeland in 1938, the nation's mood was belligerent, promilitary, and intolerant of basic liberties that did not conform to nationalistic ideals. For someone who had great respect and admiration for the United States and whose wife was an American citizen of Japanese descent, he realized that freedom of expression did not exist in Japan and that whatever he might teach and say at the podium in the classroom would have to conform to the then present nationalistic mood. Thus, he set aside his lifelong dreams and settled into a corporate career that eventually took him and his family to Manchuria.

By 1952, the Allied occupation of Japan had ended, and the nation had adopted a new Constitution that no longer recognized the emperor as the supreme ruler of the land. Japan was now forced to stand on her own two feet, independent of GHQ, to mold a new democratic society. In that year, Maruyama finally fulfilled his dream and launched his true career ambition by becoming a lecturer at Meiji University, located near the heart of Tokyo. Meiji University was founded in 1881 and was Japan's largest private university as well as his alma mater. He happily immersed himself in teaching economics and English. He also spent much time pursuing his love of Shakespeare and taught courses on the study of Shakespeare and his works. One of several books Maruyama wrote was *The Swan of Avon* (published in 1959 by Nan'un-do Company, Limited), which he wrote in English. The book was an essay on the life and works of Shakespeare.

For Maruyama, who led a Japanese students' movement in the United States in the 1930s to right the wrongs brought about by the discriminatory Immigration Act of 1924, and who escaped from Manchuria with two companions to move General MacArthur and GHQ to dispatch ships to Koroto to rescue the Japanese trapped under Soviet occupation after the war, one more battle waited. When he was hired as a lecturer for Meiji University, he was assigned to the newly created BA Department, which was responsible for the education of more than three thousand students.

After several years, Maruyama noticed that the entrance exam scores of many students who were admitted were veiled in secrecy. In fact, it became obvious that many students with high entrance exam scores were denied acceptance since so many of the limited number of slots were filled by students whose scores were kept hidden. When Maruyama brought up the discrepancy for discussion at a departmental meeting, Kyuro Kusaki, the dean of the department, who also harbored ambition to become the next university president, eventually banned Maruyama from attending faculty meetings. Because all of the other professors in the department did not want to incur the wrath of the probable next president of the university,

Maruyama was isolated and ostracized by all but one of his colleagues. That one faculty member, Professor of Ethics, Logic, and Philosophy Kenjiro Tatsuno, sided with Maruyama and stood by him, thereby drawing the enmity of his colleagues.

Maruyama brought the matter of the corruption involved in the selection of new students to the attention of Meiji University President Kojima, who paid lip service to the problem but did nothing to correct the situation. Ultimately, Maruyama took the case, with ample evidence, to the attention of Minister of Education Ichiro Kiyose, whom Maruyama had known since his student days at Meiji. The *Yomiuri* newspaper found out about the meeting between Maruyama and Kiyose and headlined the scandal in its February 21, 1956 issue. Now, the irregularity in the appointment of new students to Meiji University, one of the nation's most prestigious institutes of higher learning, became a national topic. Initially, Maruyama was subjected to severe criticism, particularly from influential alumni, for airing Meiji's dirty laundry in public. Telephone calls threatening death were received at his home, and the tires of his car were punctured on one occasion. Many editorials in national publications took up the issue of unfairly admitting undeserving children of influential and wealthy families while rejecting deserving and bright candidates.

By now, University President Kojima was forced to appoint an investigative committee to scrutinize and seek the truth in the matter. An alumni association also launched its own independent investigation. In the end, Maruyama and Tatsuno (the only professor who stood by him) were completely vindicated. Dean Kusaki was scathingly condemned, and all the other professors who did not have the courage to stand up against Kusaki and his corruption were criticized. Even before the verdict was in, Dean Kusaki was overwhelmingly defeated for the presidency of Meiji University, capturing only six affirmative votes out of 129 cast.

Maruyama continued to teach at Meiji University until 1969 when he had to step down as professor due to the mandatory retirement system in Japan. His love for teaching would not let him retire just yet. He accepted a position as professor of economics at Teikyo University while he simultaneously continued teaching at Meiji as a lecturer.

The Influence of Sir Thomas More's Utopia

Throughout his life, one book had the greatest influence on the way Maruyama lived and conducted himself. That book *Utopia*, was written in 1516 by the great English scholar and martyr, Sir (later Saint) Thomas More. To Maruyama, utopia was a place of perfection, a place or thing to strive for. Whether seeking fair treatment from U.S. legislators for Japanese students unfairly affected by the anti-Japanese Immigration Act of 1924, or seeking action from General MacArthur and GHQ to rescue the 1.7 million Japanese seemingly abandoned in Manchuria, or seeking to eliminate corruption in the admissions system at Meiji University, Maruyama was always guided and inspired by his search for utopia. Some may say he was stubborn, arrogant, or narrow-minded, but no one has said he was dishonest, insincere, or uninvolved in causes he believed in.

In personal life, he was a wonderful father, an excellent role model, and someone his children and all who knew him respected and loved. Unfortunately, he never talked about himself or about his accomplishments to his children—ever. What he did in Manchuria; how he escaped; how he worried about his family as he carried on the campaign on behalf of those left behind in Manchuria, including his own family; what emotional ups and downs he must have experienced as he pressured GHQ and the Japanese government to keep their eye on the ball regarding repatriation; how he must have personally suffered in many ways as he carried on his lonely battle against the corrupt dean at Meiji University; and how he must have felt abandoned when all his colleagues except one refused to support him—all these events and episodes he kept to himself. His wife, Mary, was the only person to whom he confided his private and personal concerns. Never one to dwell on his own ego or his own accomplishments, he lived his entire life simply following his own conscience, doing what he knew to be right.

Around 1968, Maruyama finally found the time to begin writing a book describing the three greatest challenges he had faced in his unique and remarkable life. He aptly entitled his book *Aiming at Utopia*. The book narrates the three episodes related above: (1) his battle in the 1930s as a graduate student in the United States to seek better treatment for Japanese students caught in the enforcement of the anti-Japanese Immigration Act of 1924; (2) his escape from Manchuria with two companions to Japan and the subsequent repatriation campaign that reached all the way to General MacArthur; and (3) his lonely battle to eliminate corruption at one of the most prestigious institutions in Japan, Meiji University. (Subsequently, the second episode was published on its own as a book entitled *Why Was Koroto Opened*.) Helping Maruyama with his book, editing every word, helping him recollect incidents, and researching various facts was his wife, Mary.

The Children of Kunio and Mary

By that time (around 1970), none of the Maruyamas' children were still living at home; all were pursuing various careers or were in college. Robert, the eldest, had joined the Society of Mary as a Marianist brother and was then teaching at Riordan High School in San Francisco. Joseph, the second oldest, was an engineer for General Electric in northern California and was able to return from time to time to work on GE's nuclear power plant projects in Japan. Third son Paul was an officer in the United States Air Force and was stationed with his family at nearby Yokota Air Base, then later at Headquarters Fifth Air Force in Fuchu near Tokyo. The youngest brother, Xavier, was then a candidate for a doctorate in nuclear physics at Massachusetts Institute of Technology (MIT).

Marianne, who was born in Japan after the war (in Kugayama, at the former headquarters for the Representatives to Petition for Saving Our Countrymen Living in Manchuria) had just graduated from San Francisco Women's College and was employed by Roos/Atkins Company in San Francisco. Roseanne, the youngest of the six siblings, who was also born at Kugayama, was attending San Jose City College in San Jose, California.

Never in their wildest dreams during those turbulent days in Manchuria following the end of World War II could Kunio and Mary have imagined that all their children, who barely had enough to eat to survive, would grow up as they did, to graduate from some of the most prestigious colleges (Robert, Joseph, and Xavier graduated from the University of Notre Dame; Paul started at Loyola University of Los Angeles and graduated from San Jose State University) and go on to pursue fulfilling careers as responsible American citizens.

The four Maruyama sons are fully aware that, if their father had not taken the courageous and almost unimaginable risk to escape Manchuria and work tirelessly to bring about their repatriation and the repatriation of more than one and a half million other Japanese stranded in Manchuria, they might never have survived to become what they have become. The boys also fully recognize that the pillar of strength who brought them through those dark and terrible days was their mother, who never, ever was heard to complain about the difficult ordeal she endured in raising and protecting four young boys without her husband in a brutal, dangerous, and unforgiving environment which was postwar Manchuria.

Thus it was that, even while writing his book, nothing was discussed by Maruyama about Manchuria with his children. It was not that he wanted to keep things from his children; rather, he was too modest and reluctant to talk intimately about his heroic accomplishments and contributions to anyone, even his own children. He never took himself seriously; in his estimation, he merely did what he had to do, and that was the sum of the matter. His children are more than grateful that he left them a priceless legacy—his books, which recorded the exploits that he was too modest to "brag" about to his children.

Almost all children naturally think that their own parents are special, above the ordinary, a cut above other parents. The Maruyama children, of course, have the same feeling about their parents. But they are convinced that their parents' exceptional qualities were proven beyond a shadow of a doubt in the ordeal they experienced at the end of the war: Maruyama in his heroic escape to Japan; and Mary in keeping the four young boys and the helper Toki safe, fed, and healthy in spite of living in an environment with no public order and hardly any food to eat, separated from her husband with no means to contact him. Had it not been for the inner strength and deep and abiding Christian faith of this remarkable woman who nurtured, fed, and protected her family in those frightening days of Manchuria, her children might have joined the nearly 2,500 Japanese who died each day from hunger, cold, disease, and incessant violence. The Maruyama siblings know that Kunio and Mary Maruyama were indeed extraordinary people, a cut considerably above the average.

The author (from left), his daughter Katherine (age one year) and his wife LaRae, visit with Mary and Kunio Maruyama at their home in Kokubunji, Tokyo, in the fall of 1973. The author (then an Air Force captain) had just ended his tour in Southeast Asia and was on his way to his next assignment at the United States Air Force Academy in Colorado Springs, Colorado. (Author's Collection)

Shortly after Maruyama began his career as a professor at Meiji University, in the mid-1950s, the Maruyamas sold their Kugayama house that had played such a vital part as the headquarters for the repatriation effort and moved to a house in Kokubunji, about an hour's train ride west of Tokyo. During a visit by their oldest son Robert to Kokubunji in the fall of 1981, Maruyama, Mary, and Robert made a vacation trip to their *besso* (a summer home) in the resort town of Fujimiland at the foot of Mount Fuji. To Maruyama, the sight of Mount Fuji never failed to move him and lift his spirit. He never forgot how majestic and awe-inspiring the snowcapped symbol of Japan looked when he stepped out on the veranda of his Kugayama home in the spring of 1946 after his escape from Manchuria.

Maruyama died suddenly on October 17, 1981, at the age of seventy-eight, at the *besso* in Fujimiland; this time, Mount Fuji gazed down upon him as Mary and Robert shed tears of sorrow at the passing of a selfless, courageous, and humble human being. In spite of their grief, however, Mary and Robert took comfort in knowing that God had a special place in heaven for a man like their husband and father, Kunio Maruyama. Maruyama had been a lifelong Buddhist, but shortly before his death, he had been baptized a Catholic.

After her husband passed away, Seattle-born Mary Mariko Maruyama contemplated moving back to the United States where all her children then lived, but in the end, she decided to stay in Japan among all her many friends. She died on March 23, 1991, at eighty years of age with her older daughter, Marianne, nursing and caring for her at her bedside. Mary and Kunio are interred side by side in the mausoleum of St. Mary's Cathedral in Tokyo, the magnificent structure that was designed by the famed architect, Kenzo Tange. Never will they be separated again as during their year of separation in 1946–1947, she in Dalian with her boys, he in Japan putting his heart and soul into the effort to bring his countrymen home, neither knowing whether the other was safe or even still alive.

May they rest together eternally in peace.

Notes

Introduction
1. Kunio Maruyama, *Yutopia wo Mezashite* [Aiming for Utopia] (Tokyo: Shinano Shuppan, 1970).

Chapter 1
1. William L. Neumann, *America Encounters Japan from Perry to MacArthur* (Baltimore: John Hopkins Press, 1963), 177.
2. Maruyama, *Yutopia,* 23.
3. Maruyama, *Yutopia,* 111.

Chapter 2
1. John Whitney Hall, *Japan from Prehistory to Modern Times* (Tokyo: Charles E. Tuttle Co., 1971), 336–337.
2. "Fascist states form Axis," *Chronicle of the 20th Century,* ed. Clifton Daniel (New York: Chronicle Publications, Inc., 1987), 464.
3. Maruyama, *Yutopia,* 33.
4. James L. McClain, *A Modern History of Japan* (New York: W.W. Norton & Co., 2002), 340.
5. McClain, 421.

Chapter 3
1. Richard B. Frank, *Downfall—The End of the Imperial Japanese Empire* (New York: Penguin Group, 1999), 1.
2. McClain, 514–515.

3. "Yalta: Big Three Plan Future Moves," *Chronicle of the 20th Century*, ed. Clifton Daniel (New York: Chronicle Publications, Inc., 1987), 584.
4. Frank, 221–229.
5. Maruyama, *Yutopia*, 139–140.
6. Frank, 278–281.
7. Robert S. Elegant, *Mao vs. Chiang—The Battle for China 1925–1949* (New York: Grosset & Dunlap, Inc., 1972), 104.
8. Yasuo Wakatsuki, *Sengo Hikiage no Kiroku* [The Record of Repatriation After the War] (Tokyo: Jiji Tsushinsha, 1991), 127.
9. Wakatsuki, 202.

Chapter 4

1. Yoko Tanoue, ed., *Oya to Ko ga Kataritsugu Manshu no "8-gatsu 15-nichi"* [Manchuria's "August 15" as Related by Parents and Their Children] (Tokyo: Hasuyu Shobo Shuppan, 2008), 81–85.
2. Ryounei Social Science Institute, ed., *Koroto Hyakuman Nihon Kyouryumin no Dai Sokan* [The Mass Return of 1 Million Japanese Settlers from Koroto] (Beijing: 5 State Communication Publishing Co., 2005), 40–41.
3. Kunio Maruyama, *Naze Koroto wo Hiraita ka* [Why Was Koroto Opened] (Tokyo: Nagata Shobo, 1970), 40–41.
4. Tatsuo Iiyama, *Haisen: Hikiage no Dokoku* [Defeat in War: The Lamentation of Repatriation] (Tokyo: Kokusho Kanko Kai, 1979), 17.
5. Iiyama, 18.
6. Iiyama, 19.
7. Iiyama, 20.
8. Iiyama, 21–22.

Chapter 6

1. SCAP GHQ Memo to SCAP Staff G3, 8 November 1945, *Subject: Status of Repatriation*, MacArthur Memorial Library Archives, Norfolk, VA.

2. SCAP GHQ Memo to SCAP Staff, G-3, SCAJAP, and CG Eighth Army, 16 January 1946, *Subject: Status of Repatriation*, MacArthur Memorial Library Archives, Norfolk, VA.

3. SCAP GHQ Memo to SCAP Staff and Others, 13 February 1946, *Subject: Status of Repatriation*, Record Group 5, Box 2, MacArthur Memorial Library Archives, Norfolk, VA.

4. Maruyama, *Koroto*, 47.

5. Maruyama, *Koroto*, 50.

6. Maruyama, *Koroto*, 50.

Chapter 7

1. Maruyama, *Koroto*, 12.

2. *Hikiage wa Koushite Jitsugen Shita—Kyu Manshu: Koroto e no Michi* [This Was How Repatriation Happened—The Former Manchuria: The Road to Koroto] NHK Broadcast, 8 December 2008.

Chapter 8

1. "Manchurian Pillage," *Newsweek*, 11 March 1946: 49.

2. "Russians Strip Manchurian Industry," *Life*, 25 March 1946: 27–33.

3. "Looted City," *Time,* 11 March 1946: 32.

4. "Rape of Manchuria," *Newsweek*, 18 March 1946: 49.

5. *Newsweek,* 18 March, 1946: 51–52.

6. *Washington Message to CINCAFPAC*, 23 March 1946, Record Group 9, Box 158, MacArthur Memorial Library Archives, Norfolk, VA.

7. "Generalissimo Chiang Kai-shek's Victory Message," *World War II Resources*, August 15, 1945 http://www.ibibilio.org/pha/policy/1945.

8. Elegant, 125–132.

Chapter 9

1. Maruyama, *Koroto,* 57–59

Chapter 10
1. Masamichi Musashi, *Ajia no Akebono—Shisen wo Koete* [The Dawning of Asia—Crossing the Lines of Death] (Tokyo: Jiyusha, 2000).

Chapter 11
1. Musashi, 71.
2. Maruyama, *Koroto*, 68–72.

Chapter 12
1. Musashi, 90.
2. Maruyama, *Koroto,* 40.

Chapter 13
1. Maruyama, *Koroto*, 78.
2. NHK Broadcast, 8 December 2008.
3. Minutes from "*Chubei Soho Dai Nikai Nihonjin Furyo Oyobi Kyoryumin Kenso ni Kansuru Kaigi Jiroku*" ["Record of the 2nd US–Chinese Conference on Returning of Japanese POWs and Civilian Residents"] held in Shanghai, 5 January 1946.
4. SCAP GHQ Report to Various Pacific Theater Commanders, 17 March 1946, *Subject: Conference on Repatriation,* 15–17 January 1946, Tokyo, Japan, Government Section 319, National Archives, College Park, MD.

Chapter 14
1. Maruyama, *Koroto,* 85–86.

Chapter 15
1. Maruyama, *Koroto*, 91–93.
2. Maruyama, *Koroto*, 93.

Chapter 16
1. Patrick Byrne, Letter to Father General, 31 December 1945, Maryknoll Mission Archives, Maryknoll, NY.

2. Bishop Furuya's Report as Recorded by Brother Clement, 22 June 1953, Maryknoll Mission Archives, Maryknoll, NY.

3. Raymond A. Lane, *Ambassador in Chain* (New York: P. J. Kennedy & Sons, 1955), 154.

4. Lane, 152–153.

5. Lane, 156.

6. Maruyama, *Koroto*, 99.

7. Thomas Quinlan, Letter to Cardinal Fumasoni Biondi, 27 April 1953, Maryknoll Mission Archives, Maryknoll, NY.

Chapter 17

1. SCAP GHQ Memo to Various Staff, 2 January 1946, *Subject: Status of Repatriation*, MacArthur Memorial Library Archives, Norfolk, VA.

2. State-War-Navy-Coordinating Committee Note, 26 February 1947, *Subject: Revision of Yen-Dollar Military Conversion Rate*, National Archives, College Park, MD.

3. Maruyama, *Koroto*, 100–105.

4. Musashi, 111–112.

5. Maruyama, *Koroto*, 108.

Chapter 18

1. Musashi, 113.

2. *Foreign Relations of the United States*, Vol. X (U.S. Government Printing Office, Dept. of State Publications 8562, 1946), 902–903.

3. JCS Report, 20 March 1946, *Subject: Repatriation of Civilian Japanese from China*, National Archives, College Park, MD.

4. SCAP GHQ Report, 17 March 1946, *Subject: Conference on Repatriation, 15–17 January 1946, Tokyo, Japan, NR: CFBX28789*, National Archives, College Park, MD.

5. HQ US Army Pacific Message to CG Nanking HDQS Command, 18 April 1946, National Archives, College Park, MD.
6. Gallup Memo for Record, 20 April 1946, National Archives, College Park, MD.
7. SCAP Message to COMGENCHINA, 23 April 1946, National Archives, College Park, MD.
8. CG China General Message NR29901 to SCAP, 30 April 1946, National Archives, College Park, MD.

Chapter 19
1. Musashi, 130–140.

Chapter 20
1. *Tokyo Telephone Directory*, 16 May 1946, Record Group 100, MacArthur Memorial Library Archives, Norfolk, VA.
2. Maruyama, *Koroto*, 121–123.
3. *Newsweek*, 18 March 1946.
4. Maruyama, *Koroto*, 126–128.
5. Kunio Maruyama, *Zaiman Douho wo Sukue* [Save Our Countrymen in Manchuria] (Tokyo: Koumin Kyuhonsha, 1946).
6. Maruyama, *Koroto*, 130.
7. Maruyama, *Koroto*, 131–132.

Chapter 21
1. Shigeru Yoshida Letter to Douglas MacArthur, 14 June 1946, Record Group 620, MacArthur Memorial Library Archives, Norfolk, VA. This letter is on display in the hallway of MacArthur Memorial Library in Norfolk, Virginia.

Chapter 22
1. Musashi, 130–181.

Chapter 23
1. Maruyama, *Koroto*, 140–150.

Chapter 24
1. CG USAF China Message to SCAP, 11 March 1946, *Subject: Repatriation Through Dairen*, National Archives, College Park, MD.
2. CG China Message to SCAP, 28 May 1946, NR CFB02131, National Archives, College Park, MD.
3. SCAP message to WDCSA and State Department, 19 December 1946, Record Group 9, Box 161, MacArthur Memorial Library Archives, Norfolk, VA.
4. Tatsunosuke Takasaki, *Manshu no Shuen* [The End of Manchuria] (Tokyo: Jitsugyo no Nihonsha, 1953), 192.

Chapter 25
1. Maruyama, *Koroto*, 164.
2. "Press Release 1947," 13 January 1947, Record Group 6, Box 10, MacArthur Memorial Library Archives, Norfolk, VA.
3. NHK Broadcast, 8 December 2008.

Chapter 26
1. American Consul General Benninghoff Letter, 6 June 1946, Maryknoll Mission Archives, Maryknoll, NY.
2. "Bishop Lane's Naval Order: Dairen to San Francisco," 25 June 1946, Maryknoll Mission Archives, Maryknoll, NY.

Chapter 27
1. NHK Broadcast, 8 December 2008.
2. Maruyama, *Koroto*, 170–171.
3. *Foreign Relations of the United States, Vol. VIII* (U.S. Government Printing Office, Dept. of State Publications 8562, 1946), 306–307.
4. Maruyama, *Koroto*, 178.
5. Maruyama, *Koroto*, 182–184.

6. Maruyama, *Koroto*, 184.

Chapter 28
1. SCAP GHQ Report, 7 May 1948, *Subject: Status of Repatriation*, National Archives, College Park, MD.
2. John Dower, *Embracing Defeat* (New York: W.W. Norton & Co. Inc., 2000), 507.
3. Maruyama, *Koroto*, 192–193.
4. Dower, 52.
5. Maruyama, *Koroto*, 194.
6. Dower, 52.

Chapter 29
1. Tanoue, 93–97, 101–102, 120, 127–128, 132–133, 135–141, 144–147, 151–154, 171–173, 195–203.

Chapter 30
1. Maruyama, *Koroto*, 115.
2. Masamichi Musashi, Letter to the Author, 22 February 2009.

Chapter 31
1. Maruyama, *Koroto*, 198
2. NHK Broadcast, 8 December 2008.
3. Barton J. Bernstein and Allen J. Matusow, ed., *The Truman Administration: A Documentary History* (New York: Harper Row Publishers, 1966), 317–320.
4. Minutes from "*Chubei Kaigi*" in Shanghai.
5. Takako Tominaga, *Dairen: Kuuhaku no Roppyakunichi* [Dairen: 600 Days of Vacuum] (Tokyo: Shinhyouron, 1986), 292–320.
6. Tominaga, 319–320.
7. Tominaga, 320.

References

"Bishop Lane's Naval Order: Dairen to San Francisco." 25 June 1946. Maryknoll Mission Archives, Maryknoll, NY.

"Generalissimo Chiang Kai-shek's Victory Message." *World War II Resources*. August 15, 1945. http://www.ibiblio.org/pha/policy/1945

"Looted City." *Time*. 11 March 1946: 32.

"Manchurian Pillage." *Newsweek*. 11 March 1946: 49.

"Press Release 1947." 13 January 1947. Record Group 6, Box 10, MacArthur Memorial Library Archives, Norfolk, VA.

"Rape of Manchuria." *Newsweek*. 18 March 1946: 51–52.

"Russians Strip Manchurian Industry." *Life*. 25 March 1946: 27–33.

"Yalta: Big Three Plan Future Moves." *Chronicle of the 20th Century*. Clifton Daniel, editor. New York: Chronicle Publications, Inc., 1987.

American Consul General Benninghoff Letter. 6 June 1946. Maryknoll Mission Archives, Maryknoll, NY.

Arai, Emiko. *Shonentachi no Manshu* [The Boyhood Manchuria]. Tokyo: Ronsosha, 2007.

Bernstein, Barton J. and Allen J. Matusow editors. *The Truman Administration: A Documentary History.* New York: Harper Row Publishers, 1966.

Bishop Furuya's Report as Recorded by Brother Clement. 22 June 1953. Maryknoll Mission Archives, Maryknoll, NY.

Byrne, Patrick. Letter to Father General. 31 December 1945. Maryknoll Mission Archives, Maryknoll, NY.

CG China General Message NR29901 to SCAP. 30 April 1946. National Archives, College Park, MD.

CG China Message to SCAP. 28 May 1946, NR CFB02131. National Archives, College Park, MD.

CG USAF China Message to SCAP. 11 March 1946. *Subject: Repatriation Through Dairen.* National Archives, College Park, MD.

Craig, William. *The Fall of Japan.* New Jersey: Galahad Books, 1997.

Dower, John. *Embracing Defeat.* New York: W.W. Norton & Co. Inc., 2000.

Elegant, Robert S. *Mao vs. Chiang—The Battle for China 1925–1949.* New York: Grosset & Dunlap, Inc., 1972.

Foreign Relations of the United States, Vol. VIII. U.S. Government Printing Office, Dept. of State Publications 8562, 1946.

Foreign Relations of the United States, Vol. X. U.S. Government Printing Office, Dept. of State Publications 8562, 1946.

Frank, Richard B. *Downfall—The End of the Imperial Japanese Empire*. New York: Penguin Group, 1999.

Gallup Memo for Record. 20 April 1946. National Archives, College Park, MD.

Hall, John Whitney. *Japan from Prehistory to Modern Times*. Tokyo: Charles E. Tuttle Co., 1971.

Hikiage wa Koushite Jitsugen Shita—Kyu Manshu: Koroto e no Michi [This Was How Repatriation Happened—The Former Manchuria: The Road to Koroto]. NHK Broadcast. 8 December 2008.

HQ US Army Pacific Message to CG Nanking HDQS Command. 18 April 1946. National Archives, College Park, MD.

Iiyama, Tatsuo. *Haisen: Hikiage no Dokoku* [Defeat in War: The Lamentation of Repatriation]. Tokyo: Kokusho Kanko Kai, 1979.

JCS Report, 20 March 1946. S*ubject: Repatriation of Civilian Japanese from China*. National Archives, College Park, MD.

Lane, Raymond A. *Ambassador in Chain*. New York: P.J. Kennedy & Sons, 1955.

Maruyama, Kunio. *Naze Koroto wo Hiraita ka* [Why Was Koroto Opened]. Tokyo: Nagata Shobo, 1970.

Maruyama, Kunio. *Yutopia wo Mezashite* [Aiming for Utopia]. Tokyo: Shinano Shuppan, 1970.

Maruyama, Kunio. *Zaiman Douho wo Sukue* [Save Our Countrymen in Manchuria]. Tokyo: Koumin Kyuhonsha, 1946.

McClain, James L. *A Modern History of Japan*. New York: W.W. Norton & Co., 2002.

Minutes from "*Chubei Soho Dai Nikai Nihonjin Furyo Oyobi Kyoryumin Kenso ni Kansuru Kaigi Jiroku*" ["Record of the 2nd U.S.–Chinese Conference on Returning of Japanese POWs and Civilian Residents"] held in Shanghai, 5 January 1946.

Morishita, Noriyoshi. *Hokuman: Shonenhei no Seikatsu Nikki* [Northern Manchuria: The Everyday Diary of a Recruited Soldier]. Tokyo: Ronsosha, 1980.

Musashi, Masamichi. *Ajia no Akebono—Shisen wo Koete* [The Dawning of Asia—Crossing the Lines of Death]. Tokyo: Jiyusha, 2000.

Musashi, Masamichi. Letter to the Author. 22 February 2009.

Nakanishi, Rei. *Akai Tsuki* [The Red Moon]. Tokyo: Shinchosha, 2003.

Neumann, William L. *America Encounters Japan from Perry to MacArthur*. Baltimore: John Hopkins Press, 1963.

Quinlan, Thomas. Letter to Cardinal Fumasoni Biondi. 27 April 1953. Maryknoll Mission Archives, Maryknoll, NY.

Ryounei Social Science Institute, editor. *Koroto Hyakuman Nihon Kyoryumin no Dai Sokan* [The Mass Return of 1 Million Japanese Settlers from Koroto]. Beijing: 5 State Communication Publishing Co., 2005.

SCAP GHQ Memo to SCAP Staff and Others. 13 February 1946. *Subject: Status of Repatriation*. Record Group 5, Box 2, MacArthur Memorial Library Archives, Norfolk, VA.

SCAP GHQ Memo to SCAP Staff G3. 8 November 1945. *Subject: Status of Repatriation.* MacArthur Memorial Library Archives, Norfolk, VA.

SCAP GHQ Memo to SCAP Staff, G-3, SCAJAP, and CG Eighth Army. 16 January 1946. *Subject: Status of Repatriation.* MacArthur Memorial Library Archives, Norfolk, VA.

SCAP GHQ Memo to Various Staff. 2 January 1946. *Subject: Status of Repatriation.* MacArthur Memorial Library Archives, Norfolk, VA.

SCAP GHQ Report to Various Pacific Theater Commanders. 17 March 1946. *Subject: Conference on Repatriation, 15–17 January 1946, Tokyo, Japan.* Government Section 319, National Archives, College Park, MD.

SCAP GHQ Report. 17 March 1946. *Subject: Conference on Repatriation, 15–17 January 1946, Tokyo, Japan, NR: CFBX28789.* National Archives, College Park, MD.

SCAP GHQ Report. 7 May 1948. *Subject: Status of Repatriation.* National Archives, College Park, MD.

SCAP Message to WDCSA and State Department. 19 December 1946. Record Group 9, Box 161, MacArthur Memorial Library Archives, Norfolk, VA.

SCAP Message to COMGENCHINA. 23 April 1946. National Archives, College Park, MD.

Sengo Hikiage 660 Man-nin Kokyou e no Michi [Postwar Repatriation: The Road Home for 6.6 Million]. NHK Broadcast, 11 December 2007.

Yoshida, Shigeru Letter to Douglas MacArthur. 14 June 1946. Record Group 620, MacArthur Memorial Library Archives, Norfolk, VA.

Spector, Ronald H. *In the Ruins of the Empire*. New York: Random House Publishing Group, 2007.

State-War-Navy-Coordinating Committee Note. 26 February 1947. *Subject: Revision of Yen-Dollar Military Conversion Rate*, National Archives, College Park, MD.

Tanoue, Yoko, editor. *Oya to Ko ga Kataritsugu Manshu no "8-gatsu 15-nichi"* [Manchuria's "August 15" as Related by Parents and Their Children]. Tokyo: Hasuyu Shobo Shuppan, 2008.

Taiheiyou Sensou Kenkyukai [The Pacific War Research Association], *Manshu Teikoku ga Yoku Wakaru Hon* [Book to Easily Understand the Manchurian Empire]. Tokyo: PHP Kenkyusho, 2004.

Takasaki, Tatsunosuke. *Manshu no Shuen* [The End of Manchuria]. Tokyo: Jitsugyo no Nihonsha, 1953.

Tokyo Telephone Directory. 16 May 1946. Record Group 100, MacArthur Memorial Library Archives, Norfolk, VA.

Tominaga, Takako. *Dairen: Kuuhaku no Roppyakunichi* [Dairen: 600 Days of Vacuum]. Tokyo: Shinhyouron, 1986.

Wakatsuki, Yasuo. *Sengo Hikiage no Kiroku* [The Record of Repatriation After the War]. Tokyo: Jiji Tsushinsha, 1991.

Washington Message to CINCAFPAC. 23 March 1946. Record Group 9, Box 158, MacArthur Memorial Library Archives, Norfolk, VA.

Wiest, Jean-Paul. *Maryknoll in China*. New York: Orbis Books, Maryknoll, 1988.

Yano, Ichiya and Ieson Yan. *Manshu Chinkon: Hikiage Kara Miru Senchu/Sengo* [Manchuria Requiem: Viewing Wartime and Postwar from Repatriation Standpoint]. Tokyo: Impact Shuppankai, 2001.

Index

Japanese names, which have been used in Westernized order in the text, are inverted in this index; entries for Sakae Araki, for example, appear under Araki, Sakae.

A

Changchun, 18, 28, 29, 38-39, 104, 120, 122, 123-24, 146, 149, 160, 181, 214, 251, 253, 329, 349, 354, 360
cherry blossoms, described, 236
Chiang Kai-shek, xx, xvi, xxii, 26, 31, 85, 87, 265. *See also* Chinese Nationalist forces
children
death rates among, 147
killing of, 40, 44
medical care for, 341
orphaned/left behind, 39–40, 53, 329
of refugees, 46, 47
repatriation of, 205, 209
selling of, 53
work by, 50
China. *See also* Chinese Communist Army; Chinese Nationalist forces; Manchuria
as escape route, 86
Japan and, 18, 23–24, 33–34, 85–88, 109, 307, 333–34
repatriation efforts and, 213–14
Soviet Union and, 83–84, 89
United States and, 89, 197–99
Yalta Conference, exclusion from, 26
Chinese Communist Army
about, 31
in Anshan, 339–40
behavior of, 33, 54
Japanese soldiers and, 334–36
vs. Nationalist Chinese forces, 83, 87–89, 214, 222, 251, 265, 337–38
prisoners of, 72–74
soldiers of, as prisoners, 254
Chinese Eastern Railway, 18–19
Chinese Nationalist forces. *See also* Chiang Kai-shek
in Anshan, 337
vs. Communist Chinese Army, 83, 87–89, 214, 222, 251, 265, 337–38
control of Koroto, 140–41
corruption and, 263
detention by, 111–12
escorts of, 218–20
Musashi and, 216–18, 252–64
in repatriation efforts, 251–52
support of escape plot, xx, 85–87, 90, 106, 109, 117, 354
United States support of, 89

humanitarian effort, repatriation as, 197–99, 237, 296, 353
Hungary, Soviet Union in, 25

I

Ichigayamitsuke, tribunal at, 274–77
Iiyama, Tatsuo, 42–43
immigration policies
 in Japan, 37–38
 in United States, 1–7, 10, 363, 366
Imperial Army, 11, 40, 72, 116–17, 282–83
Imperial Household Agency, officials of, 245–46
imprisonment. *See* detention and imprisonment
impudence, 146–47
Inaba, Torao, 90–92
industrial facilities
 looting of, 35–37, 63, 334–35
 technical workers, delayed return of, 333–40
infants. *See* children
intelligence-gathering. *See also* spies
 by Allied Powers, 214
 by escapees, 53, 58, 74, 107, 145
 need for, 357
interrogation, 221, 254–59
Ishiwara, Kanji, 19–20

J

Japan. *See also* Japanese citizens; Japanese military
 Allied administration of, 12–13, 118, 151–52, 169–75, 270, 273, 275
 Catholic Church in, 168
 China and, 18, 23–24, 33–34, 85–88, 109, 307, 333–34
 Germany and, 13
 government of, 192, 320–21, 356, 361–63
 history of, 6, 17–18
 imperial family, 245–46
 map, xxiv
 occupation of Manchuria, 14–16, 354
 postwar conditions in, 127–28, 213–14, 228–29, 318, 358
 recognition of escapees in, 357
 Russia and, 18
 Soviet Union and, 25, 333–34
 surrender of, 24–25, 44, 59, 170

Law No. 13, 346–48
leadership, ideals of, 136
League of Nations, 12–13, 20
left-behind orphans, 39–40, 53, 329, 341
legislation and legislators
  about loan repayment, 346–48
  immigration policies, in Japan, 37–38
  immigration policies, in United States, 1–7, 10, 363, 366
  repatriation efforts of, 245–48
letters
  from Lane, 94–95, 117, 134–35, 360–61
  to MacArthur, 243–45
  from Marella, 135
  in response to public diplomacy, 187–88, 239–42
  from Sister Roseanne, 103–4, 152
  from Takasaki, 104, 131–33
liberalists, 13–14
Liberty ships, 208–9, 244
Life magazine, 82
Lin Biao, 88–89, 265
Lincoln, Abraham, 70–72, 279
Liu (Colonel), 263–65
Liu Wanquan
  on Koroto, 111–12, 145
  reentry documents from, 214, 216
  scandal and, 218, 221
  support of escape plot, 90–92, 107
loans, for repatriation effort, 344–48
London, Maruyama's experiences in, 50–51, 153
Long, Huey, 5
looting
  of industrial facilities, 35–37, 63, 334–35
  of personal possessions, 29, 32–34, 44
  Western news coverage of, 79–85
losing face, 142–43, 235
LSTs. *See* Landing Ship, Tank amphibious vessels (LSTs)
Lytton Commission, 12–13, 20

M
MacArthur, Douglas
  authority of, 118, 247
  Byrne and, 168–69

embroidered portrait, 331–32
escapees and, 139, 159–64
Lane and, 96
letters to, 243–45
orders of, xvi, 195, 199–200, 297–99, 355–56
pictured, 165
Manchukuo. *See* Manchuria
Manchukuoan Army, 27
Manchuria
  Chinese/Japanese relationships in, 23–24, 33–34, 47, 65–66, 85–88, 329, 340–42
  industry in, 15–16, 354
  Japanese occupation of, 14–16, 17–21, 87
  Japanese population in, 37–38, 58, 120–21
  map, xxiii
  postwar lack of peace, 161, 182, 276, 279
  Soviet invasion of, xvii, 22–34
  Soviet occupation of, 35–48, 134, 238, 353, 359
Manchurian Catholic Mission. *See also* Lane, Raymond A.; Maryknoll Catholic Church
Manchurian Electric Works Company, 149
Manchurian Heavy Industry, 104
Manchurian Incident, 20
Manchurian Iron Manufacturing Company, 63
"Manchurian Pillage" (*Newsweek*), 81–82
Manchuria's "August 15" as Related by Parents and Their Children (Tagami), 342
manners and civility. *See also* manners and civility
  among escapees, 62, 108–9
  among family members, 289
  among U. S. politicians, 6, 7
  breakdown of, 47–48, 182
  face saving, 142–43, 235
  impudence, perception of, 146–47
  during meetings with leaders, 146–47, 195, 270–71
  modesty, 368
  shame and, 3, 45, 142–43, 203–4, 255, 336
Mao Zedong, 31, 87, 329
maps
  of Japan, xxiv
  of Manchuria, xxiii
  showing port of Koroto, 141–44

V

W

Y

Z

Paul K. Maruyama

LaVergne, TN USA
17 March 2010
176360LV00002B/1/P